In Defence of
THE ASHES

Testing Time: MCC in the West Indies 1974
Assault on the Ashes: MCC in Australia and New Zealand 1974/75
MCC in India 1976/77
The Jubilee Tests

In Defence of
THE ASHES

England's Victory, Packer's Progress

Christopher Martin-Jenkins

Macdonald and Jane's · London

*To Reg, June, Ian, Susan, Bruce, Ross and Wanda
Hayman, and countless other hospitable Australians*

CONTENTS

ACKNOWLEDGEMENTS

My warm thanks are due to my employers, the BBC, for sending me on another eventful tour. To British listeners I was able to report very different stories from four years before. I am grateful also to the ABC for again inviting me to join their panel of commentators. I watched most of the cricket in the wise and convivial company of Lindsay Hassett and Alan McGilvray.

All but one of the pictures in this book are by Patrick Eagar, who needs no introduction (second, third and fourth Tests and WSC night cricket), or Ron McKenzie of the *Mirror/Telegraph/Australian* group of newspapers, whose skill with the camera is equalled only by his prodigious capacity for ice-cold beer. Many thanks to both. Also to Jim Fenwick of the *Brisbane Courier Mail* for allowing me to use his picture of Derek Randall's vain airborne attempt to run out Graham Yallop.

INTRODUCTION

The Australian Cricket Board used the slogan 'The battle for the Ashes' in all its publicity for the 1978–79 series. It was a battle on two fronts. On the cricket field the Australians were determined to upset the odds in favour of England retaining the Ashes won under Mike Brearley's captaincy in England in 1977. Off the field the officials of establishment cricket were desperately anxious to see the traditional series comparing favourably with the second season of pirate cricket run by Kerry Packer's World Series Cricket organisation.

The pages which follow relate how England did indeed retain the Ashes whilst WSC gained ground in some respects on establishment cricket in the bitter conflict which continued to divide players, administrators and spectators alike. It became fashionable after the series was over to try to discredit the cricket played, as if it were not worthy of the Ashes tradition. Mr Packer himself was quoted in the British *Sunday Telegraph* as describing the cricket put on by the Australian Board as a 'joke' and the English side as 'very ordinary'. He was able only to 'shake his head sadly' over the state of the Australian side. Having bitterly attacked sections of the Australian media the previous year, he also accused the English media of 'beating a dead horse and writing us down as a failure'. Mr Packer also stated in his *Sunday Telegraph* interview that the only reason he had not signed more England players was because they were not good enough. Yet during the Headingley Test of 1977 he had approached Mike Brearley with Tony Greig and suggested to the England captain that the *whole* of England's team should join WSC. WSC has also made individual approaches to Derek Randall, Bob Willis and Chris Old. None of the players accepted because they believed they would be both happier and equally well, if not better, rewarded by staying with official cricket. In addition, towards the end of the tour Tony Greig issued an invitation to Brearley's team to visit his house for drinks and remarked that there might be some WSC contracts available. None of the players accepted the invitation.

The successes and the failings of WSC in its first two years will be noted in the narrative of this book, but it seems essential at the outset, because of statements like those quoted above, to establish very briefly the *bona fides* of the Ashes series itself. In the first place it was anything but a joke. The cricket was as fiercely but as honourably contested as any in the 102-year history of Anglo-Australian Test cricket. Secondly, Tests between England and Australia have always merited the serious attention of cricket followers because of this tradition, even when, as after the two World Wars, one side has been noticeably weaker than the other. To describe the series as a joke because one side is claimed to be weak is a little like discrediting a great building by Christopher Wren because damp has appeared on the ground floor or the roof is in need of repair. Thirdly, and perhaps most important, it is questionable whether the standard of Test cricket played in Australia in 1978–79 was as low as those with a WSC axe to grind would like to suggest. On the contrary, standards in the field on both sides were extremely high. It is nearer the truth to suggest that the balance between batsman and bowler has altered in the latter's favour.

I do not necessarily wield an axe for the establishment, only for the good of cricket as a marvellous and many-faceted sport worth preserving. But I would briefly point out here one or two themes which will be developed later. First, though batsmen struggled throughout the Ashes series for many reasons which included poor pitches, excellent bowling and brilliant fielding, low scores were an even more striking feature of WSC cricket than they were of the Test matches. This did not necessarily make them a 'joke'. Secondly, the Australian side won one of the six Tests. The 1977 side won none and lost three; they were the first Australian side to lose as many as three Tests in England since 1886. Thirteen of that touring party of seventeen were now representing the WSC Australians. Thirdly, although England would have found it still tougher to retain the Ashes against an Australian side combining the talents of both teams, England's excellence in the field would, I think, have seen them through in any case. England overcame a promising but fatally inexperienced Australian side through good leadership, team spirit, superb fielding and an ability to recover from some startling batting collapses. When England were in trouble they fought like terriers; when on top they killed like tigers. The margin of their victory was in itself extraordinary.

Five-one is something of an empty record because there have been six Tests rather than five in only three previous series; nevertheless England have never before won by four clear Test matches against Australia either at home or away. This suggests one of the greatest England sides of all time. It is doubtful if they were that good, but Brearley's team was certainly something better than just 'ordinary'.

Time may also prove Australia to have been better than they appeared to be. It is too easy to forget that they came close to levelling the series at two-all in the first two weeks of 1979. They have many talented players who are still improving: amongst them are Yallop, Wood, Darling, Border, Wright, Higgs and the record-breaking Hogg, who seemed, like Thomson four years earlier, to spring from nowhere in the great Australian tradition of finding new Test players overnight. One might ask Geoffrey Boycott, England's senior batsman, if this Australian side was really so weak. Against Greg Chappell's team of 1977 Boycott made 442 runs in five innings at an average of 147.33. Against Yallop's eighteen months later he made 263 runs in 12 innings at an average of 21.92. There were many reasons for this but amongst them was the simple fact that Yallop's team bowled better than Chappell's had done.

It is difficult to understand the social forces behind the Packer cricket revolution and the reasons for its relative success without appreciating the ethnic origins of Australia's city dwellers. Both from the enthusiastic support the England team received at the country matches and from all that was said by those connected with country cricket it was clear that the general attitude of the rural areas was conservative, traditional and hostile to the parasite which had come to feed on establishment cricket. However a huge majority of Australia's population – nine-tenths – lives in the cities.

In December 1978 Australia's official population was 14,287,000. At the time of the last census, in 1976, it was 13,548,467, of which 88.8 percent were of European origin. As many as 2,718,855 were born overseas, and of these only 1,109,240 were born in the United Kingdom and Eire. 1,089,842 came from other European countries and the remainder from elsewhere (the majority being Asian). In other words less than half of Australia's new immigrants are likely to have any understanding of cricket or, more pertinently, any feeling for the significance of 'the Ashes'.

Even amongst the longer-established Australians, a substantial proportion were likely to be indifferent to cricket traditions. Of the Australian-born population of 10,829,661 at the last census, 1,319,856 were born of parents who had themselves been born in countries other than the United Kingdom, Eire or Australia.

The cricket package which Kerry Packer's World Series Cricket was promoting was an Americanised version of the game. The very name 'World Series', the idea of night cricket and coloured clothing, and the whole approach to promoting the game had baseball connotations. The old game, dressed up as something new, was becoming a fashionable, colourful and exciting interest for young Australians, including those who could not be expected to have a real feeling for the deeds of a Bradman or a Grace. But the feeling of being a part of a great tradition has always been at the heart of Test cricket both for players and spectators, and it would be tragic for the game if the 'new Australians' do not learn to appreciate its history, its legacy of great characters and great matches fought for honour rather than for money, in a spirit of patriotism and tough but fair competition.

It would have been better for 'traditional' cricket if England had not won by the margin they did. In fact, as the story of the Test matches will explain, the series was less one-sided than the results suggest (this has often been so in the past too), and if the Australian team had possessed more experience and more nerve at critical points, or the England team had been less spirited and resilient, the result could easily have been three-all. But it would have been contrary to the meaning of Test cricket for any player to have given an inch to an opponent at any stage in the interests of wooing more spectators.

One must have faith that spectators of the future will recognise the value of a truly fought contest played in a great tradition, just as one trusts that those who guide traditional cricket will change the game according to modern tastes and economic demands but without altering its essential character. It is because the World Series organisers have endangered its traditional character that one fears for the game's future if the war goes on. The great hope, however, remains the fact that the leading cricketers themselves, of both camps, do have a feeling for the traditions of cricket and most would agree in their hearts, whatever their pockets might dictate to them, that Test cricket ought to remain the highest form of the game.

Chapter One

PACKER
BACKGROUND

The story is now well known of how many of the world's greatest players defected from established cricket and signed, most of them secretly, to join the ruthless but enterprising Australian businessman Kerry Packer. Bitter because he was refused the right to televise Test cricket in Australia due to the Australian Cricket Board's loyalty to their traditional supporters, the Australian Broadcasting Commission, Packer exploited the fact that not enough of the proceeds from a sustained boom in international cricket had been getting through to the players. He now offered them instant big money, which no more than a handful of men could resist, to set up a jazzy form of 'Super Cricket' in Australia. With the players as bargaining weapons he next offered to scale down – or even abandon – his plans if he could be guaranteed the right to televise Test cricket. However, at Lord's in June 1977 the delegates of the Test-playing countries meeting as the International Cricket Conference refused him this guarantee. The Australian Board's assurance that he would be given an equal chance to bid for a new contract when the ABC agreement expired in 1979 was not accepted by Packer, who promptly declared war with his often quoted assertion that it was now 'every man for himself and the devil take the hindmost'.

The cricket establishment was sure that a devil was indeed in its midst, and the authorities countered with proposals to bar the Packer players from all first-class cricket. This was the impasse at the end of the 1977 cricket season in England, and since the 1978–79 defence of the Ashes, won by England that momentous Jubilee year, can only be seen against the background of developments in the Packer revolution it seems logical to recount briefly how the cricket authorities were thwarted in the High Court and how, despite massive publicity and almost unlimited capital outlay, and despite also some interesting and worthwhile experiments, the first season of space-age cricket failed to capture the imagination of either old or new cricket followers.

Because its organisers were prepared to learn from their mistakes and because Mr Packer's company was prepared to use apparently unlimited money, which might otherwise have disappeared in tax, to buy advertising, new players, new grounds and anything else that would make the grandiose plans effective, the initial failure of World Series Cricket was not fatal. It certainly would have been so, however, if the case in the High Court had gone in favour of the cricket authorities. The lifeblood of World Series Cricket was provided by the players who had made their name in the traditional game. If the Packer men had been comprehensively banned the supply of new players must gradually have dried up and World Series Cricket would sooner or later have frozen to death. The High Court case was therefore of climactic importance in the history of cricket.

It began in London on 26 September 1977 before Mr Justice Slade, with Michael Kempster, QC defending, on behalf of the TCCB and the ICC, actions brought by World Series Cricket and three of its new employees, Tony Greig, Mike Procter and John Snow. Mr Kempster has been criticised both for the advice he apparently gave at the outset that the authorities had a reasonable case and for his handling of the trial itself, but to this observer his bedside doctor manner, gentle but clear voice and clinical method were sometimes as impressive in their way as the more dramatic brilliance of Mr Packer's Counsel, Robert Alexander, QC, the man who was to enjoy the ultimate triumph. Alexander is a tall, imposing, beaky-nosed figure with a slight hunch in his back, and throughout the trial he revealed a sharp wit and a great feel for dramatic effect. When he put a particularly loaded question he would lean forward onto the ledge in front of him, his shoulders rounded – no doubt from repeating the gesture so often over the years – and look up at the high ceiling of the crowded court room, savouring the moment when the witness wriggled uncomfortably as he wrestled for an answer. If there was anything dubious in the reply Alexander was on it like a flash, and he liked nothing better than for his first question to be misunderstood, so that he might repeat it with still greater deliberation.

Mr Alexander's opening speech outlined the entire Packer case and lasted more than a day. He had many strong points to make. The Packer players would be earning a minimum of £12,000 as opposed to the £3000 which the MCC team had earned the previous winter in India and Australia during an arduous tour. The players concerned in the case were not contracted anywhere else in the winter and were therefore legally free to sign for Mr Packer. The proposed bans amounted to a 'nineteenth-century lock-out'. They were, he claimed, illogical in that they would deprive English cricket of leading players, penal because they deprived players of a summer living, and dictatorial because the defendants were asserting a monopolistic control of cricket. Yet these authorities, Mr Alexander claimed, had quite failed to ensure adequate rewards, or any real security, for cricketers. Mr Packer's arrival, however, had already stimulated an enormous rise in the earnings of English Test cricketers.

These opening blasts of thunder clearly weighed more heavily in the judge's mind than the donnish responses of Mr Kempster, who was unable to bring home with sufficient force the various counter points such as the immense value of the benefits awarded to cricketers who lasted the course in the county game (nowadays massive tax-free sums approaching six figures in some cases, though at the time of the trial the largest declared figure was Basil D'Oliveira's £45,000); the various perks such as free travel and hotels, sometimes free cars and income from endorsement of cricket equipment; and the increasing prize money offered, before Packer's intervention, by sponsors both in England and Australia. Mr Packer's assertion that most of the players had signed with an alacrity he had found 'frightening' was apparently more convincing.

The judge clearly accepted the defence's assertion that World Series Cricket was essentially a parasite skimming off the cream from milk it had not paid for and that a private promoter such as Mr Packer had no responsibility to finance and nurture the game of cricket at all levels. To most of those who understand the game, this was the essential point. But, unfortunately for the ICC and the TCCB, this was not the question on which he was called to judge. Mr Justice Slade was concerned solely with the justice or otherwise of the proposed bans, and in coming to his decision he said that he was particularly influenced by the evidence of Peter Short from Barbados who, representing the West Indies Board, had expressed grave reservations about making the bans retroactive and who had supported the other ICC members only so that they might be seen to be presenting a united front.

The court case itself lasted 31 days. The hearing ended on 7 November and on 25 November Mr Slade delivered a judgement which filled 221 foolscap pages and took five and a half hours, virtually a full day's play, to deliver. Moreover, as no newspaper could resist saying, Mr Packer won by an innings. The judge ruled that the proposed rule-changes by the ICC and the TCCB which would have effected the bans were void and *ultra vires* because they were an unreasonable restraint of trade and also amounted to an unlawful inducement to the players to break their contracts with World Series Cricket. Costs, amounting to about £200,000, were to be paid by the defendants, which in effect meant largely the TCCB and partly the other Test-playing cricket authorities. The defendants, the judge said, acted in good faith and in what they considered to be – although Mr Justice Slade made it painfully clear that *he* did not agree – was in the best interests of cricket. The official line had been that no one wanted to ban anyone, but that the proposals were necessary in order to protect the game in the long term, a point strongly argued also by the English players through their official 'union', the Cricketers' Association.

The effect of this momentous judgement was to give World Series Cricket an enormous morale-booster at a time when it was struggling to win spectators for contests which seemed empty in more senses than one, as well as making a large hole in the then healthy financial reserves of the TCCB. The Packer players were now free to play in their own domestic competitions when these did not clash with World Series matches, and they were also in theory free to continue playing in Test cricket; before long, expediency dictated that first West Indian and later Pakistan cricketers would indeed do so, although, ironically, the England and Australian Packer players who had opposed each other in 1977 *before* the judgement have never represented their countries in Test matches since.

England, minus Greig (who alone amongst the Packer players had been criticised by the judge for signing on players on Mr Packer's behalf whilst still captain of England) as well as Knott, Underwood, Amiss and Woolmer, toured Pakistan and New Zealand after their home triumph against Australia, whilst Australia themselves, deprived of more than twenty of their leading cricketers, played India. This turned out to be a fascinating series between India's always vulnerable but subtly skilled team and a brand-new Australian eleven captained by Bob Simpson, who came out of retirement to lead the home team to a narrow victory by three Tests to two. The crowds exceeded the expectations both of the Australian Board and of World Series Cricket officials, some of whom apparently had a scant understanding of the traditions of the game. Indeed one senior official illustrated the point by issuing a statement claiming that World Series Cricket had proved it was superior to Test cricket because there were more fours and sixes scored. When the press ridiculed the statement, he lost his job. The truth of the matter was that empty stands proved, even if promising television ratings did not, that Australian cricket followers were more interested in supporting their national team playing 'fair dinkum' cricket than a parade of more than fifty star players in unfamiliar coloured caps struggling to stimulate attention as they batted and bowled for big prize money ($100,000 Australian) but titles and honours which meant nothing.

There were other reasons for the failure. None of the major Test grounds was available to WSC, and instead the organisers chose to rent two huge grounds which had never before been associated with cricket and which were situated well away from the city centres. Melbourne's VFL Park is not directly served by public transport and is seventeen miles out in the suburbs; Adelaide's Football Park is seven miles from the centre. Moreover, not only was the Australian public largely in favour of traditional cricket but the cricket press of the world, nurtured on official cricket, able from an objective viewpoint to see the damage that was being done to it, and believing that there was not a great deal wrong with the *status quo* (indeed, had there not been a boom in the game Mr Packer would never have wanted to be involved), were largely hostile to the brash new product being forced onto the market.

World Series Cricket did, however, make some important experiments in their opening season. John Maley, the curator of the Gabba ground at Brisbane, would have stayed there if the Queensland Cricket Association had been able to find more money for him. Instead he was lured away and, faced with the apparent impossibility of making good cricket pitches in the middle of rough football grounds, triumphantly solved the problem by preparing mobile pitches under glass and having them lifted into a hole in the middle in time for the new grass to marry with the old. In addition, experiments with a white cricket ball proved successful and so did the decision to start some matches in mid-afternoon and continue them under floodlights at night.

It took time, however, for the innovations to be widely appreciated. For a long time it looked as though World Series Cricket was destined to become the most expensive flop in sporting history, but Mr Packer, who had been on the defensive since his High Court victory, suddenly found the battle going his way again in January. The second successive heavy defeat of the new Australian side by the resurgent Indians, who had won by an innings at Sydney to level the series, coincided with two events which gave the sleeping giant a chance to rise again from his corner. The World Series chairman, Brian Treasure, had the bright idea of canvassing those Australian players under contract to see which of them would be available to go to the West Indies if the official selectors should choose them. Seventeen players said they would be prepared to go, although most, no doubt, were aware of the fact that they were very unlikely to be asked. When the news of their availability was announced and drew no response from the Australian Board, Mr Packer wasted no time in suggesting that if some of his players were not chosen the Board would be in contempt of the High Court decision. 'If they are not picked on ability', he said, 'it amounts to a barring of these players.' Referring to Mr Justice Slade he said: 'The umpire has given the Cricket Board out and it won't leave the wicket. What sort of men of principle are the Board members? Are they going to stand by their word or are they not?'

The Board, it is true, had agreed in the High Court in London to abide by the decision of the court. But the judge, for all the heavy weight of his judgement against the establishment, had drawn a clear distinction between the retrospective action which the authorities had sought to take, by banning players simply for signing with Packer, and any prospective action against players who made themselves unavailable for Test cricket because of their involvement with World Series, which might be more reasonable. At the start of the Australian season the Board had required their own cricketers to sign two-year contracts which bound them to play only for official Australian teams if they were selected, in return for large rewards (according to Bobby Simpson, the most humble of his 1977-78 team earned between thirty and forty thousand Australian dollars), and they pointed to the obvious fact that since the Packer men had not been available to play against India they could not expect to go to the West Indies. How can a Test team be built if players are available for only *some* series? This had been one of the main arguments on the establishment side all along, although it was now made to seem weaker for Packer's oft-expressed desire to compromise so that his cricket could live with Test cricket rather than conflict with it.

Not surprisingly the Australian Board stuck by their new team. It had, after all, won a Test series, which is more than Greg Chappell's side in England, described by Trevor Bailey as a 'track-suited shambles', had done. But in the Caribbean it was a different story. The West Indies Board had always been against banning their players until such time as they made themselves unavailable for Test cricket. Their percipient President, Jeffrey Stollmeyer, tried in vain to explain to his unsophisticated public, who cared only that the West Indies should be represented by the star names, that they must try to see the problem in global terms. He asked what the reaction would be if a private promoter were to stage a series of matches in the West Indies during a Test series there, enticing away the best home players to play in competition with the official series. In other words he tried to put himself in Australian shoes. But expediency triumphed, partly no doubt because of the volatile reaction which was likely to be aroused from cricket followers in the West Indies. It was not long, in the event, before Mr Stollmeyer's hypothetical situation became fact, with the World Series Cricket tour to the West Indies in March 1979 replacing the official Test series which had been planned between the West Indies and New Zealand.

Back in 1978, the West Indies selected their Packer players for the first two Tests against the fledgling Australian side and, with their fast bowlers rampant and hostile, won both in three days, the first by an innings and 106 runs, the second by nine wickets. The West Indies Board then tried unsuccessfully to get an assurance that the Packer players would be available to tour India with the official West Indies team at the end of 1978. The Packer West Indians have since tried to maintain that there was a chance of dates being changed – by agreement between WSC and the Indian Board – to enable this to be possible. To me this seems to have been wildly unlikely. The Packer players were never likely to play in India when a new World Series season was planned simultaneously in Australia. The West Indies Board, though one understands the public antipathy they faced, should have grasped the nettle earlier. As it was, amidst bitter acrimony they dropped some of the Packer men for the third Test, and the remainder

withdrew in protest. A completely new West Indies side lost the
third Test, won the fourth and with it the series, and would probably have lost the final one at Sabina Park had not a disgraceful
crowd invasion resulted, after much debate, in the abandonment
of the match.

The bitter political battle in world cricket was by no means con-
fined, however, to Australians and West Indians. Before their
series began in the Caribbean there was an abortive attempt to
bring three Packer men into the third and final Test in Karachi in
January, where Pakistan were playing England. A splinter group
of the Pakistan Board, led by the manager of the 1974 tour to England, Omar Kureshi, claiming to act with at least the tacit blessing
of Pakistan's Chief Martial Law Administrator, General Zia-ul-
Huq, invited three of Pakistan's finest cricketers, Mushtaq
Mohammad, their former captain, Zaheer Abbas, and Imran
Khan, back from Packerland to play against England.

Mr Packer made what he hoped would be interpreted as a mag-
nanimous gesture when he released the three and travelled with
them as far as Singapore. Whether he was doing this in a genuine
spirit of compromise or to drive in the thin end of the wedge is
uncertain, but it clearly suited him to keep his men in the public
eye by getting them back into Test cricket. In Pakistan, however,
the three returning exiles received no rapturous welcome. Unlike
the Indians and West Indians, the Pakistan masses are largely
apathetic to cricket, and the young players of both the England
and the Pakistan teams were bitterly opposed to any of the Packer
cricketers returning to the Pakistan side. Mike Brearley, at this
juncture abruptly relieved of his job as tour captain because of a
broken arm sustained in an unimportant one-day match, issued a
statement on behalf of the England team deploring any possibility
of Packer cricketers playing in Tests. They had made their choice
and good luck to them, but they could not expect to have it both
ways. On the eve of the Test there were strong rumours that England would refuse to take part in the match if Mushtaq and company played, although there were instructions from Lord's that
they would be breaking their tour contracts if they did not meet
the commitment to play. In the event the Pakistan selectors did
not select the Packer men, who returned to Australia with their
tails between their legs, no doubt feeling like pawns in somebody
else's game. Not until the following winter did Pakistan, chafing
from heavy defeats in England in 1978, select several World Series

cricketers to play against India. Again, as in the case of English county cricket, expediency triumphed over principle.

It was late in January 1978 that the Kerry Packer enterprise was really able to claim an unqualified success for the first time. The first match played with a white ball under floodlights had proved instantly attractive. Now in three nights of cricket at the VFL Park in Melbourne 52,831 people travelled to the distant suburb. Since this success followed the previous best figures of 35,424 over the four days of the 'Super Test' at the Sydney Showground a week earlier, there was no questioning now the immediate future of the venture, and the two main spokesmen, Tony Greig and Packer himself, were as usual quick to capitalise. Both tended to play down the fact that it was the sheer novelty of cricket under floodlights, and the exciting spectacle which it was proving to be, which had attracted the spectators. Greig claimed that 'sponsors will be queuing up to become part of the scene following the last three nights at Melbourne'. The large crowds told the players that 'they were finally accepted'. It was a reward, he said, 'for the fifty players who took the punt to leave the traditional ranks to try something new and exciting'.

Packer himself stuck to his constant theme, namely that the people would pay to watch the best. He said that he had disproved the theory that Australians would only go to watch their national team, and in his latest hour of triumph he even admitted that he had miscalculated at first: 'It took a little longer than I had hoped. At the start there was a lot of interference by certain groups and bodies who have made it cost more than it should have done, but most of these things are behind us now.'

The actual cost of the whole gigantic gamble was still something of a mystery. Mr Packer's organisation claimed that his outlay was six million Australian dollars. But a team of diligent researchers from Melbourne University put the amount at no more than 3.8 million dollars, breaking it down as follows: SALARIES 1.3 million; HIRE OF GROUNDS AND PREPARATION OF PITCHES 700,000 dollars; BROADCASTING COSTS 360,000 dollars; GROUND OPERATIONS 400,000; ADVERTISING AND ADMINISTRATION 500,000; TRANSPORT 250,000; LEGAL COSTS 200,000; HOTEL BILLS 100,000. The team conceded, however, that 'ongoing commitments', including the long-term salaries, would have put the total outlay nearer to the Packer estimate of six million. The research team estimated the loss after the first year of World Series Cricket to be about one and a half million dollars.

Other estimates, based on the higher outlay figure, made the loss nearer to three million dollars, but all the WSC statements suggested that they were as determined to continue in their brave new world as were the authorities to ignore them in the hope that they would gradually freeze to death.

The spotlight switched temporarily back to England in late January when Tony Greig spoke out once too often even for the tastes of his own county Sussex. (The International Cricket Conference, meeting at Lord's on 1 February, decided finally that they would not attempt an appeal against the High Court decision.) Greig lost the support of his county committee when he published some sharply critical comments in the Sydney *Sun* about the temporary new England captain Geoff Boycott. After blaming him unfairly for leading the England team's resistance to the attempt to introduce the Packer players in Karachi, Greig added that Boycott was the last person in the world to comment about whom he should play against. 'His ability to be where the fast bowlers aren't', he wrote, 'has long been a talking point amongst cricketers. By some stroke of good fortune he has steered clear of the world's best fast bowlers for the past five years.'

This was one of Greig's last public statements in England. The Sussex committee deprived him of the captaincy for breaking TCCB rules about making derogatory statements. He was suspended for six weeks by the Board itself and then made a brief and unsuccessful reappearance in county cricket before announcing his retirement and emigrating to Australia. Not long afterwards, under their new captain Arnold Long, Sussex, who had won nothing under Greig, won the Gillette Cup.

In July 1978 there was another attempt by the ICC and WSC to resolve the tragic split in the game, of which the personal argument between Greig and Boycott was but one small example. David Clark and Jack Bailey, respectively Chairman and Secretary of the ICC, held secret discussions in New York with Andrew Caro and Lynton Taylor, two high-ranking WSC executives. The proposals for a compromise solution put by WSC at this meeting were discussed at the ICC meeting at Lord's on 25 and 26 July. Although the ICC statement which followed expressed a desire for the dialogue to continue, they found the proposals, which suggested that WSC cricket should be played somewhere in the world in every month of the year except July and

August, unacceptable on the following grounds:

1. Any 'official' tour to Australia by a Member Country would be disrupted by having to release some or all players for a number of days in December and January. The leading Australian players would also be unavailable for their domestic cricket in this period.

2. No 'official' tours allowing free selection of teams could be arranged between Member Countries during the period mid-December to mid-March (the prime period in most countries) because it is considered essential for national touring teams to remain intact during the course of a tour in another country.

3. It would be virtually impossible to arrange any worthwhile 'official' tours prior to mid-December, bearing in mind the proposed WSC commitments of India, New Zealand and Pakistan and the 'Supertest' champions' tour to Pakistan.

4. 'Official' tours between Member Countries after mid-March are not feasible other than in West Indies (until end-April) and in England (May–August). The WSC programme involves the 'Supertest' champions visiting West Indies in March/April and England in May/June.

5. The game throughout the world largely depends on the successful promotion of Test matches and tours, and any scheme which interferes so fundamentally with this vital aspect of cricket cannot meet with the approval of Member Countries.

WSC were asked to reconsider their proposals, and within forty-eight hours Mr Caro was summoning the cricket press to the penthouse suite at the Dorchester Hotel to explain that the original proposals had only been intended as a working guide. He now proposed that from 1979/80 the WSC five-day matches should not start in Australia until 1 February, but that they should be accorded first-class status on the understanding that WSC Australians would be available for official Test matches earlier in the year. At the end of the WSC 'series' the champions, who in WSC examples are always apparently presumed to be Australia, would undertake a tour of 'West Indies, England, Pakistan and India to enable the cricketing public in those countries to see the home challenge'. Short tours of approximately twenty days were envisaged in the West Indies in March/April, in England in May/June or September, and in Pakistan and India in October/November.

With the official calendar getting busier year by year, one's impression was that these proposals were still far too vague and ambitious ever to win acceptance by the ICC. Thus, with the impasse as wide as ever, the situation stood when England began their tour of Australia in October 1978. The most profound issue at stake now was not (if it ever had been) whether cricketers would be paid a fair wage; it was whether first-class cricket as it had been known for years would in future become a breeding-ground for a glossier version of the game run not by devoted administrators who had played the game and understood its traditions, but by businessmen, television companies and the players themselves.

Chapter Two

OF BREARLEY, BOYCOTT AND OTHERS

The sixteen players chosen for Australia at the beginning of September toured under the name of England rather than MCC, a 1977 decree of the Cricket Council which seemed both petty and unnecessary. The party contained one player whose choice had not been expected, Roger Tolchard, and two others who, though they had always been likely candidates, cannot have listened with complete lack of anxiety to the announcement of the party on BBC Radio: Geoff Miller and Derek Randall. Neither of these two had played for England in the last Test of the summer; Randall indeed had not played a Test since the previous winter tour. One man was disappointed despite being selected: Geoff Boycott. The position he had held as vice-captain on the last tour was given instead to Bob Willis. Boycott had captained England in four Tests only six months before.

Mike Brearley had already been chosen to lead the side in Australia and had played a major role in selecting it, along with the official selection committee of Alec Bedser (chairman), Ken Barrington, Charlie Elliott and John Murray. They were joined for the meeting to pick the side, held at the Victoria Sporting Club in London, by Peter May in his capacity as chairman of the cricket committee of the Test and County Cricket Board, and in a non-voting capacity by the TCCB secretary Donald Carr and by George Mann, acting as the nominee of Freddie Brown, Chairman of the Cricket Council. Shortly after the announcement J. T. Murray resigned as a selector. It was said in some press reports that he disagreed with the choice of Tolchard as reserve wicket-keeper and preferred Bairstow of Yorkshire, who had widely been considered more likely to get the job. It was also said that he wanted Boycott rather than Willis to be vice-captain. In fact, I understand that Murray resigned because of a number of small disagreements he had had during the season, because he felt that Boycott had been kept out of the side for too long, and because he felt that, rather than Bairstow or Tolchard, the reserve 'keeper should have been Downton of Kent, who had toured as Taylor's youthful understudy in Pakistan and New Zealand the year before.

The tour management had been chosen before the team was. Doug Insole, a player and later an administrator of great experience, took over the role of 'front-man' from Ken Barrington, who had done an excellent job as manager on the two previous winter tours. The 'Colonel', as he was affectionately known by his players, was assistant manager this time, with the playing affairs of the team now his primary responsibility. Bernard Thomas, as usual, took charge of physical training and all medical matters, not to mention numerous other odd jobs. Alec Bedser, who attended three Tests as Chairman of Selectors and who had been manager of the previous MCC tour to Australia, had been keen to go as manager again. He loved Australia and Australians loved him. But Insole was preferred, partly no doubt because of his previous close involvement in the ramifications of the Packer affair (he only resigned as chairman of the TCCB shortly before the tour began). It was always likely that there would be developments in the relationship between WSC and the cricket authorities of England and Australia, and although he no longer held an official TCCB post the new manager was an ideal person to have on the spot for consultations.

The partnership between Insole, with his blunt, honest approach, and Brearley, who tends to react against anything pompous, worked well from the start. Brearley's selection as captain had been far from automatic. The question as to who should lead an England side in Australia is traditionally a topic for debate in both public bar and private parlour. Brearley suffered more than his fair share of speculative gossip, however, and if he had not already developed a skin as thick as a cabinet minister's he surely did so during the course of 1978. Cricket mirrors life faithfully in the way it doles out its rewards and punishments. Brearley was happy to admit his good fortune the year before when Greig's defection led to his own elevation to the England captaincy after playing in only eight Test matches. Yet he had played an important part in the winning back of the Ashes and in the achieving of England's best home record (3–0) against Australia since 1886. His high intelligence, shrewdly applied to both strategy and tactics, his sympathetic approach to players and his coolness and resource under pressure had served himself and his side outstandingly well. He went on the tour to Pakistan and New Zealand as a well-established captain, with Geoff Boycott as his vice-captain. If the combination worked well together it was hoped that the tour would prove a successful dress-rehearsal for the defence of the Ashes in Australia a year later.

The cricket in Pakistan was, generally speaking, dull and wearisome for players and spectators alike. Brearley batted reasonably well as opening partner to Boycott, who was by some margin the side's most successful batsman although he could not rise above the funereal tempo of the cricket, largely because of the lifeless pitches. Then, late in the tour and playing in what on paper seemed to be the least significant match on the itinerary, a Sunday fixture against a Sind XI at Karachi on 15 January, Brearley had his left forearm broken by a lifting ball from Sikandar Bakht (promptly christened 'Sickunderthebat' by Brian Johnston) and had to return home to have a metal plate inserted in his arm in a Birmingham hospital. He later went to New Zealand as a journalist and British Airways representative and watched Geoff Boycott leading England in his place. The reports of respected first-hand witnesses suggest that Boycott handled the side well in the field but set an exaggeratedly pedestrian example with the bat, and that he did not always do the right thing off the field. One of the selectors, Ken Barrington, was manager of the team and it was, no doubt, partly on his evidence that Boycott was not retained as captain when Brearley became fit again and that he was later overlooked even as vice-captain in Australia. Of four matches under Boycott's command England drew two, won one and lost one – the first defeat ever recorded by England against New Zealand.

At home Brearley's success as captain continued, but his ability to hold a place in the side as a batsman was soon being questioned up and down the land. During the summer he took his record as Test captain to eight wins and five draws in thirteen Tests. Yet against Pakistan and New Zealand (in England) his scores were 38, 2, 0, 2, and 11 as opening batsman, and 58, 33 and 8 not out when he dropped down the order to number five. 'They should pick a side on merit first and then pick the captain, like the Aussies do', wailed his critics. Many people were viciously anti-Brearley, just as others were viciously anti-Boycott. It is extraordinary how vitriolic cricket-followers can be sometimes: almost always the misinformed who do not understand the game. The outstanding reason for Brearley being chosen to captain England in Australia

was the exceptionally successful fist he had made of the job so far,
granted of course that he had won against a somewhat demoral-
ised Australian side, a promising Pakistan team which had never
played anywhere near its potential, and a New Zealand team
undone by superb England bowling and fielding. Brearley had,
however, first been chosen to represent England as a batsman, not
as captain. It is true that he did not look a Test-class batsman in
1978, and indeed that he had never looked likely to be outstanding
in the highest company. But his form in 1978, for reasons which
may have included subconscious reaction from his broken arm as
well as the extra worries of his benefit season for Middlesex, was
far worse than normal. The 'normal' Brearley was an effective, in-
dustrious and brave batsman, more naturally gifted than some
would care to admit, but with the good sense to play to his limi-
tations. His first-class career average when the tour of Australia
began was higher than that of any of the other players in the side,
except only for Boycott's. He had a great opportunity not only to
become the third England captain since the war to return home
with the Ashes but also to improve on a modest Test batting
record.

Geoff Boycott had missed the traumatic 1974–75 tour of Australia for personal reasons, so one can only guess at how he
might have fared against the all-conquering Thomson and Lillee.
He could never have redressed the balance between the two
sides, but it would have been surprising if he had not done better
than most of the other England players on that tour. Under
Mike Smith in 1965–66 and Ray Illingworth in 1970–71 he had
been a conspicuous success, and now he was fully expected to be
so again after his phenomenal series against Australia at home in
1977 when, after missing thirty Test matches by his own choice,
he came back to score 107, 80 not out, 191, 39 and 25 not out.
Yet the disappointment of hearing that he had been overlooked
as vice-captain had been followed by much more shattering news
on his own doorstep. First he was obliged to return home from
his end-of-season holiday because his mother had died after a
long and miserable illness. Yorkshire had several weeks earlier
called a meeting of the cricket committee for the following day
and according to the testimony of their secretary, Joe Lister,
Boycott was rung up and asked whether he still wanted to attend
the meeting. He said that he would do so. At the meeting Boycott
was asked to leave the room when the question of the captaincy

arose. He returned to hear that he had been dismissed as captain and replaced by John Hampshire, but that he had been offered a two-year contract to continue playing for Yorkshire 'in the ranks'. To any man who had captained his county for eight years this would have been a severe blow; to Boycott, a man of intense personal pride, it was, coming so quickly after the news that he had lost the England vice-captaincy and that his mother had died, a disaster.

One must deal briefly with the unsavoury question as to whether the cricket committee should have postponed their decision. Boycott commented on television that they 'could not even wait until my mother was buried', so determined were they to get rid of him. It would certainly have seemed more civilised if the cricket committee, whose decision was soon ratified by a majority of Yorkshire's general committee, had waited until after the funeral. Their meeting had been arranged some time before, however, and Boycott had agreed to attend it. As to whether the decision should have been withheld, it is dangerous sometimes to make a decision and then to postpone an announcement. Something is nearly always leaked and a story of this significance would almost certainly have been so. It may also have been true that as John Hampshire was leaving the day after the meeting to have a holiday abroad on his way to playing for Tasmania during the Australian season the committee were anxious to let him know he had been appointed before he left. It is understood that Hampshire had told the committee that he would not have continued to play for Yorkshire under Boycott's captaincy, and that Ray Illingworth, who was to take over as Yorkshire's coach in 1979, had asked the club to settle the issue between Boycott and Hampshire before he arrived. Illingworth had privately made it plain that his preference was for Hampshire to be appointed. A majority of the Yorkshire team seem to have supported this view. They had often done well under Hampshire's captaincy in Boycott's absence due to injury or to Test match appearances.

Boycott himself, as he made abundantly clear in his controversial interview on the Michael Parkinson programme a few days after his sacking, and in a subsequent letter to the editor of *The Times*, felt that there had been members of the committee who had been eager to remove him almost from the moment of his appointment to take over from Brian Close during the 1970–71 tour of Australia. Under Close Yorkshire had been successful. Under

Boycott they had won nothing in eight years, though they had several times come close to victory. Boycott's personal performances certainly had nothing to do with this failure, because he was as prolific as ever. In the passionate self-defence which he now mounted he claimed that because he had never had the loyalty of the full cricket committee he had never been given a chance. He had lost several senior players such as Philip Sharpe, Tony Nicholson and Richard Hutton soon after taking over the captaincy, and he felt that the young players now in the side were reaching maturity and on the verge of bringing the county the success which it had come to regard as traditional. He was unwise enough to add, on the Parkinson Show, that he had no great players. He did not actually say 'apart from myself', but this was implicit. He is, of course, a great player. But in addition Chris Old has been a key member of the England side for many years now, and in Kevin Sharp and Bill Athey Yorkshire have two young batsmen whom everyone hopes *will* become great. That Yorkshire had disadvantaged themselves vis-à-vis the other sixteen county clubs by their praiseworthy policy of refusing to engage anyone not born in Yorkshire is also true. This is one reason why so many people outside the three Ridings sincerely hoped the county would win something again.

A certain discontented feeling in the Yorkshire dressing-room that Boycott did not always put his side's interests before his own, as a good captain must try to do, came to a head in a match at Northampton in July when Hampshire and Colin Johnson pointedly blocked for several overs after Boycott had taken up most of the permitted 100 overs in the first innings over a slow century. There was plenty of time for Yorkshire to have secured maximum batting bonus points if Hampshire and Johnson had batted at normal speed. They did not, however, and Yorkshire lost a point they should have won. Most public sympathy at the time was with Boycott. It was felt that if Hampshire had a complaint against his captain this public demonstration was not the way to go about changing things. At the time the Yorkshire committee backed their captain, issuing a severe reprimand to Hampshire and Johnson and saying that this was the end of the matter unless Hampshire transgressed again. As later events proved, however, it was definitely not the end of the matter.

Boycott refused to take his dismissal lying down. He fought back with all the stubbornness and tenacity he shows at the crease, supported by a pressure-group of members calling themselves the 'Reform Group', who succeeded in acquiring enough signatures on a petition calling for Boycott's reinstatement. They forced the convening of a special general meeting of the club for 9 December in order to express 'no confidence' in the cricket committee which had dismissed Boycott and to call for his reappointment as captain. (More of this in Chapter Four.)

If the Yorkshire committee had wished to react strongly to the things Boycott had said publicly about them they could almost certainly have punished him for breaking the TCCB regulation about not making derogatory public statements. They chose, however, to remain as silent and dignified as possible. On the day before the England team left for Australia, 23 October, Boycott put his case to the general committee; he was aided by his solicitor, who had advised him on many matters for several years. The committee would not alter its decision to dismiss him as captain, though it re-emphasised its offer of a two-year contract to remain as a player. I understand that the statement issued after this meeting was almost word for word the same as one the committee had prepared a week earlier but had decided against releasing. In other words, Boycott had been wasting his breath trying to convince the members that he was the victim of a conspiracy and that the decision should be changed. However, the statement seemed to me to be a succinct and sensible one which put the issue into proper perspective. Boycott, it said, was being replaced as captain 'because of what he is, not because of anything he has done'. His admirable dedication makes him a wonderful batsman, but his introspection does not enable him to inspire players to play to, or sometimes even above, their potential. It was, or should have been, as simple as that.

All this was not, of course, the ideal preparation for a cricket tour. However, Boycott was clearly relieved, when he got to Australia, to be free of the domestic pressures which had dominated his life in the preceding few weeks.

It was clear that Boycott was going to have a major role to play during the tour. He had scored more Test runs when it began than all the rest of the team put together. The figures are worthy of mention: Boycott 5675, the Rest 5435. In this century at any rate such an instance had happened only twice before in Anglo-Australian Tests – Walter Hammond in 1946–47 and Don Bradman in 1948 being the players concerned.

The only serious question-mark over the England side, as-suming that the faster bowlers remained fit and bowled to their potential, concerned the remainder of the batsmen. Brearley, as has been mentioned, had been forced to drop to number five in the order in the final Test of the 1978 season against New Zealand, and the only other opener in the party was Graham Gooch. He had first played for Essex as a middle-order batsman and in that role acquired a 'pair' against Lillee and Thomson in his first Test on a nasty wicket at Edgbaston in 1975; after making 6 and 31 at Lord's he was then dropped. At 21 this must have been a demoral-ising experience and he struggled for some time even in county cricket to look again like the confident, powerful player who had made a brilliant 77 for MCC against the Australians at Lord's earlier that summer. But in 1978 his county captain Keith Fletcher decided to ask Gooch to open in place of Brian Hardie, who was having a bad run. He quickly found a consistency he had previously lacked and two early-season centuries for Essex helped him back into the England side against Pakistan. He did well for England for the rest of the summer and when he made runs he did so in an attractive and positive way which started the innings on a much more adventurous and confident note than had been the English fashion in recent years. If there had been any doubt about his selection it was dissolved by his 91 not out in the first Test against New Zealand at the Oval. Then he im-pressively stepped up the scoring rate after tea when imminent rain seemed to threaten England's chances of completing their victory.

Gooch, however, was not the major 'discovery' of 1978: this was David Gower, the six-foot, fair, curly-haired left-hander who eased his way into Test cricket as a mature 21-year-old after scor-ing 33 and 114 not out in the Prudential Trophy matches against Pakistan. His first ball in Test cricket (against Pakistan at Edgbas-ton) was short and on his leg-stump. On the evidence of what had gone before, none of the other batsmen in the England side would have done anything but think: 'Good, that's a fairly friendly first ball. I'll go back and play it carefully back to the bowler. Nice to get such an early indication of the bounce of the pitch.' Gower's automatic cricketing thought process was different: 'Ah, a long-hop, good; smack!' With a swift sure pivot of the feet the ball was hooked effortlessly for four. Blessed with some luck at times, notably when he tended to chip the ball lazily through the hands of some obligingly butter-fingered mid-ons, and also when he played the occasional airy shot near gully, he continued to play gracefully, responsibly and successfully at the top level for the rest of the summer, making 58, 56, 39 (a fine innings on a difficult pitch at Headingley ended by a debatable ·l.b.w. decision which went in favour of Sarfraz Nawaz), 111 (at the Oval against New Zealand), 11, 46, 71 and 46. From the moment that this impressively self-assured, phlegmatic and balanced young man played his first innings for Leicestershire in 1975 it was clear that Kent, where he had been born and educated (at King's Canterbury), had let a special talent slip away from them. His form for his county in three-day cricket has, oddly enough, been very inconsistent but in whatever type of cricket he played he remained a potential matchwinner.

Clive Radley is in every way a contrast. With his stumpy figure and highly functional if unorthodox batting technique he could never be described as graceful, nor does the game come as easily to him as it appears to come to Gower. Yet throughout his career, which began in 1964 after he had gone to Middlesex on trial from his native Norfolk, Radley had been constantly underrated. When Brearley broke his arm in Pakistan Radley was summoned to Karachi from Australia where he was coaching in the employment of Kerry Packer. He did not play in the final match against Pakistan, but his chance came in the second Test against New Zealand when England won at Christchurch to avenge their historic defeat at Wellington. Radley made 15 in his only innings here but retained his place and revealed much of the grit and ability to concentrate in an extraordinary marathon in the third match at Auckland where he reached his first Test hundred in eight hours and seven minutes, going on to make 158 in only a little less than eleven hours at the crease. He was, it should be added, playing to orders and he showed the other side of his batting nature with some rapid scoring for England in the Prudential Trophy matches the following summer. He also scored a second hundred in the first Test of the English season, and although many people had doubts about his ability to control the high bounce of the ball in Australia he made it very difficult for the selectors to leave him out because of the consistency of his batting for the remainder of the season. However his inclusion, along with that of Miller and Randall, meant that Chris Tavaré, a brilliant slip fielder and clearly a player of high class as the most successful of the many outstanding Kent batsmen in 1978, had to be content with a position as first reserve. He travelled to Australia instead as one of the lucky recipients of the laudable Whitbread scholarships, along with Wayne Larkins of Northamptonshire, Mike Gatting of Middlesex, who had also come close to selection, and Jonathan Agnew, the 19-year-old fast bowler on Leicestershire's staff who looked to be the only young cricketer in England who might develop into a bowler of the highest pace.

Derek Randall was making a welcome return to the England team after a season in the wilderness. He had begun his Test career so promisingly in India in 1976–77, concluding his first tour on a euphoric note with his 174 in the Centenary Test at Melbourne. An unfortunate injury to his elbow prevented him getting more runs than he did against Australia at home in 1977, but no one was expecting him to have such a miserable tour to Pakistan and New Zealand. He was dropped from the side when he got home, and apart from one successful appearance in the Prudential Trophy against New Zealand (41 off 40 balls) he could not force his way back in. This was due more to the success of Gower and Radley than to any lack of form on Randall's part for Nottinghamshire. Indeed he had an outstanding season for them, scoring more runs (1525) than any other member of the touring party in first-class matches in 1978. Randall, the fidgety little comic with his effervescent fielding and cheerful mien, was sure of a welcome in Australia and especially in Melbourne where his great innings had saved the Centenary Test from anti-climax and made it instead into an unforgettable match. However, the very first comment I overheard when he went in to bat in the first match of the tour was: 'Come on, Randall, you great Sheila; you couldn't get a kick out of an electric chair.'

Like Gower and Gooch, Geoff Miller was a product of representative England schools cricket. Mainly because of his off-spin bowling he had got his chance for young England but despite playing eleven consecutive Tests for England in 1977 and 1978 (three each in Pakistan and New Zealand and the first five in England in 1978) he had still not established himself as a Test all-rounder. Unlike the other two all-rounders in the side, Botham with his boisterous self-confidence and Edmonds with his quiet assurance, Miller played his cricket with a certain diffidence. But in the last Test of the summer Miller's absence had been noticeable because the England tail had begun dangerously high with

Taylor at number seven, and he was therefore being pencilled in to the Test side when the tour began. But this, he knew, was likely to be his make-or-break tour. It was a worry that despite making 98 not out for England against Pakistan at Lahore he had still not made a first-class hundred when the tour began (despite having batted high in the order for Derbyshire for three seasons), and his best bowling figures in Test cricket to date were a modest three for 99 against New Zealand at Auckland. But he was a useful 'bits and pieces' cricketer with a sound temperament – a capable enough off-spinner in favourable conditions and a batsman who, though he lacked any great power, had a definite talent which everyone was hoping he would develop in Australia.

About Ian Botham there were no such doubts, except that one feared he might be unable to live up to the immensely high standards he had set himself in his eleven Test matches. It is really only necessary to quote his phenomenal figures when the tour began to underline the point. He had already scored three Test hundreds (in fact, he scored three in four Tests, one against New Zealand at Christchurch and two at home against Pakistan) and was averaging 41 in Tests with the bat despite a modest start against Australia in 1977. As a fast-medium bowler of immense hostility, stamina and strength, with a priceless ability to move the ball late both ways but primarily towards the slips, he had taken 64 Test wickets at an average of sixteen apiece, and he had already taken five or more wickets in a Test innings on eight occasions. Against Pakistan at Lord's he made 108 and took 8 for 34 in a humid atmosphere in the second innings when the Pakistan batsmen found him virtually unplayable. After his eleven Tests, indeed, he had either scored a century or taken five wickets in an innings on nine occasions. In addition he had clung on to every slip chance that had come his way. It was Ken Barrington who had first described him as a new Keith Miller, but at the rate he was now going there would be few to compare with Botham himself.

Botham had enjoyed a season which quite apart from his Test successes was outstanding. He took a hundred first-class wickets for the first time, mainly for Somerset, although he also opened the season at Lord's in April with a hat-trick for MCC against Middlesex (all bowled) and in both first-class and one-day matches he scored 1024 runs and took 138 wickets. After all this he needed a long rest, so it was not the disaster it might have been when he injured his wrist just before the start of the tour.

Apart from Botham, no one had made greater progress in quicker time than Phil Edmonds. When he first played for England against Australia in 1975 he had a sensational spell of bowling to start him off (5–28 at Headingley) but he would have been the first to admit that fortune smiled on him that day, and the renowned skill of Derek Underwood kept Edmonds out of the side until Mr Packer came along to open up some gaps in the England side. In Pakistan and New Zealand in 1977–78 Edmonds developed a more rhythmical flow in what was already a classical left-arm spinner's action, thanks to some assiduous practice and sound advice from Geoff Boycott and Ken Barrington. Already a very good bowler he became as reliable as Underwood himself, a formidable opponent to any batsman even on good wickets, and since his batting was more than useful and his all-round fielding was brilliant he was very soon looking an indispensable member of the England side.

Chris Old, when fit, had long been one of the best fast-medium bowlers in the world. Two things about him had changed in the past two seasons. In the first place, one had given up hope that his batting would ever be effective enough in Test cricket for him to be considered a serious all-rounder at that level. His Test batting average when the tour began was a mere 14. However his bowling, now a little gentler in pace, had acquired an almost perfectly grooved rhythm. Having abandoned the idea that he could get many batsmen out through sheer speed, he now seemed to be able to cut or swing the ball even on the sunniest days and the best wickets. He was still sadly prone to injury, such as the trouble in his shoulder and neck which caused him to miss the last two Tests of 1978 after he had begun the first series of the summer by taking four wickets in five balls against Pakistan at Edgbaston.

The tour to Australia was his second full visit there, after a disappointing one four years earlier under Mike Denness, and his sixth major tour overseas. With Botham and Willis apparently certain to be in the Test side Old knew that he faced the sternest competition from Lever and Hendrick. On the other hand he was now, after 40 Tests, at his peak, and if he was ever going to have a really successful tour this was the time to do it. There was a distinct feeling amongst his fellow-players that given his natural ability and physique 'Chilly' ought to have achieved even more than he had done. But Old was not blessed with the single-minded dedication of a Boycott or a Willis. He plays his hardest on the field and then likes to relax with a beer off it. Perhaps it is hopeless trying to make someone what he is not. Still, one cannot help recalling the rueful comment Bob Willis once made about him: 'If I only had half Chris Old's ability . . .'

Willis, perhaps, was doing himself a disservice, for though his action has never been a thing of beauty and his build, at nearly six feet six inches, is nothing like the idea of the classical, squarely constructed fast bowler, he has nevertheless always possessed the ability to bowl fast and bounce the ball awkwardly. But he too had changed and improved since the previous tour of Australia. His performance then, with injured knees, had been a worthy example of his courage and determination. But he has no sterner critic than himself, and after having operations on both knees, which he likened to a 20,000-mile service on a motor car, he came back into the England side against the West Indies in 1976 and did not look back. The match in which he returned was the extraordinary game at Leeds in which the brilliant West Indies batting side began with 147 for no wicket (Greenidge and Fredericks) before lunch off only 27 six-ball overs, reached 330 for two by tea and 437 for nine off 83 overs at the end of a dizzy day in which they therefore averaged five runs an over *on the first day of a Test match*. But Willis, with three for 71, escaped the worst of the carnage, and he took five for 42 in the second innings to bowl out West Indies for 191 so that in the end England came close to winning. On this one very rare occasion he had the support of genuine speed at the other end because John Snow and Alan Ward were also playing, along with Willis probably the fastest bowlers England had produced in a decade. In that series the West Indies bombarded England's batsmen with an almost ceaseless barrage of speed from Roberts, Holding and Daniel, and Willis, convinced that Tests could be won by speed alone, has always longed for a bowler of equal pace at the other end. But Snow was now past his peak, Ward was hopelessly plagued by injuries, and 'Big Bob' had to soldier on alone. 'I finally got it through my thick skull', he says, 'that you have to be really fit to bowl fast.'

Henceforward he set himself even higher standards of physical fitness. He began to go on daily five-mile runs and allied this to a programme of exercises developed by a German doctor. Thus he built up his stamina and the niggling injuries which once used to keep him out of cricket several times a season disappeared. He felt mentally fresher and more confident that he would not break down. The rehabilitation was completed during the Centenary Test in Melbourne early in 1977 when he learned a semi-hypnotic method of mental relaxation and self-motivation from an Australian specialist. The Australian cricketers felt the full force of Willis 'mark two' in England the following summer, and when he got to Australia again Willis could look back to that Test at Headingley in 1976 and realise with pride that he had not missed a Test since then and had taken 104 wickets at twenty runs apiece.

He was also given a new responsibility for the tour, the vice-captaincy. His sense of humour and his ability to encourage other players made him an ideal deputy to Brearley, although his experience of captaincy itself was scant. One guesses that he had no desire to find himself suddenly captaining his country in a crucial Test in Australia as John Edrich had done on the previous tour when Denness decided to rest himself.

One of the fascinating questions about the team when the tour began was whether Old, Lever or Hendrick would share the new ball with Willis. Lever and Hendrick had been friendly rivals for several seasons, with Lever having the better record overseas and Hendrick, whose natural environment always seems to be wind-swept Derby on a cold, grey day in May, usually being preferred at home. Hendrick indeed, who shared with Willis and all the Derbyshire side a belief in the need to keep fit by a hard programme of physical training, was determined to show that the formidable qualities of his bowling at home *could* be transplanted overseas. He still remembers with remorse the worst moment of his career when his hamstring snapped as he was walking back to bowl at the start of the third Test in Melbourne in 1974–75.

John Lever had no such painful memories, or, if he did, no one remembered them. He never seems to break down; he never stops trying; he swings the ball if there is any possibility of it swinging; and if he is not getting any help from the pitch or the atmosphere he will still bowl tidily for long periods. Yet since his remarkable Test debut in India in 1976 when he took seven for 46 and scored 50 to boot he had only played for England twelve times, such was the competition for a place in the side. He began the tour, however, quietly confident after a very successful season in which he had taken 106 first-class wickets at a cost of fifteen runs each and been awarded a cheque by the Lord's Taverners for being 'the cricketers' cricketer'.

Brearley's strong hand of bowlers was completed by his own county off-spinner, the tall, quietly spoken, dry-witted cockney who was making his first official overseas tour at the relatively advanced age of 26. His opportunity would certainly have come sooner had he not been kept out of the Middlesex side by the little maestro Titmus. But John Emburey was no tyro. He had been recognised on the county circuit as one of the steadiest and most dangerous spinners in the game almost immediately after putting on the Titmus mantle, and his experience and reputation had grown after a successful season of grade cricket in Melbourne in the last Australian season. Oddly enough, however, it seemed likely that he would only attain a regular place in the England side if he could develop his batting enough for him to be considered an all-rounder. Largely due to the fact that Bob Taylor, the best wicket-keeper in the world, was not at Test level half the batsman Alan Knott had been, there was a greater need in the present England side for the bowlers to make runs. Emburey had taken over as England's off-spinner from Miller in the last Test against New Zealand and had made a good impression. He was indeed widely considered to be a better bowler than Miller. But the selectors had resolved never to go into another Test match, at least until the series was safe, with a tail starting at number seven. So to get into the side Emburey needed not only to make a case for himself as the off-spinner but also as a man who could get useful runs lower down the order. Curiously enough his chances would also be increased if his Middlesex spinning partner Edmonds could also develop further his considerable batting potential. The more genuine all-rounders a side can have, the better.

So, finally, to the wicket-keepers. Taylor had Kerry Packer to thank for his belated recognition. He had for many seasons been one of the most polished craftsmen in the game, an exemplary sportsman and professional. If he had only been a batsman of Knott's class, or if the front-line England batting had been more reliable, he would have had many more Test caps than the thirteen he had collected by the time the tour began. At the age of 37 he had grasped his belated chance with both hands, as he had 'grasped' almost every chance that had come his way behind the stumps in eighteen years of keeping wicket for a living, and there were still a good many days of his Indian summer to run.

His deputy Roger Tolchard was a better batsman, good enough indeed to have played a vital part in winning for England the first Test he played in, against India at Calcutta. The critics of his selection for this tour did not deny his ability as a batsman, nor the likely usefulness of his role as a utility player. They agreed that he would be a capable enough wicket-keeper in the less important matches who could come into a Test match in an emergency and do a sound job. If things went as well as they had for him under Greig in India he might again even challenge for a batting place in his own right. There were, after all, only six specialist batsmen in the party and on every tour someone is bound to fail. But Tolchard's was an expedient selection which took no account of the fact that Taylor could not go on for ever. It would have been more informative for the future had Bairstow of Yorkshire or Downton of Kent or any of the other young wicket-keepers bidding to take over from Taylor been given experience from the outset of the tour. The selectors, however, believed that their primary job was to pick a side to bring back the Ashes. They were justifiably confident, after England's recent run of success and Australia's vast upheaval following the Packer earthquake, that they had a side capable of doing so. They were a settled combination, used to success.

Australia in sharp contrast had only a few players considered to be certain selections when the tour began. Bob Simpson, who had come out of retirement to captain an untried side against India and West Indies the season before, retired a second time when the selectors told him that he would not be guaranteed a place against England. Simpson had served the cause well, leading Australia to a 3–2 success in the fascinating series against India and passing on the qualities of dedication and concentration to his young side during a traumatic tour of the West Indies. Although Simpson himself no longer had reactions sharp enough to cope with the furious speed of the West Indies fast bowlers, who had been too good for all comers in the inaugural World Series matches, several of his players – notably Yallop, Wood, Toohey, Clark, Higgs, Yardley and Laughlin – had emerged with credit from the tour. The optimists in Australia believed that this nucleus had been given a crash course in Test cricket, first by the best spinners in the world, the Indians, then by the best fast bowlers, the West Indians. 'We are more experienced than the "Poms" think', the argument went. 'We'll have the right attitude, which is more than Greg Chappell's mob did in England, and we don't think much of the England batting. All those typical English seamers will be brought down to earth out here, too.' Events would tell whether they were whistling in the dark or whether the odds of four-to-one on England were ridiculously unbalanced.

Chapter Three

EARLY UPS AND DOWNS

'She's a lovely ship', Walter Hammond once said as he looked over the rails of the SS *Orion*, Australia-bound in the merciless heat of the Red Sea, 'but I wish she-well-had wings.' Sir Neville Cardus quotes the remark in his description of the outward voyage of Gubby Allen's MCC side in 1936. He evokes marvellously the somnolent, artificial life which was led on board, the way that C. B. Fry would hold court on deck to admiring audiences, how Verity read *The Seven Pillars of Wisdom* from beginning to end, Duckworth danced the night away, and Cardus himself saw Australia for the first time through his port-hole.

How different in 1978! If Walter Hammond had been a passenger on the jet which finally landed the England team in Adelaide after 29 wearying hours he might well have sighed for those leisurely days when the arrival at Fremantle after several weeks on the sea was followed by a gentle build-up to the serious business of Test cricket. In Hammond's day the team would spend three weeks acclimatising in Perth; the journey across the continent, some three thousand miles, which can now be done in a few hours, then involved three days' journeying by train. Instead of five Test matches in five months the present team would play six in four. There would be less time spent in private homes or in seeing the country, much more spent in hotels and the big cities. Cricket was now as much a business as a sport.

It is commonplace perhaps these days, but nevertheless a minor miracle even to the most seasoned traveller, to move from autumn in one country to spring in another in little more than a day. The autumn of 1978, in the south of England at least, was a particularly beautiful one and the mellow warmth of the weather we left behind actually compared favourably for once with that which greeted the England party in South Australia. Not long after Brearley and Insole had played the first barrage of questions from press and broadcasters with cautious straight bats it was raining hard and the 'Poms' were being gently chided by the glib, fast-talking disc jockeys, whose words flow like fountains all day be-

tween the records on the commercial radio stations, for bringing
their dirty weather with them. This is not to say that the welcome
accorded to the party, players, officials and press alike, was anything other than friendly. There are few people more hospitable
than Australians.

All that anyone wanted to do at first, however, was to sleep.
When I awoke the first thing I saw in the broad park beyond the
road opposite the hotel was the lone, track-suited figure of Bob
Willis jogging his way round the perimeter with long strides, his
head bent, in contemplation no doubt of the responsibilities
which lay ahead of him. It was an exaggeration to say that
England's chances depended upon Willis remaining fit but he,
more than any other player, Boycott possibly excluded, was the
most feared man in the team in the eyes of the Australian cricketers. Boycott, incidentally, was inevitably the first to pick up a
bat and don his pads, having his first knock of the tour in front of
the Members' Stand at the Adelaide Oval whilst most of the rest of
the team were in the showers at the end of an opening session of
running and muscle-stretching under the experienced eyes of Bernard Thomas. Boycott was obviously delighted to have a bat in his
hands again.

The only absentee from the practice which gradually developed
in intensity over the first few days was Ian Botham, who had been
the victim of an unfortunate accident shortly before the team had
left England. He had been given a farewell party by friends at a
pub near his home in North Lincolnshire (an interesting place, incidentally, for someone Cheshire-born and Somerset-bred to
choose to live) and was visiting the lavatory before leaving. The
lavatory door swung back at him on its spring and Botham in-
stinctively put up a hand (fortunately his left one) to stop it
swinging back and hitting him. Sadly his fending-off movement
propelled the hand through a glass partition in the door and as he
withdrew it he severely lacerated his wrist on the jagged glass. He
was taken to hospital and ten stitches were inserted into the
wound. Luckily for Botham the tendons of the wrist were not
harmed, but he was forced to travel to Australia with his hand
and wrist swathed in a large bandage and his arm in a sling. Perhaps it was a blessing in disguise, for no one had needed the rest
at the end of the season in England more than he did. It was too
much, however, to expect all the Australians (some of whom
knew the story of Botham's belligerent public argument with Ian

Chappell two years before at a bar in Melbourne) to accept this innocent explanation of the injury. 'Botham', wrote one journalist with a sense of humour, 'injured his arm in a fracas with a pub: the pub won!' Botham himself was unworried and uncomplaining. There were four months ahead in which to conquer Australia, so a few weeks of inactivity could be cheerfully borne.

Whilst the remainder of the team practised assiduously in cool but pleasant weather, spending almost as much time sprinting, jogging and stretching muscles as they did in the nets (as good as any in the world, reckoned Ken Barrington, who had experience of plenty), many Australian eyes were fixed on the New South Wales Equity Court in Sydney, where a judgement was expected any day after a twelve-day hearing in which the Australian Cricket Board were contesting the right of Jeff Thomson to play for World Series Cricket. Thomson, in fact, had already signed for Mr Packer's company after a sad saga. He had originally been one of the mass of Australian players who signed for World Series, but he then withdrew during the tour of England because he was already contracted to a Brisbane radio station and he was, of course, a vital member of the Test side which played under Bob Simpson against India in Australia. In common with all the other cricketers who played in State cricket in 1977–78 Thomson was required to sign a contract which was intended to bind him to official cricket in return for his share of the sponsorship money available so long as he played for Queensland. When he was picked to tour the West Indies Thomson also signed a tour contract.

Thomson did not handle his own financial affairs successfully. Despite a healthy income, well-deserved after all his success for Australia, he got into debt, mainly because of a sports shop in Brisbane which went bust. He was, therefore, ripe for the plucking and World Series offered him a three-year contract for 90,000 Australian dollars – in addition, it was widely believed, to buying his house in Brisbane and leasing it back to him at a nominal rent.

In the action brought against Thomson and WSC the Board sought an order declaring that the two contracts signed by Thomson, in November 1977 and February 1978, were valid, and also an order prohibiting WSC from inducing him to break the contracts. In the decision made by Justice Kearney on 3 November the first contract, known as the Standard Form of Agreement, was found to be an unreasonable restraint of trade, and therefore unenforceable. The tour contract, however, was found to be valid and in force and Thomson was therefore ordered not to play for WSC until 31 March 1979.

Thomson, whose evidence had been described by the judge as unreliable, said at first that he would leave cricket alone for the rest of the season. He had played just one game for Queensland in which he produced record figures of six for 18 against South Australia. It was less than four years since he had played in his second Test match, the momentous game against England at Brisbane which had so radically altered the course of his life. Altogether he had taken 145 wickets at a cost of 27 runs each in his 32 Tests for Australia.

One felt after the trial that this was certainly not the last that would be heard of the man known throughout the cricketing world as 'Thommo'. But for the moment he told waiting journalists that he was 'going fishing'. He would, he said, 'go out with some mates of mine and go after reef fish; I'll catch any fish which brings a dollar.'

As far as official cricket was concerned, the most significant fact was that World Series Cricket would not be able to boast of an emotional counter-attraction to the Ashes series: the nostalgic reunion of Lillee and Thomson. Thomson's solicitor Frank Gardiner later said in a newspaper interview that 'people claiming to act on behalf of the Australian Cricket Board' had offered Thomson the captaincy of the Australian team in succession to Simpson, plus certain guarantees on the composition of the team to play England. The assertion might have carried some genuine weight if Mr Gardiner had been able to say who these 'unofficial emissaries' were. The Board denied any knowledge of all this.

In the end the Board magnanimously allowed Thomson to play for WSC in the West Indies in February and March 1979 before his contract expired. In return WSC abandoned their attempts to appeal against the judgement.

Thus the sordid story unfolded in the early weeks of the England tour. Now that it was known for certain that Thomson would not be playing in the official Test series the Australians could begin to look for an opening pair to unsettle the long odds being quoted against their regaining the Ashes, and the first month of the tour was to see a series of virtual trials for those aspiring to the famous baggy green cap. To a good many cricketers that cap still meant more than all the dollars which its possession now guaranteed.

For Brearley's team the first week of acclimatisation had been gentle, pleasant and uneventful. The matches began with a visit to the South Australian River Country, the river being the Murray, the longest in Australia, which meanders its wide, ponderous way from the Macpherson mountain range in Queensland down to the sea in South Australia. Renmark, where the opening fixture was played, is a prosperous little country town with a population of some 6000, who are almost exclusively involved in the growing of grapes and citrus fruit and in the production of wine and dried fruit. The prosperity owes everything to the Murray and to irrigation, because the basic property of the terrain in these parts is flat desert. No one was quite prepared for this and the passengers on the Ansett Airlines Fokker Friendship which landed in Renmark on a fine, sunny morning were a little surprised to look out of the port-holes and see not the familiar tarmac of a runway but red dust pitted with a variety of weeds which would have outdone even my own vegetable patch.

The mayor of Renmark met the plane himself and soon explained that the airstrip was no longer in regular use because of the roaming kangaroos which tended to be a hazard for aircraft trying to land. He may have been pulling our legs, but I don't think so. The plane, in any case, was in good hands. The pilot, Alan Crabb, had been an Australian rules football champion and was renowned as one of Ansett's best. Some apprehension was expressed when it was known that he would be watching the cricket all day, but he must have resisted the temptation to refresh himself too much with the local wine or beer because he made an exemplary take-off in the evening by the light of a row of kerosene flares, having been guided out to the 'airstrip' by the tail-lights of a lorry.

The whole day had a pleasantly old-fashioned, parochial ring about it. The visit of the England team was the biggest event in the area since the Duke and Duchess of Kent had visited in 1969, and those who could remember far enough back still talked about the visit of Freddie Brown's team to Renmark in 1950–51. A local bowler called Lou Curtis took all but one of the ten MCC wickets on that occasion, when MCC won by an innings in a two-day match. Nine for 60 in 14.3 overs was his remarkable analysis on that distant day, and as a reward Curtis was put straight into

South Australia's Sheffield Shield side. A medium-pace bowler, he was given very few overs, playing with ten men he had not met before, and he never represented the state again.

There were no such heroics this time on either side. The pitch was a true one but it did not have much life or bounce, which made it difficult for batsmen to entertain the enthusiastic crowd of a little under 4000 as much as they would like to have done. From England's point of view, however, there was some useful practice for both batsmen and bowlers in an uneventful drawn match. Brearley, Gooch, Radley, Gower and Randall all had at least fifty minutes at the crease and no one played better than Radley, whose 64 was by some margin the highest score of the day. Poor man, he was soon to be brought painfully to earth with a reminder that not many Australian pitches are as lifeless as this one proved to be.

The serious cricket began in the magnificent surroundings of the Adelaide Oval on 3 November. Brearley lost a toss he would greatly like to have won on a beautiful day, and there was a suitably peaceful start to the first-class cricket with even the hostile opening sallies of Willis unable to steal the glory from the ground itself, with the cathedral, the tree-covered hills beyond and the elegant botanical gardens which border half the perimeter all shimmering under a cloudless blue sky.

Willis gave the Test opener Rick Darling plenty of bouncers in an opening spell which was not particularly impressive, but he had read his man correctly because having hooked him well for two and four in his fifth over Darling tried to repeat the shot to a very high bouncer. He made contact with both feet off the ground but merely succeeded in lobbing a catch to square-leg. It was England's sole success before lunch, although Old bowled well without luck and survived one nasty moment when in fielding off his own bowling he dislocated a finger. He came off in agony and with everyone wondering how serious the injury might be, only for Bernard Thomas to meet him at the picket gate, put the finger back into place in five seconds flat, and with a quick slap of the face send Old back to finish his over.

Old, as it turned out, was the only England bowler (one over from Gooch excepted) not to take a first-innings wicket, but until the last session of the day the honours went mainly to the stocky right-handed opener John Nash, who once played for Hampshire 2nd XI and had taken several seasons to establish himself in the South Australian side. He scored most of the 29 runs which came off Willis in two overs after lunch and he continued to cut and drive his way to a chanceless hundred, his second in succession for the state. Good impressions were also made by Ian McLean, who pronounces his name like the toothpaste, and by the 21-year-old all-rounder Peter Sleep, who batted positively in the first innings and later bowled his leg-spinners well with a good, high action.

England, for all their intense practice, were a little rusty in the field for a while. Someone who is considered in England to have a good arm can suddenly find himself struggling to reach the stumps with his throw from the more distant parts of a large Australian field, and at Adelaide there are 208 yards from sightscreen to sightscreen. (The width, 138 yards, is on the other hand rather less than the average.) In addition the ball comes faster through the air in Australia, especially in the dry atmosphere typical of Adelaide, and this probably accounted for the fact that Lever was unable to reach a lofted hook, Miller was slow to react to another half-chance at short-leg, and the normally unimpeachable Gower missed quite a simple catch at cover.

The bowlers, too, Willis in particular, were inclined to bowl either too short or too full a length, but there was plenty of time in hand to sort out the best length to bowl in Australian conditions. In any case, they worked their way through the bulk of the South Australian batting and after losing the toss the state's close-of-play score of 281 for nine represented a fair start for the touring team. No one shone more brightly in the field than Bob Taylor, about whose 'keeping the only suitable adjective is 'impeccable'. The only remarkable feature of his performance on this occasion, indeed, was not that he took four catches and a stumping but that he let through two byes.

It took forty minutes for England to finish the South Australian innings in the morning. Willis was unable to bowl because of a blistered toe, and the last-wicket pair added thirty comfortable runs before Miller had Attenborough l.b.w. sweeping. Miller finished with figures of three for 41, possibly a little flattering, but he had bowled generally tidily and been more prepared to give the ball air than he sometimes is.

At ten to twelve on Saturday morning the first and eagerly awaited confrontation between Geoff Boycott and Rodney Hogg began. Boycott turned the first ball to fine leg for a single and did not face another for three overs. In that short time Hogg bowled his way to a likely first Test cap and catapulted England back four years to the time when they first faced Jeff Thomson. This fair-haired 27-year-old milkman turned insurance salesman is squarely constructed, the ideal build for a fast bowler, and from the moment that he approached the wicket with a crouching run-up and unleashed his first ball from a long final delivery stride it was clear that he possessed exceptional pace. He dismissed Gooch in his second over as Gooch went back to a lifting delivery and got an outside edge to the wicket-keeper. Radley got off the mark with an involuntary four through the wicket-keeper's gloves off a no-ball, then was beaten for pace by the next one which lifted off a length and struck him a fearful blow above the left eye as he moved into line and vainly tried to fend the ball away. He staggered back dislodging the bails, and was taken off the field with blood streaming from his forehead. His first words in the dressing-room, after checking that he was out, were: 'If they all bounce like that out here, I'm b . . . d!' Seven stitches were inserted into the wound in hospital. Gower came in, looking cooler than he can have been feeling, and was very nearly caught third ball in the gully by Sleep, who in truth was wide awake and did well to get two hands to the chance before the ball popped out.

From this nadir, Boycott, calm, correct and sound, and Gower, sound enough in defence but dangerously inclined to spar outside his off-stump, took England to 42 for one at lunch. In the afternoon both prospered, Gower still getting away with some firm-footed wafting outside his off-stump but also timing his offside strokes beautifully in hitting Hogg for five fours in the course of two overs. Boycott looked in no trouble and England seemed well on the way to a big score when three wickets fell in the last quarter of an hour before tea. Gower was l.b.w. to the medium-paced left-arm bowler Attenborough after scoring 73 in 150 minutes of in-and-out batting which nevertheless included 12 fours, almost exclusively through the covers. Then Hogg, brought back to welcome the new batsman Brearley by Blewett, the South Australian captain, got the unexpected scalp of Boycott, whose flawless innings ended when he went back instead of forward to a ball of full length and was given out l.b.w. Boycott lingered long enough to indicate that he was disappointed, more with himself at missing the ball than because of any dissatisfaction with umpire French. Remarkably after batting for three hours this was only the seventh ball from Hogg that Boycott had faced.

Miller faced five balls before turning Hogg to short leg, and the

new hero thus went in to tea with figures of four for 38. Brearley
drew his sting for a while afterwards and batted soundly, if without much attacking intent, for nearly two hours before being
yorked for 27. Had it not been for some powerful driving by
Edmonds England's position would have been worse than it was
on the Saturday evening. However, it had been a most encouraging two days for the wider cause of Australian cricket. The
'defector' Thomson had been defeated in the Equity Court; Hogg
had looked like a genuine replacement for him – even if doubts
existed about his stamina because of a minor asthmatic condition;
and, simultaneously in Sydney, Peter Toohey was putting an indifferent start to the season behind him with a sparkling innings of
153 against the Sheffield Shield champions Western Australia.
One could hear, and almost feel, the interest in the coming Test
matches starting to build.

Phillippe Edmonds, who had made such vast strides as an all-
round cricketer in the past year, was largely responsible for keeping England in the match on the third day. He took his overnight
32 not out to 38 not out before losing Old, caught in the deep off
Sleep for 4. Willis could neither bat nor bowl because of a poi-
soned toe on his left foot, so with England out for 232, 79 runs behind, South Australia had a great opportunity to strike an early
blow both for the Australian cause generally and for their own as
well, since they were tired of being called the weakest cricketing
state.

Old quickly removed Darling in the second innings, but Nash
and McLean played well until the spinners came on. Miller again
bowled well and had Nash stumped by Taylor, who finished with
five catches and three stumpings in the match, but it was
Edmonds, with his perfect action and control and his ability on
this pitch to get some considerable turn at times, who did the main
damage. McLean stayed longest for a very promising 52, but two
run-outs due to direct hits on the stumps (one by Randall, the substitute for Willis, the other by Edmonds) helped towards the lowly
total of 149 which left England only 229 to win.

They first had to contend with Rodney Hogg, however, and in
his third over he had Boycott l.b.w. for the second time in the
match, this time for only six. Boycott was moving across his
stumps and Hogg's first Test cap seemed assured. Radley, bravely
but possibly unwisely, came in with seven stitches still in his cut
forehead and was caught third ball off Sincock for three. He had

never looked like buckling down in true Radley fashion. But the admirable Gower joined Gooch, who had dealt with Hogg's early burst well enough, and these two took the score to 67 before Gooch was bowled for 23 sweeping at a leg-spinner from Sleep which turned a long way. Gower, driving and pulling with great authority, and Brearley took England to within 141 runs of victory with one day to go. It seemed a straightforward affair. If Gower could get going again on the cloudy, cooler fourth morning of the match England would win. If he were out early they would struggle, and very probably lose.

In the event Gower reached a faultless fifty with a few more thoroughbred strokes but then drove on the up at a wide delivery from Hogg's opening partner, Sincock, and edged a comfortable catch to first slip. England's score was 100 for four. Their captain was in residence, defending stoutly but not doing anything to suggest that he was capable of taking on the dominating role that was now required of him. His new partner, Miller, had a great opportunity to stress his claims for a Test place which had already been enhanced by the five wickets he had taken with his steady off-spinners. His method, generally speaking, is to play back rather than forward, contrary to most English players, and this in theory equips him well to cope with Australian conditions. Ironically, it was in playing half-forward to Sincock that he was struck on the back foot by a ball which moved and kept low.

The decline now gathered momentum. Taylor played an indifferent half-cut and was well caught by an outstanding fielder, Jeff Langley (nephew of the former Australian wicket-keeper Gil Langley, who is now Speaker in the South Australian state parliament). Edmonds was greeted with some dangerous out-swingers by Attenborough, who had him caught behind fourth ball, and then Brearley took a risky single to Darling, the fastest fielder in the South Australian side, and just failed to win the race to the stumps.

Old and Lever therefore came together with two wickets left and 109 runs still needed. Five wickets had fallen for 24 and negotiations about an early plane to Melbourne had already started. The situation, however, brought the best out of Old and Lever, who played with tremendous spirit and enterprise to make an interesting game exciting to the last. At lunch England were 176 for eight and it took a particularly good yorker from Hogg afterwards to get rid of Lever after the doughty pair had put on 68 entertaining runs in even time.

Willis joined Old and stayed with him until Old's fine innings ended with a catch off 'Sounda' Sleep to give South Australia victory by 32 runs. It was the first time since 1925, when Arthur Gilligan's side had lost, that an MCC (or England) team had gone down to South Australia, and the sixth in 45 meetings between the two. It was, one felt, a happy result for several reasons. It gave South Australian cricket an uplift it badly needed. Narrowly avoiding the wooden spoon in the Sheffield Shield the previous season, the state had been bottom in the two years before that, and it was the only state team not to have found a local business to sponsor it. They had thoroughly deserved to beat the touring side. For England, on the other hand, defeat was certainly no disaster at this early stage of the tour and may even have been a blessing in disguise in that it proved to the players that they could not afford to be complacent. On the contrary, the suspected brittleness of the batting had been underlined by the failures of all but Gower and Boycott, and even these two cannot have been entirely happy with their performances. Gower knew that if he had batted for another hour or so England would probably have won. Boycott knew that he had twice been l.b.w. to Hogg. The latter was only the first, indeed, of a number of aspiring Test fast bowlers still to be faced during the approach to the first Test. Callen, Hurst, Lawson and Clark, to name but four, were in the queue waiting to unleash themselves at what some Australians were now beginning to believe was an overrated side.

On the credit side Edmonds had enjoyed an excellent first match in Australia, Miller had supported him well with his off-spin, and Gower had shown Australians what a gifted batsman he was, and how dangerous he would be once he learned to resist temptation outside the off-stump. Certainly the team was quite unworried by the defeat. There was still plenty of time in hand and they would be immensely strengthened once Ian Botham was fit to play.

Botham had some recompense for his misfortune in missing the first few games within a few hours of the team moving east from Adelaide to Melbourne. November the seventh was Melbourne Cup Day, when the whole Australian nation goes racing mad and when virtually every Australian adult has a wager on one of the entries in the competitive two-mile handicap at Flemington. The race combines the national involvement of the Epsom Derby with the fashionable aspects of the Ascot Gold Cup, and Melbourne was full of visitors from all over Australasia – some from even farther afield. 77,000 people went to the races at Flemington despite the fact that the Melbourne Cup was being televised in Victoria for the first time and despite a showery day. Botham not only drew the winner in the team sweepstake, to win fifty dollars, but added about five times that amount to his winnings backing the same horse in a separate bet.

Australia certainly lived up to its reputation for being gambling mad on these occasions. On the Victorian Tote alone 7.2 million Australian dollars (about £4.2 million) were invested. As always, Melbourne was alive with sporting activity, and apart from one or two famous names from the racing world several of the world's best golfers, amongst them Nick Faldo, Sevriano Ballasteros and Johnny Miller, were staying at the same hotel as the touring team. They were in Melbourne for the Australian PGA Championship at Royal Melbourne, which was won a few days later by the American Hale Irwin.

England's first match in Victoria took place against another country eleven at Leongatha, and it brought the team their first victory. The opposition was weak but it was a timely success for all that, following the defeat at Adelaide and preceding the important game against Victoria. Leongatha is set in pretty, rolling, pastoral country only eighty miles from Melbourne. The area, South Gippsland, is renowned for its dairy produce, and Leongatha itself, which has a population of some 3500, boasts the largest dairy factory in the southern hemisphere, producing mainly butter and milk powder from a huge building claimed to be almost half a mile long.

Sadly for the enthusiastic locals a goodly proportion of the area's generous annual rainfall had fallen on Melbourne Cup night and the ground was very damp when play began, but the England team were as keen for practice as they were not to disappoint the townsfolk, who had a public holiday for the occasion. A school brass band introduced a proper sense of importance to the occasion by greeting the English openers, Gooch and Miller, with a rendering of Rule Britannia as they walked out to bat. They responded with a stand of 41 which was by some distance the largest of of the match. Miller made 30, Gooch 29, Gower and Taylor 21 each and the local team held some magnificent catches, notably three by Macnamara, a 21-year-old batsman. But conditions became even more difficult and unpleasant after a torrential downpour early in the afternoon, and only Bob Willis's laudable decision to play on in recognition of all the hard work which had been put into the game enabled another enthusiastic crowd to get their money's worth.

Willis was rewarded for his generosity because after Hendrick had taken two quick wickets Emburey's off-spin was too tricky for the Victorian country batsmen and they were bowled out for 59, with Emburey returning remarkable figures of five for ten in eleven overs. The two-hour coach-drive home, through first the rolling green hills, then the long ribbon suburbs of the city, was made in cheerful spirits.

The four-day match against Victoria, the Sir Robert Menzies Memorial Match, was obviously an important one. England could hardly afford to lose to another state side, but they were up against a captain, Graham Yallop, determined to show that he was the man to lead Australia into battle three weeks later, and three bowlers, Alan Hurst, Ian Callen and Jim Higgs and an all-rounder, Trevor Laughlin, who all aspired to places in the first Test team.

The most significant conflict in the match was the one between these three Test bowlers and the top five batsmen in the England eleven. With Boycott being rested, though he would have preferred to play despite continuing anxiety about the bursitis on his left knee, Brearley moved up to open the innings with Gooch; Randall was promoted to number three, the position in which he had made his famous 174 in the Centenary Test, and Radley, needing runs to re-establish himself after his nasty hit on the head, was lowered to number five. 'How much lower can you put him?' Brearley was asked. The knives were out early for Radley.

It was Victoria's batsmen who were tested first, however. Graham Yallop, their personable young captain, who had played in the same MCC side as Brearley against Scotland in 1973, won the toss and batted first on a bare-looking strip which contrasted sharply in colour with the vivid green of the vast outfield and the black of the Merri Creek soil scattered liberally over the rest of the square which a mere six weeks before had been a quagmire churned up by the boots of the rules footballers.

Any fear that the vast stadium might be lacking in atmosphere was quickly dispelled. The Victorian Cricket Association
had organised a mammoth coaching session before play began
for more than 13,000 schoolboys, and the first day's play took
place before a constant high-pitched cacophony which echoed off
the semi-circular roof of the southern stand all day. It felt like
being inside an aviary or a packed municipal swimming-pool
during a school gala.

Once the Victorian opener, Julian Wiener, a correct fair-haired
right-hander, had survived an excellent opening spell by Old he
enabled Victoria to make a steady start, despite losing Hibbert to
an injudicious hook. But the general pattern of the day was one of
cautious batsmen being tied down by very accurate bowling and
excellent ground fielding. There was little to choose between the
three England seamers fighting for one Test place, whilst
Edmonds and Emburey both bowled their spinners well and the
former held three catches, including a beauty diving to his right at
mid-wicket to give Lever the first of two well-deserved wickets. It
was Edmonds, too, who took the important wicket of Yallop,
who came down the wicket to hit across the spin and was bowled
off his pads as he tried to take the initiative away from the miserly
England attack.

Towards the end of the day, however, the two left-handers,
Moss and the vigorous Laughlin, prospered, notably against the
second new ball, and Victoria ended the opening day at 205 for
five. One's first impression of Laughlin, who has played in league
cricket in both Scotland and Lancashire, was of a determined and
zestful all-rounder looking something like Jimmy Connors, the
American tennis star, but built more along the lines of Eddie
Barlow of South Africa.

Victoria could add only 49 more runs on the Saturday morning
for the loss of their last five wickets. Once Laughlin had been
unwise enough to try and take a short single to Gower, to be comfortably run out for 37, Edmonds and Emburey made short work
of the tail. Moss played some more good strokes to reach 73 but
the Middlesex spinners prospered on the slow, turning pitch,
given as always the right kind of attacking field by Brearley, and
they both fully deserved their three wickets.

Hurst and Callen were given 35 minutes before lunch to throw
all that they could at the England batsmen. Hurst was yards
quicker than Callen or any of England's three seamers in this

match, and in his early overs he also swung the ball as much as anyone. Brearley survived one confident l.b.w. appeal in his first over but Gooch, going back across his stumps to a ball of full length, much as Boycott had done to Hogg the week before, was not so lucky. Enter Randall along the long path from the western stand which he had last travelled in the opposite direction with the cheers of a vast crowd (indeed it had seemed at the time like the cheers of the whole cricket world) ringing in his ears. The ball was soon ringing off his bat with equal clarity, and before long on this docile pitch he and his captain were making batting look a very comfortable business indeed. Victoria soon had to settle for a policy of containing cricket – tight bowling to largely one-saving fields – which met with the approval of the state coach Frank Tyson. But on this pitch a patient batsman who got a start ought to have been able to look after himself, and although Higgs had some moral successes against both with his leg-spin Randall and Brearley scored a steady 100 together in 152 minutes and Brearley reached only his fourth fifty since the start of his difficult 1978 season with a solid square-cut off Higgs. Randall was dismissed rather unexpectedly, bowled driving at the occasional off-spin of Wiener for 63, and Wiener added to the good marks against his name both with the bat and in the field by persuading Gower to give him a return catch after making 13 fluent runs. Surprisingly Yallop did not bring back Hurst or Callen to confront Radley, as Higgs continued a marathon spell of 25 overs of tidy leg-spin, which cost him only 54 runs.

Heavy overnight rain, which seems almost as natural in Melbourne as it does in Manchester, prevented any play starting on the Sunday, and a further downpour on Sunday night meant that a moribund match could not recommence until two o'clock on the final afternoon. The man who had most to gain from the dying hours was Brearley, and with infinite patience and admirable soundness he reached the important landmark of the first hundred of the tour. There was plenty of moisture in the pitch, which enabled Higgs to turn the ball a little more sharply than he had two days before, and he was rewarded with a heady little spell of three for three in 32 balls. Radley, Tolchard and Edmonds were his victims, all three caught trying to drive on the hopelessly stodgy pitch. Brearley, however, was not to be tempted into anything indiscreet, and after battling soundly away for more than six hours he pulled Higgs to square-leg to reach his first hundred since one against Gloucestershire in July 1977. He was still not timing the ball as well or playing his attacking strokes with as great a degree of conviction as he had when he won his first Test cap against the West Indies in 1976, but this substantial score, which reached 116 not out before he declared, must greatly have helped his confidence. Although he would be more vulnerable, the runs would also flow more freely on the faster wickets to come. His innings was a minor personal triumph after all the disappointments he had suffered at the crease since he had broken his arm, and a lesson in application which not even the inactive Boycott could have improved upon.

The great man, however, was not to be upstaged for long. To assuage his disappointment at missing an innings on the MCG (the one Australian Test ground where he had not hitherto scored a century), he arranged for a net to be erected in the middle of the square on the morning that the team departed for Canberra. There he played for more than an hour against the willing if not exactly youthful attack of Doug Insole and the former Australian captain and off-spinner Ian Johnson, augmented by the exciting young English fast bowler Jonathan Agnew, who had already made a big impression in district cricket in Melbourne. Agnew later played as a member of the England Under-19 team which toured Australia in the New Year. In Melbourne he came under the keen eye of the Victorian state coach Frank Tyson, who obviously shared the general view that England had not produced a faster bowler since Willis.

Thus sharpened, Boycott promptly produced his first hundred of the tour against the ACT District XI at Canberra. The issue of the Yorkshire captaincy and the special meeting to express 'no confidence' in the cricket committee had only the day before been the subject of a High Court order (cricket was rapidly, it seemed, becoming an important source of legal income) but there was no doubting Boycott's concentration on the job in hand as he mercilessly dealt with the country attack. Roger Tolchard's century was, I am told, a sparkling innings too and the prelude to an impressive piece of fast bowling by Bob Willis as the touring team turned on the heat for the first time. Alas, I was not able to see all this because on a perfect summer's day I was in bed in a hotel room, the victim of a particularly vicious virus. I did my best to convince myself that there could have been worse plights than lying miserably ill in unfamiliar surroundings, unable either to sleep or eat, but until the admirable Bernard Thomas bestowed some of his miraculous antibiotics I was not very successful. This is the nature of touring overseas: for almost everyone in a long stay away from home there are moments of loneliness and depression, just as there are many of great enjoyment amongst convivial people. Fortunately the good times far outnumber the bad, and this England team as a whole was certainly one which was visibly enjoying itself. Their approach was positive, relaxed and businesslike without forgetting that, though they were in Australia to win, there was more to the tour than just doing that.

The cricket took precedence again when the New South Wales match began on a hot mid-November day at the much-altered Sydney cricket ground. The government-appointed trust which now had control of the ground had decided to open up its facilities not only to World Series Cricket but to other sports and activities, including pop concerts. The old Brewongle Stand had been torn down and a new one was in the process of construction. There was also a long scar across the turf where the Channel Nine microphones had been inserted, ready for showbiz cricket. But the most radical change bludgeoned one between the eyes in whatever direction one happened to look. Between the elegant old Victorian stands with their green corrugated-iron roofs topped with fretted wrought ironwork and billowing flags, between the palm trees and the purple jacarandas, on either side of the green hill which for more than a century had been the ground's hallmark, six hideous chimneys soared towards the sky. Some 240 feet high, battleship grey in colour and topped by eighty powerful lamps, they dwarfed everything else, the living and omnipresent reminder that commercialism had triumphed over tradition. The day before, I had seen some of Mr Packer's Channel Nine coverage of the Australian Open Golf Championship. Technically the transmission could not be faulted, but at every tee a huge placard dominated the scene, a little advertising message floated across the screen as the players drove off, and the commentator referred to the '15th hole, 420 metres, dog-leg right, sponsored by blankety blank and blank'. Perhaps it was my BBC upbringing, but I found it very disturbing. Sponsors, not golfers, seemed to be running this show.

Fortunately, though one could not ignore the grotesque monuments to Packer-power, the cricket on the first day was absorbing enough to hold the full attention of every spectator. Willis called

correctly and after an excellent morning's play England were 86
for one when the first interval came. The 21-year-old fast bowler,
Lawson, tall, raw-boned, fast, bouncy and at first erratic, hurried
and harried both Gooch and Boycott. Watson, who seemed faster
on his home pitch than on his adopted one at Worcester, had little
luck either in a good opening spell. Gooch looked much the more
likely to go early on, but he needed luck and he had it. He was well
aware that his place as England's opener was in jeopardy if he did
not make a big score this time. Instead it was Boycott, most unexpectedly, who was out when he edged a wide half-volley to third
slip.

Lawson was almost at the end of his tether when he took this
wicket but he deserved it, and the thought occurred that it was the
pace and bounce of some of his earlier deliveries, rather than the
one which took the wicket, which had got Boycott out. In other
words he was half looking for something venomous and was not
in the right position to drive or stroke the ball through the covers
as he would normally have done. According to Boycott, it was a
slower ball.

Randall, as ever, took no time to make his presence felt and
before long he had made his Test recall a certainty. He glanced his
first ball from Lawson for four and was glanced himself – on the
side of the head – by the following one. It was one of the few
moments of anxiety which he suffered. He was soon driving the
ball sweetly both through the covers and wide of mid-on. Gooch,
too, soon shrugged off the shackles which had bound him and
drove, cut and forced his way into something like his true form.
He scored the faster after lunch, one commanding hook off
Lawson and a lovely off-drive against the orthodox left-arm spinner Border staying in the memory.

It is typical of cricket that the unorthodox left-armer Hourn
should have caused all the batsmen problems but that Border
should have dismissed not only Gooch, as he aimed a savage
square-cut, but also the hapless Radley, who gave a catch to short
leg and walked out knowing that he had probably lost his Test
place.

Gower was soon in full flow and Randall was now stroking his
way irresistibly towards a memorable hundred. They added 77 in
fifty exhilarating minutes, Gower on one occasion pulling Border
first bounce over the mid-wicket boundary where the ball was lost
for several minutes amongst the piles of bricks waiting ready for

the new stand.

But the romp ended rather abruptly with a wild shot by Randall, who had hit 17 fours and, although he clowned far less than he had in India, had charmed the crowd with his perky manner and cheerful presence as well as with the perfect timing of his strokes. Then Gower too, as he does so often, got out when well set. Hourn, who so richly deserved a wicket after beating the bat an embarrassing number of times, twice deceived Gower, then bowled him as he shaped to force a shorter, quicker ball, probably the top-spinner.

Botham thus came in for his first innings of the tour, needing to consolidate. He soon got going, but Miller, intent on defence, could make only five in 43 minutes before Rixon stumped him very smartly off Hourn. One felt sorry for Miller, who alone amongst the batsmen with serious pretentions (Botham as yet excepted) had not made a fifty, but also pleased for Hourn who thoroughly deserved another wicket. The coming Tests would not be dull if he were to be selected.

Botham, like everyone else, needed a little luck against Hourn but he made very few errors for one playing his first innings of the tour and he finished a thoroughly satisfying first day of the match 28 not out.

The next morning, a glorious summer's day, he was confronted with a new ball and a fresh Lawson and Watson. He hit the latter for three magnificent offside fours, plus another through square-leg for good measure, and when Lawson removed Taylor and Emburey to catches in the slips in successive overs he off-drove Lawson too, imperiously, for four. It is difficult to imagine that anyone has ever hit the ball much harder than Botham, who reached an admirable fifty and found in Willis a steady and resolute partner.

Botham soon skied a shot to mid-off, but Willis and Hendrick took the innings up to lunch with their own brand of long-handled driving before returning to their more familiar trade. Life was harder for them, for once, with ball rather than bat in hand, although both had good opening spells and Willis dismissed the young New South Wales captain, Andrew Hilditch, with his sixth ball. But Toohey, restraining himself admirably at first, and Dyson, a Test player the year before and looking a well-organised player in his midnight-blue steel cap-shaped batting helmet, which with its peak, and no front grille, looked much less conspicuous than the type used in England, got their heads down and steadily worked the shine off the new ball.

Toohey, built very like Doug Walters, had also taken on some of his mannerisms and technique, no doubt unconsciously. He looked an equally neat mover of his feet and an equally crisp striker of the ball, and he also appeared to be vulnerable around his off-stump. Two gullies were soon posted for him as they always had been for 'Dougie'. The differences, on this evidence, were that Toohey did *not* accept the first invitation to hook and also disciplined his attacking offside strokes better until, cutting at a high bouncing delivery from Hendrick, he presented Gower with a rasping head-high catch at cover-point.

This slightly unlucky dismissal (though Hendrick had bowled well and deserved a wicket) brought in Allan Border, a chunky left-hander with hopes of a Test cap, who was just starting to look settled when he hit a strong cut off Miller which struck Gooch low on the back of his right leg at close gully and bounced up for Taylor to catch.

Miller had another success when Johnston edged low to Hendrick, who took an excellent slip catch, and then ended Dyson's solid innings when the batsman drove back over the top of the bowler's head. Boycott ran from long-on and caught the ball as he pitched headlong amongst a flock of seagulls. Dignity and corpus may have been a little bruised, but the catch was safely held. With Emburey, given only seven overs on the Saturday, soon taking a wicket with the help of a typically deft piece of work by Taylor, New South Wales ended the second day still needing 68 runs, with four wickets in hand, to save the follow-on.

No one quite expected them to fold as rapidly as they did, however, on the third morning. In just six overs and four balls the two England off-spinners, Geoff Miller and John Emburey, finished the innings. Miller took three of the wickets to give him the splendid figures of six for 56 after a spell of three for two in 28 balls in the morning. Since two of his wickets were catches by Hendrick close to the wicket, Derbyshire, in the persons of Miller, Hendrick and Taylor, had a hand in nine of the ten wickets.

New South Wales fared better at the second attempt. Dyson, their most resolute batsman in the first innings, fell to a fine low catch at first slip by Gooch off Willis, but Hilditch offered some solid defence and Toohey, after a quiet start, cut and drove Botham for ten in one over before rain appeared two overs after lunch and stayed in Sydney for the rest of a dismal afternoon. So dismal was it, indeed, that play was held up in the Open Golf Championship a couple of miles away, but nothing could put Jack Nicklaus off his imperious stride as he took his sixth Australian Open title.

The bad weather disappeared as quickly as it had come and the final day was played in glorious weather. England were made to work for their first win against a state side. The 22-year-old captain, Andrew Hilditch, with very little first-class cricket behind him and under criticism from the press after three early failures, obviously relished the back-to-the-wall situation and produced his highest first-class score, 93, to ensure that at least his side did not go under without a stern fight.

It took half an hour for England to break through when Toohey nibbled outside the off-stump to give Botham his first wicket of the tour. Botham wasn't swinging the ball as he usually does at home, but he banged away with his customary strength and perseverance, and two more wickets came his way in an eight-over spell of more than an hour. It was not especially impressive to watch: yet he took three for 18 in eight overs and when two more wickets fell smartly after lunch, one to Emburey, the other to yet another fine throw at the stumps by Gower, it was no longer a question of whether New South Wales would go under but when.

Rixon held England up for some time, surviving a chance off Miller to Gooch at slip, though since Gooch had taken three slip catches he could easily be forgiven. Emburey eventually took his wicket and although Hilditch was still there at tea and Taylor actually missed a possible leg-side stumping, the taking of the new ball after the interval hastened the end. Willis, not at his most menacing, and Botham, relishing the work, took the wickets leaving Hendrick feeling perhaps a little hurt at missing his last chance to demand inclusion in the first Test.

Although England needed only two runs to win Lawson ended the match on a vindictive note by bowling four bouncers at Boycott in five balls. The third brought an official warning from Tom Brooks, and when Lawson ignored it and bowled another which Boycott managed to edge over the slips for the winning runs Brooks gave Lawson a furious talking-to. The raw young fellow had made his point though. Boycott could expect plenty more rough treatment and if the selectors gave him the chance Lawson was ready.

The smoke from these last-minute fireworks could not, however, hide the fact that New South Wales had now lost three times in a row to a representative side from England. The wins against New South Wales had been two of the high-points during Mike Denness's ill-fated MCC tour four years before.

This very fact urged one to be cautious about England's chances this time. The victory, in only a fraction over three days, was well-earned, and the key cricketer in the team, Ian Botham, had made a fifty and once again taken five wickets. However, Boycott's dismissal by Lawson was another reminder that the batting might still be vulnerable if Australia were to find the right bowlers for the right pitch, and Hilditch, who looked a promising player batting with great determination, had shown that Willis and Botham could be resisted. It was far too early for celebrations.

Willis, by winning the match, continued a highly successful run since he had first taken on the captaincy of a touring side, by default, the previous winter in New Zealand. He was working hard at the difficult business of controlling a cricket team in the field, and he did the job well. Only his decision not to give Hendrick any bowling at all on the last day mystified me. It can hardly have encouraged Hendrick, and there were times when the two off-spinners had looked in need of a rest. In every other respect Willis was starting to prove to the unbelievers that just because he is a big fast bowler whose slow drawl does not immediately suggest a second Einstein this does not mean that he does not think deeply and intelligently about the game. He does.

Celebrations, I repeat, were premature, as everyone realised, but the party drove through a golden Sydney evening to the airport with Brisbane and the first Test the next exciting stage. There, by chance, they bumped into the party of World Series cricketers returning from a 'warm-up' fortnight of cricket in New Zealand where small crowds had watched pathetically low-scoring matches on what were obviously difficult pitches. There were some poignant reunions: Derek Underwood meeting Phillippe Edmonds and perhaps wondering whether he might still have been wearing the blue touring blazer and pressing on to a record number of Test wickets; Alan Knott, accompanied by the wife and child he always wished he had had with him overseas in the past, talking to Bob Taylor and Roger Tolchard; and in the true spirit of the game, whatever else they might have felt, Geoffrey

Boycott and Tony Greig shaking hands. The two who had attacked each other in print smiled and did their best to look each other in the eye. 'How are you, Fiery?' said Greig. 'Not too bad, apart from my left knee', said Boycott. And off they went in conversation, like some latterday Stalin and Churchill talking off-duty niceties at Yalta.

Englishmen, Australians, West Indians and South Africans mingled cheerfully for a few minutes, then went their separate ways, official cricketers to Brisbane, 'defectors' to Perth. 'It was nice to see all those people again', Brearley said later. Doug Insole could not think how to reply. It was indeed an extraordinary situation: two sets of friendly warriors fighting a war in which, like most wars, none of them wanted to be involved but which all were obliged to fight because the statesmen could find no way out of the impasse, and because the leaders of neither side could afford to lose. At least the soldiers in this particular battle were not going to die. On the contrary, they were all, in a financial sense, winners.

But the old game – cricket itself – was still bleeding from the wound which Kerry Packer opened up when he drove his iron wedge through its defenceless body. The healing process was taking a painfully long time, and the scar would never disappear.

Chapter Four

BRISBANE: THE HOSTILITIES REOPEN

Brisbane was, as Brisbane usually is, hot and sunny. The thriving city centre, a happy jumble of skyscrapers, Victoriana, churches, parks and bridges, has developed even further in the last four years, but the essential character of the place is still based on its broad, weaving river and the surrounding hills. Brisbane, largely because of the heat, moves at a more relaxed pace than most Australian cities, yet the pulse-rate of the tour quickened from the moment we touched down. The Test series was now approaching fast, and everyone was looking towards 1 December.

Australia's selectors declared their hand ten days in advance whilst England were in the middle of a country match at Bundarburg; they named a new captain, Graham Yallop, a new vice-captain, Gary Cosier, and three new caps, Rodney Hogg, Philip Carlson and John Maclean. Carlson, tall, straight-backed, fair-haired and good-looking in a Scandinavian way, heard the news in the middle of his innings against England as captain of the country eleven. He had been on the verge of national selection since making a century for Queensland at the age of eighteen. Now, ten years later, newly married and with his greatest ambition apparently about to be fulfilled, life had suddenly turned rosy for him. As a cricketer he had grown in stature since Greg Chappell left the Queensland scene for Packerland. But despite a good season in 1977–78 he had not been picked for Australia's tour of the West Indies, and he had been on the verge of 'giving the game away' until his brother, who shared with him a business selling fertilisers to the sugar-cane farmers near Childers, persuaded him to go on. 'Boy, am I glad I did!', he said when he heard the news in the tea interval at Bundarburg. In the event, sadly for him, he became Australia's 12th man.

For John Maclean, recognition had come even later in life. The first Test, indeed, was to be his 100th first-class game and at 32 he had virtually given up hope of being picked. It was at least as unusual for an Australian to be chosen when he was over thirty as it was for an England player to be selected in his early twenties, although Maclean had an encouraging precedent in Wally Grout, who had first been chosen to keep wicket for Australia when he was thirty and had held the job for nearly ten years. Maclean owed his selection both to his consistent record as a wicket-keeper for Queensland for eleven years and to his batting, which was reckoned to be half a class better than Rixon's. He heard the news during a birthday party for his third child, his one-year-old son Nicholas. A few minutes later, Rixon was unable to speak for disappointment when a journalist phoned him in Sydney to tell him the worst. In the next New South Wales match he broke a hand while batting.

Rodney Hogg, of course, had been half-expecting his chance. He had done quite enough at Adelaide for England to know that he must be treated with the utmost respect, and the partnership of Hurst and Hogg would be one of genuine speed. After two isolated Tests Hurst had much to prove, though it was obvious that one weakness of the side was that there was no specialist support for these two bowlers. Wayne Clark, discarded partly because of back trouble after taking 43 wickets in nine Tests the previous season, Geoff Lawson, Ian Callen and Geoff Dymock must all have hoped to get into the side at Brisbane where the pitch was expected to be grassy, but the selectors clearly felt that the inclusion of any one of these would give the side too long a tail. They therefore included in their twelve three capable batsmen who also bowled seam-up: Cosier, Laughlin, and Carlson. They also kept faith with the two spinners who had each taken fifteen wickets in five Tests in the West Indies: Bruce Yardley and Jim Higgs.

To Cosier fell the important task of opening the batting with Graeme Wood, which did not worry the England fast bowlers, who felt they could cheerfully deal with Cosier at any time. Wood, one of three batsmen in Australia's first four with a Test average in the upper forties, was more of a worry, and he, Toohey and the new captain Yallop seemed to hold the key to their side's chances.

Yallop, given the captaincy initially for one Test only at the age of 26, knew at least that he had nothing to lose. 'Perhaps it will be like 1958 when everyone thought May's bunch would wallop us and the Poms were hammered four-nil:' this was one hopeful comment I heard. Yallop, though, was hardly cast in the Richie Benaud mould. Coming from a well-to-do family he had been educated at the traditional Melbourne school Carey Grammar. There had been suggestions that after a successful start to his Test career against the West Indies in 1975–76 he might not prove competitive enough for the hurly-burly of international cricket. All that had happened, in fact, was that he had started the following season poorly and lost his place in the side. His record suggested that, though he was neither a showman nor a colourful extrovert of the type preferred in WSC circles, he was by no means soft. He had been belatedly recalled against India at Adelaide, where he scored a fine hundred, and later emerged with credit from the stormy and tough West Indian tour. He averaged 45 in four Tests in the Caribbean and 55 in first-class matches. As a batsman, therefore, he unquestionably demanded a place. Whether he was the right man to captain the side only time would tell. One's own impression from a brief meeting in Melbourne and a first look at his captaincy was of a pleasant and composed young man who would not flap under pressure but who might lack a certain flair and imagination when it came to leading the side in the field. From playing cricket in the Birmingham League and also for Glamorgan 2nd XI (he was married to a girl from Wales) he at least had the advantage of knowing how British cricketers think.

The England team did nothing during their first week in the sub-tropical warmth of Queensland to suggest that their role as favourite was not a fitting one. At Bundarburg they did all that a touring team should do in a match against a country XI – except for twice laying out the local opening batsman, which was more the unfortunate victim's fault than that of the two bowlers concerned. The match started later than scheduled after the Fokker Friendship which conveyed the team northwards from Brisbane to the sugar-cane and rum-producing district twenty miles inland from the coast had arrived late because of mechanical trouble. This had not stopped the pilot from doing a couple of aerial circuits of the Oval to show the ground to the team and the team to the five thousand or more people who were packed round the perimeter looking at their watches.

England's batsmen made up for lost time, scoring 259 for five in their thirty-five overs on a pitch which was as fast as mercury. Roger Tolchard, unabashed at being hit on the head when trying to hook, again played the leading role, making 74 in as many minutes. His batting was all hustle, bustle and fleet-footed enterprise. Brearley made 59, a good many of them off the edge, but it was no longer a surprise to see him get runs. Randall and Gooch, who wound himself up for three sixes over deep mid-wicket in four

balls, each picked up on the half-volley, enjoyed themselves heart-
ily at the end, and only the hapless Miller and Radley missed out
on the fun.

In the field, despite Carlson's presence – he made a solid 31
before holing out in the deep – the country XI were outclassed,
although Kevin Maher made a highly meritorious 48. His opening
partner, Scott Ledger, who had represented his state, received
painful justice after escaping a confident appeal for a catch behind
the wicket. In the same over from Lever he was hit a horrid blow
on the side of the head and retired hurt to have six stitches inserted
into a gory wound. He returned from hospital and bravely went
out to bat again. Unfortunately he ducked into the first ball he
received from Hendrick, which bounced from just short of a
length to strike him on the other side of the head. Since he had
already come off the field earlier in the proceedings after damag-
ing a hand when he hit the picket-fence whilst trying to prevent a
four it was hardly his day, but he reacted with remarkable good
humour to all the setbacks. Good humour, indeed, was the key-
note of the day on the ground where Don Tallon had played some
of his early cricket and was still a famous local figure.

Tallon, Grout and now John Maclean formed a proud line of
Queensland wicket-keepers, and there was a special cheer for
'Macca' as he walked out with Mike Brearley to toss on the opening day of the state game. He called right and decided to bat first.
England were playing what was almost certain to be their first
Test side, and Willis and Old could scarcely have asked for a more
responsive pitch on which to bowl. It was hard, fast and liberally
covered with a thick matt of grass. Not surprisingly, the early
overs were full of incident, with Broad being dropped by Gooch
off a hook to deep backward square-leg, his opening partner Walters getting caught off a lifter in the gully before he had scored,
and Broad surviving a concerted appeal for a catch behind the
wicket. Willis showed uncharacteristic fury when the appeal was
turned down, and two vicious bouncers whistled over Broad's
head before the over was out. The pitch was reminiscent of the one
on which Thomson and Lillee had wrought havoc four years
before, and whilst Willis, Old and Botham were enjoying it the
batsmen must have been looking ahead to Messrs Hurst and
Hogg with apprehension.

Willis, however, possibly still a little incensed, bowled too short
and gave way to Botham who, on his 23rd birthday, with his

young wife Kath and 15-month-old son Liam in Brisbane to support him, was eager to celebrate with a good performance, despite the fact that he had been up in the night in agony from food poisoning. In the event it was neither Botham's morning nor anyone else's in the England side. Two more catches went down, Taylor and Brearley being the unlikely culprits, and Queensland ended the first two hours with Ogilvie and Broad well set and a healthy-looking total of 86 for one.

England's luck changed after lunch, however. Old at last induced Broad to get a touch outside the off-stump and Ogilvie ducked into a short ball from Willis and departed the field with a cut on the back of his head, the latest in a disturbing succession of similar accidents. This brought Carlson to the wicket but he lasted only a few balls before edging Old to Miller, the finer of two gullies. Whatever England had eaten for lunch (good Queensland fruit as likely as not) seemed to have restored their true abilities. The left-handed Hohns tried to hook Willis with fatal results, and at 100 for four Maclean and Cosier came together in the knowledge that a psychological advantage was there to be gained by one side or the other.

Maclean survived for a time whilst Cosier, with his ultra-short backlift but considerable strength of forearm, attacked anything short, once pulling Old some twenty yards over the fine-leg boundary. Both, however, fell to Botham who, without being quite at his best, was bowling at a slightly slower pace than usual and was swinging the ball more as a result. Three good slip catches, two by Brearley, one by Boycott, helped Old and Botham to make short work of what remained and soon after tea England were batting.

The spotlight was more than ever focused on Geoffrey Boycott when the innings began. Before play started he had heard that the Yorkshire committee had finally launched an all-out attack on the issue of the county captaincy. They had circulated club members prior to the special meeting on 9 December with a statement saying that Boycott had been too preoccupied with his own batting and had not given enough attention to the younger players. They claimed that two senior players (Hampshire being one of them, though this was not specified) had stated that they would not play again under Boycott's captaincy, and they distributed a letter from Ray Illingworth to the committee in which the new Yorkshire coach made it plain that he had canvased all

the Yorkshire players. Most, he said, were 'wholeheartedly behind the committee's decision' and none of them were against it.

Boycott was not giving in easily. He issued a statement before
he left the team's hotel for the Gabba in which he accused the
committee of conducting a smear campaign against him and of
professing a sudden interest in players' opinions which had meant
nothing to them in the past. As an afterthought he added that if he
should be reinstated as a result of a vote of no-confidence in the
committee on 9 December he would give himself two years, and if
Yorkshire had not won a major trophy in that time he would
stand down to play under any other captain. The cynics might
have replied that he had already had eight years.

To what extent this trauma was affecting him no one knew, but
having made a brisk and efficient start to his innings against
Queensland he succumbed to the eleventh ball delivered in first-
class cricket by a tyro named George Brabon from Rockhamp-
ton, who had only found a place in the Queensland side because
three senior opening bowlers (Thomson, Schuller and Maguire)
had been ruled out for one reason or another. Brabon moved the
ball around at no more than lively medium-fast, but Boycott
would normally have expected to handle him without undue difficulty. The edged catch to slip earned Brabon a wider fame and a
share of a thousand Australian dollars (about £700) which a local
ceramics firm had offered the team if they should dismiss Boycott
for less than 20.

Randall and Gooch, however, were soon making batting look a
thoroughly enjoyable way to earn a living. Randall played some
blissful drives, and he hooked with tremendous certainty and
power. Gooch, who hit some magnificent shots himself, might
well have learned from the way that his partner deliberately
hooked the ball down. In contrast he suddenly seemed intent on
giving the legside fielders catching practice. His first skied hook
fell between two scrambling deep fielders; then he hit a very fast-
travelling chance to deep fine-leg where Balcam somehow allowed
the ball to go straight through his hands just below the waist with
the most painful possible consequences. Twice bitten, thrice foolish, Gooch top-edged another hook and departed to an inspired
one-handed catch by Brabon at deep fine-leg.

England nevertheless were well-placed at 89 for two when the
second day began, but only Randall and Brearley played innings
of substance. The humid warmth of the day helped the ball to

swing more than it had the day before, and it continued to move off the seam so that the majority of players were out caught behind the wicket. The veterans Geoff Dymock and John Maclean were the chief destroyers. Dymock made intelligent use of the conditions, generally pitching the ball on a good length around off-stump, moving it either way and from time to time throwing in a surprise bouncer. Maclean, with five catches, two of them out of the top drawer, amply demonstrated why he had long been considered Australia's most reliable wicket-keeper after Marsh.

Randall passed fifty for the third successive time in first-class matches but fell disappointingly when he chased a wide delivery. From the moment that he was out batting began to look a struggle, although Miller regained some of his confidence by making 18 and Brearley played a fine innings. Just occasionally he was hit on the pads but generally his bat looked disconcertingly broad to the Queensland bowlers and on the quicker pitch and outfield he was able to keep the runs ticking over. The man who had been openly laughed at a few months before by people who seemed unable to recognise that a cricketer's form is as fickle as a Hollywood affair, was now averaging 121 in first-class innings on the tour.

England's lead of 82 was always likely to be enough to assure them of victory but Willis soon made certain. He took wickets with the fifth and seventh balls of his first over and not long afterwards struck the bespectacled opener Max Walters a sickening blow on the forehead. The ball leapt off little short of a length and split his glasses in two. On this pitch Walters was just not good enough to deal with a bowler of Willis's pace and bounce. He was taken to hospital with a horrid gash low on the forehead, requiring ten stitches. This was the fifth time in three days that a batsman had been hit on the head and the trend was becoming alarming.

Queensland were now effectively 21 for three but they were rescued by some spirited batting by Hohns and to a lesser extent by Carlson, whose place in the final Australian eleven probably rested on his performance. His technique was an interesting one which did not inspire much confidence in those watching him. He gave himself a good deal of room – and the bowlers a good deal of hope – but he hit the ball hard, almost exclusively off the back foot. He made 37 before being bowled by a ball from Botham which came back a long way and Botham took another wicket in the same over with an equally good ball.

Queensland, however, prolonged the issue on the Sunday morning when Ogilvie, batting in a helmet after his first-innings 'sconning', contributed a solid 45 and shared in substantial stands with both Hohns and Maclean. Hohns was missed at second slip by Botham off Old before being caught in the same position by Old off Botham, a charitable catch if ever there was one. Hohns had played a fine innings. Ogilvie looked well-established when he drove at a ball of full length from Willis with his weight on the back foot and lifted a comfortable catch to cover.

Maclean, not a graceful player but a watchful, determined and effective one, continued the fight and reached his fifty to warm applause forty minutes into the afternoon session. He proved himself capable of cutting practically anything and also of hitting ruggedly on the onside. He found useful partners in both Dymock and Balcam, and for the first time on the tour Brearley was forced to go completely on the defensive against him. England had begun the day looking as if they were in no great hurry to finish things off – there was a long gap before the first Test and they were not yet over-burdened with match practice – but Maclean's splendidly defiant innings reduced them to a state of some anxiety. He eventually perished six short of what would have been his third first-class hundred when he skied Old to deep backward point in the first over with the new ball.

England were left with 208 to win on a pitch which, after two and a half days in the sun, had lost all its fire and movement. Boy-cott and Gooch made a confident start to England's second innings and it was a surprise when Gooch played a rather loose steer shot to gully off Carlson. Randall, however, quickly settled. With Boycott in assured control and Randall playing some more resounding hooks (his first scoring shot was played so early that it almost seemed he had made up his mind to hook as the ball was being delivered) England were nearly halfway to their target by the close of the third day.

The final day began in humid heat before a small crowd with just 114 runs needed for victory. Boycott and Brearley with their sound, patient and methodical approach played the major roles and insured that there were no alarms. Randall looked in a carefree, even at times careless mood, and he drove over a well-flighted delivery from the reputable-looking off-spinner Whyte to be out three short of what would have been his fourth successive score of fifty or more.

Boycott was content to take his time and collect runs whenever they presented themselves without doing anything to force the issue, but after batting a minute under four hours he played a very fine leg-glance to the lively left-arm over-the-wicket bowler Balcam and was caught by Maclean with an agility which quite belied his not inconsiderable bulk.

One felt that Brearley might have wanted Gower, Miller or Botham to go in ahead of himself – all three were in much greater need of time in the middle – but he himself went in again at number four and played in his usual quiet and steady way until England won, an hour after lunch. Unfortunately Gower, when he did get in, wasted his opportunity, cutting loosely at the leg-spinner Hohns to be well caught by Cosier at slip for only one. Miller, however, confirmed the impression he had given in his first innings that his period of self-doubt had passed. He batted confidently and assertively for his 22 not out and although Brearley received more hostile short deliveries from Balcam than he would have wished he was 38 not out when he pushed the single which gave England their second successive win against a state side. His first-class average on the tour was now 140 and he once again set an example to some of the younger players in application and concentration.

The team celebrated their victory with a rare day off from cricket. Some chose to play in a pro-am golf match, others to relax at the hotel rooftop pool amongst the great skyscrapers of Brisbane's bustling city centre. A few took on the more demanding water of the sea at Surfers' Paradise on the Gold Coast where the mountainous waves can test the nerve of the strongest swimmer and the bikinis would stir the imagination of the chastest monk. I was fortunate enough to play a round of golf at the Royal Brisbane Club and can seldom remember playing in more delightful conditions, in the merciful cool of the evening. The respite, however, was brief, and if Brearley, Yallop and their teams had any doubts about the vital significance of the series on which they were about to embark they were removed by the remarkable events at the Sydney Cricket Ground on 28 November. Skilful advance publicity and the sheer novelty of a cricket match under floodlights at one of the world's great grounds drew an immense crowd for the inaugural World Series match. It was officially estimated at 44,374, although many claimed that the number was still larger.

The match, a limited-over game between an Australian eleven and a West Indian eleven, was an ordinary one in itself, although extravagant claims were made for it by those commentators and journalists who were obliged to sell their glossy new product. It was won by the Australian eleven and this was highly significant because the Australians in their WSC guise had been heavily mauled in the majority of matches in the first year of the Packer venture by both the West Indian and the 'World' teams. The lavish and relentless publicity which preceded the second year's programme had been aimed at building up Ian Chappell's side as superfit 'masters of cricket', and a highly catchy tune 'Come on Aussie, come on' had captured the minds of most who had seen the advertisement over and over again on Channel Nine. The clear intention was to make the Australian public identify with WSC Australia rather than with the official team. This, of course, was doubly menacing because not only were the Chappells and Lillees more familiar to the public and better promoted by their paymasters but also they would attract the fringe cricket supporter all the more if they were seen to be winners and if Yallop's young side should be defeated.

That there was a truly dramatic atmosphere for the first night match at Sydney, which began at 2.30 p.m. and ended at 9.30 in a comfortable five-wicket victory by the Australian eleven, cannot be questioned. But the political overtones of the evening were much more significant than the match itself. Novelty was still WSC's main strength and a lack of tradition its main weakness. The West Indians were without two of their best fast bowlers, Holding and Daniel, and very few bouncers, certainly no dangerous ones, were bowled. There was doubt about batsmen being able to see the white ball well enough, particularly at dusk when neither the sun nor the lights held sway. There were artificial restrictions on bowlers' run-ups and on field placings.

The attraction of the match was similar to the attraction of Sunday cricket in England. It was novel, and as with all one-day matches a result was guaranteed. Just as in England on Sundays the family can all go and watch, so here it was possible for the eight till four workers to go along to the SCG, where free parking had been guaranteed. It was exhibition cricket, spectacular and drawing a new kind of audience; Mr Packer's organisation was certainly not apologising for that. For them it was an undiluted triumph, to be trumpeted abroad at maximum volume.

Whilst Ian Chappell's team were winning a second night match, this time against a 'World' eleven before a crowd of 20,134, the final preparations were under way for the Brisbane Test, now even more vital to the future of traditional cricket, the 'real thing'. The Woolloongabba Oval, known universally as simply the Gabba, was once Australia's shabbiest ground but is now its smartest and best appointed. There is in Queensland a fierce local pride, and the work of men like Brisbane's former Lord Mayor, Clem Jones, and some far-sighted and enterprising members of the Queensland Cricket Association helped to encourage lucrative sponsorships for the players – in advance of Packer – and also to create a comfortable modern stadium with a true cricketing atmosphere.

In its relatively short history the Gabba has seen many famous firsts and many decisive Test matches. Here Don Bradman played his first Test as captain, in 1936, after playing his first Test at the old Brisbane Exhibition Ground in 1928 when England under A. P. F. Chapman won by the margin of 675 runs. It was at the Gabba in 1960 that the West Indies and Australia fought to the most exciting Test finish yet seen, the unique Brisbane tie. (Not many people realise that the last-day attendance was less than 500.) Here too in the days before covered wickets desperate excitement would be caused by a heavy tropical downpour and the resultant 'sticky dog' which made batting a virtual impossibility, as in 1950 when both Lindsay Hassett and Freddie Brown declared with scores of less than 100 to get the other side in and 22 wickets fell in a day.

Here England packed their side with fast bowlers in 1954 only to lose by an innings – the deceptive prelude to the dominance of Tyson and Statham later in the series; here Doug Walters scored 155 on his Test début in 1965; Keith Stackpole made 207 against England five years later; Dennis Lillee and Jeff Thomson first began their destructive partnership against England in 1974, and a year later Greg Chappell marked his first Test as captain by scoring a hundred in each innings.

The name of Bradman will always be most closely linked with great deeds at Brisbane. He scored 200 not out against South Africa on the very day that Test cricket at the Gabba began in 1931, going on to make 226, still the highest Test score on the ground. A year before he had also scored a double hundred against the West Indies at the Exhibition Ground. His 226 at the Gabba took him past 2000 Test runs after only 22 innings, the fastest any man has reached that landmark.

The last decade has seen the bulk of the changes which have transformed the Gabba. Two spacious new stands, a comfortable modern members' pavilion and a glass-fronted building which acts as the headquarters for the greyhound racing which takes place on a grass track between the boundary fence and the stands, all give a pleasing impression, and there are plenty of trees and flowers to soften the abundance of concrete.

England were long overdue a victory at the Gabba. Australia had won there five times since England's last success in 1936–37, but the visitors were clearly the favourites on this occasion. The Queensland Cricket Association made the most of the fiftieth anniversary of Test cricket in Brisbane. On a cloudy morning, mercifully cooler than the 90° heat which had made the final day of practice for the two teams an arduous experience, the day was launched with a champagne breakfast at the Gabba at half-past seven. Two hours later a Gurkha pipe band accompanied a march-past of a thousand schoolboy cricketers. At exactly 10.25 three sky-divers, trailing orange smoke, descended onto the ground to present a special coin, which was used by the captains to toss. Five minutes later the Queensland Governor, Sir James Ramsay, presented commemorative medallions, organised by the sponsors, Benson and Hedges, to the two teams.

It was a spectacular start but quickly superseded by the beginning of the match itself. Yallop won the toss and chose to bat first. Brearley would have taken the same decision, but on such an overcast day it was not an easy one to make. Willis, bowling downwind from the Stanley Street end, delivered the first ball of the match to the left-handed Wood. The two had never faced one another before. The first ball of the series was short on the off-stump and Wood pushed it five yards out on the offside. He called immediately for an extremely risky single and Cosier only just made his ground. If Edmonds, running from gully, had hit the stumps with his throw he might not have done so. Cosier scored a single off his second ball and then, to the fifth ball of the opening over, Wood repeated his attempt at a short single. This time Gower swooped in from cover and with an underhand throw scored a direct hit on the stumps. It must have been a very close decision but umpire Max O'Connell instantly raised the finger of judgement and Cosier, who had the day before signed a contract worth some £30,000 a year to work for a development company and so to stay with established cricket in Queensland, was out for one.

Peter Toohey came in at number three and might well have been caught behind off two perfect outswingers from Old before he drove outside the third ball of Willis's second over and lost his off-stump. So Graham Yallop walked out in his first Test as captain with his side already desperately placed at five for two. He was wearing a relatively discreet green jockey-style fibreglass helmet with perspex ear-muffs, soon to become familiar equipment in this series. He batted with reassuring solidity but neither he nor Wood could do any more than defend and push for the occasional single. Old, swinging the ball considerably in the overcast conditions, was the major threat and in his fourth over he found the outside edge of Wood's bat to give Taylor his first catch of the series.

After an hour of what must have been agonising watching to home supporters, Australia were 15 for three, but they had their first piece of luck when Yallop edged a bouncing delivery from Old between Brearley and Gooch at first and second slip. Gooch dived to his right and dropped the catch at just above shoulder height. One's impression was that Brearley, going left, would have taken the ball.

A second and harder chance was not taken in the following over. Hughes, then one, edged Willis low to fourth slip and Old, diving to his left, was only able to get his left hand to the ball, dislocating the top joint of his left little finger. The miss was painful but inexpensive. Old was replaced by Botham after his fine spell of one for seven from six overs and the change had an immediate effect because Hughes was unwise enough to drive at a late outswinger with fatal consequences.

Laughlin started with a solid stroke for two but then received one of the very few bouncers which Willis bowled and top-edged his attempted hook into the safe hands of Lever, fielding substitute at deep fine-leg where he made ground with customary athleticism to get into the right position for the catch. Australia were then 26 for six and it began to look as though they might not exceed their lowest Test score of 36 against England at Edgbaston in 1902. This particular statistic was easy enough to recall. It was not so easy to remember when last the first six in a batting order had all been out for single-figure scores.

The solid Maclean, however, was now at the crease and first with Yardley, then with Hogg, he comfortably denied the more lugubrious record-keepers. He played exceptionally well, seldom looking in any trouble against the outswinger which had worried more reputable batsmen. Yardley's 17 was a lucky but more than useful contribution. He received more bouncers than anyone else and became the third man to be dropped in the slips, Gooch the unfortunate offender again and Botham the bowler. For a third time, however, the miss was not expensive because one run later Yardley edged an intended drive off Willis into Taylor's gloves.

Hogg held England up still longer. Wearing a white motor-cycle crash helmet, complete with front grille, he scored 36 out of a fighting partnership of 60 with Maclean. Both men were playing their first Test innings. Hogg cut the ball hard and well and also began to drive powerfully, but he did not appear to have convinced umpire French who asked Willis politely not to bowl any bouncers at Hogg when the latter looked discomforted by the first one that he received. Willis seemed to ignore the advice because he gave Hogg a second bouncer which the batsman managed to edge over the slips. Willis, however, was now at the end of his excellent spell and he temporarily retired to the pavilion for attention to the sore toes which had plagued him throughout the tour. Despite bringing five pairs of boots with him and acquiring still more since his arrival, he could not avoid blisters and chafing skin. He had bowled a perfect line, swung the ball more than he usually does, and had been rewarded with four for 44.

Botham now had his first bowl downwind from the Stanley Street end and he quickly cut short Hogg's useful innings with a late outswinger. A local paper claimed the next morning that Hogg was the victim of a 'Pommy plot'. A British Airways pilot had been at the ground in the morning and just before Hogg's demise he flew his Jumbo twice over the ground as a salute to the England bowlers. Diabolical! Hurst went the same way as Hogg, giving Taylor his fifth catch, and then, appropriately, Old finished the innings by bowling Higgs with the perfect outswinger which began on a leg-stump line and knocked back the off. The clock showed a quarter-past three. The innings had lasted only three hours 35 minutes and 37.7 overs.

A total of 116 represented a brave recovery from the perilous position of 26 for six and the sturdy Maclean was the main reason for it. England were all the more delighted now that Brearley had changed his usual call of heads and disproved the old theory that 'tails never fails'. The conditions, cloudy and despite a stiff breeze

Rodney Hogg, the outstanding individual performer in the series. By bowling fast and straight, and possessing the ability to bring the ball back sharply from the off, he took 41 wickets in his first Test series, more than any other Australian in an Ashes series. Umpire Bailhache watches this round-the-wicket delivery.

Above left David Gower—poetry in motion. *Above right* First blood to Hogg. Clive Radley is struck on the side of the head early in the opening first-class match of the tour at Adelaide. Batsmen later discarded the traditional cap in favour of the new fibre-glass helmets. *Below* Hogg bowls to Taylor in the Brisbane Test. Umpire O'Connell calls 'no-ball'.

Above In the first over of the first Test match Gary Cosier is called for too sharp a single by Graeme Wood, and the deadly Gower strikes. *Below* Nearly another one. Graham Yallop just defies the acrobatic Randall during his determined century in the second innings at Brisbane.

The second Test at Perth. Mike Brearley tries to lift the England scoring rate—
with fatal consequences. The veteran Queenslanders Geoff Dymock and John
Maclean have shared many a wicket like this.

also humid, had been ideal for swing bowling and in Old and Botham the redoubtable Willis had formidable support. It had been, for much of the time, an unequal struggle between very good bowlers using suitable conditions to the full and a determined but inexperienced batting side who were given very little chance to settle.

There was still time to hit back, however, and England's innings began on a distinctly uneasy note. Boycott needed all his wits to deal with some hostile early deliveries from Hurst, one of which whistled past his eyes as he rocked back inside the line. Gooch, after clipping two runs off his toes, was soon in difficulties against Hogg, who put all his might into his opening spell. He was within inches of having Gooch caught in the gully by Laughlin, who took the ball on the half-volley. But in the same over Gooch played back to another lifting delivery and the ball was caught by Laughlin, who jubilantly claimed the wicket. After a slight hesitation umpire O'Connell lifted his finger. Gooch looked amazed and the television playback, that unremitting foe of umpires the world over, appeared to show clearly that the ball had come off the top of the pad, not the bat. Gooch was wearing the modern plastic pads which are so much lighter, but off which the ball often bounces long distances. Hogg had taken his first Test wicket and England, like Australia before them, were two for one.

This brought Randall to the wicket in the fourth over, which suited him because he loathes the nervous wait in the dressing-room. He looked edgy enough in the middle, too, and played and missed more than once, but the fact that, of his first 13 runs, 12 came from crisply struck hooks, showed that he was, as usual, seeing the ball earlier than most.

The light deteriorated towards the end of the day and play was held up for ten minutes at the start of the last hour. When play resumed Hogg got a ball to lift more than Boycott expected and, playing an undistinguished shot with the bat away from the body, he edged a catch low to Hughes at third slip. Randall's reaction was to pick up an off-spinner from Yardley with the minimum of effort and to despatch the ball onto the greyhound track over mid-on. He hit a second four off Yardley between mid-on and the bowler with exquisite timing and before the umpires again decided that the light had become too bad he hooked Hogg in the air forward of deep square-leg for his seventh four of the day. England finished a dramatic opening day of the series powerfully placed at 60 for two, Randall 43 not out.

The Nottingham imp reached his fifty after a quarter of an hour on the Saturday morning, first slicing Hurst over the top of the slips with a deliberate uppercut, then surviving an appeal for a catch behind down the legside next ball, before glancing Hurst for the single which took him half-way to a hundred after facing 89 balls and hitting eight fours and a six.

In the following over, however, Australia missed a vital chance to get back into the game. Hogg produced a ball almost identical to the one which had dismissed Boycott. Randall, like Boycott, was surprised by the extra bounce and edged the ball high to Yallop's right at first slip. After an agonised juggle Australia's hapless captain lost the ball. Randall, clearly chastened, ventured nothing else before lunch and with thirty minutes being lost because of a sharp tropical shower England managed to score only 30 runs in an hour and a half before the interval. The crowd of nearly 12,000 were not particularly amused, but the shower had freshened up both the pitch and Australia's fast bowlers.

Frustration got Randall in the end: that, and a superb gully catch by Trevor Laughlin. Cosier and Laughlin himself had begun the attack in the afternoon and Randall was lucky again when he edged Cosier off the inside edge for four. Not long afterwards an authentic, beautifully struck on-drive off Cosier summed up the good and bad in his innings. It was his tenth and last four because Hurst, returning to the attack after a long rest, continued the policy of bowling wide to Randall. After leaving two deliveries outside the off-stump he could not resist driving hard at a wide half-volley and the ball flew fast and low to gully's left. Laughlin hurled himself like a porpoise and held the ball at full stretch in his left hand, a catch to rank with the very best in Test cricket.

Randall's departure ushered in a period of crisis for England. Yallop, with commendable aggression, called back Hogg for another onslaught and Brearley, after getting off the mark with an edged four, was caught down the legside by Maclean as he played at a ball which whistled through at chest height. In the next over Taylor, after defending stoutly for ten minutes less than three hours, was l.b.w. to Hurst for 20.

The result of all this was a guaranteed injection of urgency into the proceedings. Australia, having taken three wickets for nine runs, were alive again, and England now had Gower and Botham, sent in at number six ahead of Miller, together at the crease. If this did not produce some exciting cricket nothing would.

It was not long before the cricket reached a higher plane. Botham, bursting with aggression and joie de vivre, hooked Hogg for two as soon as he received a short delivery, then in the next over drove him imperiously towards the long-off boundary. Toohey made ground like a whippet to catch the ball just inside the fence and from the furthest corner of the ground hurled a perfect throw into Maclean's gloves over the top of the bails.

Gower, although he nibbled dangerously outside his off-stump several times, settled down with some fluent strokes whilst Botham made it plain that he would live or die by the sword. When he was 10 he aimed a hook off Hogg, the ball hit him on his helmet and spun in a lazy arc over the top of his stumps. The Australians thought the ball had touched the bat, but Maclean, a little late to react, could not make ground quickly enough to reach the ball before it landed. At 26 Botham was missed by Maclean, who had a badly bruised finger on his right hand. This was a straightforward chance, off Laughlin, and at 28 Botham gave another when he drove Yardley high towards the long-on boundary. Higgs raced in and just failed to hold on to an extremely hard chance. Since Botham had also square-cut Hurst through the upstretched hands of Laughlin in the gully early in his innings he was lucky to be still in residence, 30 not out, at tea, when Gower had reached 20 rather more calmly.

The new ball was taken after one over from Higgs after tea and for a time Botham and Gower prospered with some excellent strokes and less need for good fortune. Botham with strong hooks and drives and Gower with some perfectly timed square-cuts had added 95 at only a little less than even time when Botham, looking for his fifty, was caught off his glove hooking at Hogg. Soon afterwards Gower fell to a bad shot outside the off-stump against Hurst and then Edmonds was out to one of the best wicketkeeping catches that can ever have been seen in a Test match. He hooked, the ball deflected off the glove a long way down the legside, and Maclean took off to catch the ball at full stretch in his left glove.

Miller and Old denied Australia any further success on the second evening and both hit some pleasing strokes, but although England had built up a lead of 141 by the time bad light ended play early (as it so often does at Brisbane because of the Queensland government's resolute refusal to change to summertime), the Australians could be quite pleased that they had taken six England wickets – all to the two fast-bowling H's – and restricted England to 197 runs in the day.

Brisbane's weather found its true form again on the third day of the match and conditions looked perfect for batting with the pitch as good as at any time in the match and the sun burning down. England's last two wickets added 29 in just over an hour. Old batted effectively for 29 not out despite his dislocated little finger, but it was Miller who got going first, deflecting and driving with a tidy assurance before being beaten for pace by Hogg as he shaped to leg-glance and falling l.b.w.

Old and Willis squeezed a further 20 runs from the last wicket, with Old taking the brunt of the bowling. Yallop called on Higgs to try to break through, but it was Hurst who finally persuaded Willis to nick the ball to Maclean whose fifth catch earned the Australian side $A 2500 from the PGH Ceramics company. The same firm handed out a similar reward for Hogg's career-best bowling return of six for 74.

Australia had thirty-five minutes to bat before lunch. Wood and Cosier tossed for the privilege of facing Willis first. Cosier won, played tentatively forward to the first ball of the innings and lost his off-stump as the ball burst through between bat and pad. Nought for one became two for two in the second over when Toohey went half-forward to Botham, who had taken the new ball, and, having survived an appeal off the ball before, was given out l.b.w. by umpire O'Connell.

The two left-handers – Wood, small and neat in a gymnastic way, and Yallop, taller with a free backswing and an air of self-belief – guided Australia to lunch at 20 for two. Afterwards, as so often happens, Yallop looked more likely to get out but it was Wood who went first. Yallop might twice have been caught off Willis by Edmonds, fielding intimidatingly close at silly-point, and when 19 he was first caught by Brearley at first slip off a no-ball, then given not out when he hooked at Willis and the England players confidently appealed for a catch off the glove. The television playback tended to suggest that umpire French was wrong to say 'not-out', but the captain survived and instead Wood, who had been proceeding in singles after one crisply hooked four off Botham, was the one to go, playing back to Old and being hit high on the pad in front of his wicket. Whether or not it was too high must have been the main question in umpire O'Connell's mind before he lifted his finger. Wood, certainly, felt himself hard done by. Once again, after these two questionable decisions, one felt sympathy for Test umpires whose job is to make split-second decisions without the aid of a slow-motion camera.

At 49 for three Australia were near to the point of no return but Yallop stayed to make the most of his luck and to play a fine fighting innings. With Hughes he added 50 in 64 minutes and Yallop was always the senior partner, twice hooking Old for four and twice more square-cutting Botham with complete authority when Botham pitched short to him on the off-stump. At tea Australia were 102 for three and the resistance continued afterwards when Hughes, whose determination and concentration had been admirable, raised the loudest cheers of the day from a crowd of 12,250 by hooking Willis gloriously over deep square-leg.

The struggle was becoming both tense and absorbing. The occasional ball was starting to keep low and England knew they would be in for a struggle if they had anything more than 150 to get in the fourth innings. It was a tribute either to the strength of Australian beer or to the dumbness of some of the spectators on the Gabba's own grass hill that they should have resorted to a can-throwing contest at the height of the battle in the middle. The 'okkers' did, however, have some provocation. An intrepid young man had sorely tempted them by climbing onto a rostrum in a T-shirt marked 'Boycott: King Pom'. It was too much for loyal Aussies to stand, especially those who had been making up for time lost during a recent strike at the Brisbane brewery: they hailed the man with cans, then wrestled him down off his pedestal, ripped off the T-shirt and, to loud cheers, publicly burnt it. To add further insult to injury, the representative of the Boycott fan club was then bundled into a police van and escorted to the cooler, possibly for his own protection.

Miller continued a long and tidy spell of off-spin in the hour after tea, drifting the ball into the breeze and conceding only 19 runs in 13 overs, but although he had the occasional success outside the off-stump against Yallop he was generally played without great difficulty. Willis again bowled with great spirit after tea but the edge had gone from his pace and his line was not quite so perfect as it had been. Nevertheless he was unlucky again when Yallop edged a lifting ball between Brearley and Gooch at first and second slips. Gooch dived to his right and just failed to grasp a low, hard chance. Yallop was then 64. The magic had departed from England's slip fielding, with serious consequences.

If Yallop and Hughes could stay together now until close of play Australia would have a genuine if outside chance of winning the match. Willis limped off with sore toes; neither Botham nor Edmonds could get much past the bat, and the partnership exceeded 100 before bad light once again brought a premature close to the proceedings. Hughes had reached a well-deserved first Test fifty just before the players came off, driving Edmonds through extra-cover for his fifth four.

The gods were merciful because the heavens opened on the rest day and cricket then would have been out of the question. Tales of the famous 'stickies' which followed the tropical storms during the 1946 and 1950 Tests were retold as the players relaxed and gathered themselves for the crucial struggle at the start of the fourth day. One heard again how the stumps were carried away in the floodwater in 1946 and how Syd Barnes went to the fridge during the height of the storm, when freak hailstones were already amazing onlookers, and dropped a huge block of ice from the balcony. It must have seemed to the uninitiated that Armageddon had come.

This, of course, was in the days before Test wickets were covered. The pitch this time was untouched, and although the outfield looked a little greener a few hours of hot Queensland sun on the Tuesday morning was enough to ensure a prompt start.

From the outset the cricket was tense and fascinating. Miller began the bowling from the Vulture Street end and proved a testing proposition as he floated the ball in from the legside on a strong westerly breeze. Hughes and Yallop, however, continued to bat with admirable discretion. After a quarter of an hour a leg-glance for two by Hughes off Miller brought the scores level and Brearley summoned Willis as soon as the new ball became due after 65 overs. Botham shared the new ball but the magic touch had deserted him and Hughes drove him for four through mid-off, square-drove him for two and glanced him for one off successive deliveries to underline the inconsistency of Botham's line and length.

Willis was, by contrast, accuracy itself, but his venom was drawn by the lower pace and bounce of the pitch and his pace was lessened by the injuries to his toes. Nevertheless the quality of the cricket was high. Yallop showed no nervousness as he entered the nineties, although a square-cut off Botham, beautifully struck, gained him nothing as Gower dived in the gully to deny him. Later in the over, however, he off-drove for four to get to 96 and a few minutes later a quick legside single took him to his hundred in his first Test as captain of Australia. It says something about the quality of the Australian character that five other Australian captains had made centuries in their first Test as captain against England: Murdoch, G. H. S. Trott, Noble, Armstrong and Collins.

Yallop's fine innings ended rather unexpectedly. He drove at Willis without quite getting to the pitch of the ball, lofting it at knee height straight back down the pitch. Willis, following through, stuck out his right hand in a reflex action and took the catch with an almost casual air.

Yallop and Hughes had added 170 for the fourth wicket. They had given their side a belief in itself, saved the match from being one-sided and, to a large extent, made the series by establishing it in the minds of the Australian public as a worthy and authentic new chapter in the long history of Anglo-Australian Tests.

The fight-back was far from finished yet. Hughes knew he now had to become the senior partner and was more than equal to the added responsibility, proceeding steadily towards his maiden Test hundred. Laughlin, however, did not stay with him long, falling l.b.w. to Old when a swinging yorker struck him on the boot. At lunch Australia were 232 for five, still only 62 ahead, with Hughes 78 not out.

Hughes pulled the first ball after the break for three, Botham again being the sufferer, and settled in with the same watchful determination, his defensive strokes a model of straightness and technical rectitude. The worthy Maclean, meanwhile, was soon in the thick of the fight, shuffling across in front of his stumps and holding the fort with a forward prod, developed during a hundred first-class matches, which served him as reliably as the engine of a faithful old car. He also hooked Botham for two and four in successive balls to show that he was not merely there to defend.

England began to look weary again. Brearley called on Miller to resume his off-spin, with the breeze helping him to drift the ball across from leg to off to the right-hander. Occasionally a ball would turn back in from the off and it wasn't long before Maclean was removed, swinging across a drifter and being caught in front of his stumps after holding England up for a precious hour. Maclean had been lucky to get away with another l.b.w. claim two balls before.

Hughes had not long been joined by Yardley when, with a leg-glance off Old, he reached his maiden Test century more than six hours after arriving at the crease when Australia had been 49 for three. It was a sudden and triumphant coming of age. At only 24 Hughes had already been on three tours with official Australian teams yet had played in only three Tests, one in England and two against India. His aggregate from five previous Test innings was a mere 65 with a highest score of 28 against India at Perth. However he had been unlucky to have received so little opportunity as one of the non-Packer men in the ill-fated Australian team for the Jubilee Tests; and on tour with Bobby Simpson in the West Indies he had missed the first five weeks because of an appendix operation. Now, at last, the sun had shone for him and all that promise, so long in bud, had suddenly flowered.

It was a happy moment for Australian cricket. Hughes was not yet so complete a player as Yallop and a chart of his scoring strokes showed that the majority of his runs in a patient innings based on watchful but stylish defence had come from glances behind the wicket on the leg-side. The hook for six off Willis had, however, shown what he was capable of and, after Yardley had celebrated the century by crisply cutting Old for four, Hughes produced the shot of the match, moving two paces out to Miller with a classical criss-cross of the feet and hitting the ball, on the up, high over the greyhound track beyond mid-on.

Again the balance was starting to shift back towards Australia and the home supporters were starting to grip their seats: if these two could just stay together till tea . . . if England could be set 200 . . . Yardley pushed out at a ball from Edmonds and the unfortunate Gooch, too close at silly-point, grasped in vain as the ball bounced out of his hands. Yardley had made ten at this point. He was eleven and Hughes 117 at tea when Australia were 303 for six.

Yardley, lean and dark, a cheerful humorist off the field, grimly determined on it, had reached 15 and batted for 79 minutes when he tried to run a ball from Miller down past slip. Brearley, one of the finest slip catchers who has ever worn an England cap, caught the ball low to his left with lightning reactions. Yardley held his ground. It had looked to some as though Brearley might have taken the ball on the half-volley, although the fielder invariably knows in a case such as this whether he has made the catch cleanly or not. Brearley exultantly held the ball above his head in his left hand. Umpire French consulted O'Connell at short-leg, then lifted his finger and the England fielders swarmed around Brearley and Miller with relief.

Still England were not through to the tail, because Hogg had shown in the first innings, when he top-scored, that he was no pushover, and he soon confirmed the impression. He belted Miller unceremoniously over mid-off for a four which, given a few more yards in the air, would have been six. Then he hooked and chipped Botham for twos. But this, as it turned out, was the final decisive move of the innings. Botham had not bowled well. His line had been wayward and when he pitched short on this now tired pitch he had been comfortably dealt with. Yet to be hit by Hogg was too much for his competitive spirit. He suddenly found a new burst of energy and added an extra yard of pace. He bowled Hogg with an inswinger of full length, then shattered Hurst's flimsy defences with a full-toss two balls later.

Higgs has no batting pretensions and Hughes, understandably weary, was obliged now to attack. He aimed a pull-drive at Willis, and Edmonds, who had bowled disappointingly in the short spells he had been granted, redeemed himself by balancing perfectly at mid-wicket and taking a brilliant left-handed catch above his head.

Australia, 170 behind on first innings, had by coincidence left England with exactly 170 to win. At 26 for six in their first innings and again at two for two in their second it had not looked as though the match would go into the fourth day, let alone the fifth. It was particularly pleasing that the recovery had been achieved not by poor opposition bowling and fielding but by thoroughly determined batting. The pitch, except for the occasional ball which had kept low, had lost its early pace and bounce and this had taken the sting out of the England attack. But they were left to wonder what sort of score Australia might have achieved if the openers had only been able to keep Willis, Old and Botham at bay with the new ball. In the light of the later recovery Cosier's first-ball dismissal assumed an even greater significance. For England Willis and Miller had been outstanding, Willis never giving an inch and Miller using the breeze intelligently in his longest and best bowl in Test cricket so far. In the field Randall and in particular Gower were outstanding and the standard of ground fielding and throwing was remarkably high, underlining the value of all the hard physical work which had been put in at the start of the tour. Some slip catches had gone down, and this was a worry, but Bobby Simpson summed up the impression which the England side was giving at this stage: 'They are easily the best-drilled and most enthusiastic England side in the field I have ever seen, but their batting looks brittle, and because, unlike many England sides, they have so many strokeplayers, they are vulnerable. They will always give the bowlers help.'

Just how brittle the batting was would be tested as England set out in the last 45 minutes of the fourth day to get the 170 runs they needed, but the proof – or otherwise – of the assertion would come later in the series. For England now had only to play sensibly to win. On a luckier day Hogg might have had Boycott l.b.w. first ball and Hurst might have had Gooch l.b.w. before he had scored. But these two survived to make 16 before the close, and the final day of the match was gloriously sunny when they took guard again, needing 154 to take the first important step towards the retention of the Ashes.

They faltered at once, however. Boycott survived a confident shout for l.b.w. to the second ball bowled by Hurst; then Gooch pushed out to the first ball from Hogg and edged it low to the left of third slip where Yardley dived to take an excellent catch. England 16 for one.

Randall opened his account first ball, leaning into the ball and stroking it through cover-point for two. The battle was on again. Boycott gave every sign of digging in for the day and Randall was stroking the ball freely when Australia had a second success. Randall played Hurst off the back foot, called for a sharp run, and Toohey, moving in from extra-cover, picked the ball up in his right hand and with a brilliant throw hit the stumps at the non-striker's end with Boycott still short of his ground.

Randall's riposte was to sweep Yardley savagely for four, picking the ball up off his off-stump. But against Hurst he was less certain and two inswingers rapped him on the pads as he shaped to hit through mid-wicket, both appeals being turned down.

One felt the arrival of Brearley should have been the time for the introduction of the leg-spinner, but Higgs had to wait and watch whilst Brearley played himself in against some steady but innocuous medium pace from Laughlin. When he did make a belated appearance, after 90 minutes of the morning's play with England needing only a hundred to win, Higgs immediately dropped the ball onto a length and, bowling into the breeze, caused some problems. It was Yardley, however, who sent Brearley on his way, when after batting for 55 minutes in reasonable comfort the England captain cut at a ball which kept low and Maclean took an excellent catch off the bottom edge of the bat.

Gower had time to get off the mark with a powerful pull against Higgs before England took lunch at 82 for three, with Randall 37 not out and 88 runs still needed. But the atmosphere of slight uncertainty as to the result, which still lingered during the morning's play, was soon dispelled after the interval when Randall and Gower quickly established a comfortable ascendancy. Both played some commanding shots, although Gower once cut Cosier airily past Yallop's left hand at slip. Randall's 50 came with a firm sweep off Yardley, and Higgs, after being hit for 22 in his five afternoon overs, gave way to Hogg for a final burst of fire and brimstone.

It was, of course, a gesture only. Gower hastened the end by swinging Higgs over mid-wicket to bring up the 150, the ball bouncing full-toss against the pickets. Australia gave nothing away but some fluent drives from both players took England to within two runs of their deserved but, in the end, hard-won victory, and Gower hit Hogg to deep third-man to score the two runs which settled it at a little before quarter-past three on a glorious summer's afternoon.

England had won in style with Randall and Gower batting at their best, and the team had taken an important first step towards retaining the Ashes. But the manner of the Australian fight-back and the fact that it had been achieved through sound batting rather than through any lack of quality in England's cricket showed a sceptical Australian public that the young and inexperienced team representing their country was well worth supporting.

For England the magnificent form of Derek Randall, the return to form in the second innings of David Gower, and the bowling of Willis, Old and Miller were all particular reasons for satisfaction. But as Brearley relaxed at last after his 14th Test match without defeat, the fact that Boycott, Gooch and himself, the three openers in the team, had all failed to get to twenty in either innings must have been only one of many reasons why he was feeling far from complacent. 'Australia have shown themselves to be a very good side', he said, 'and they can only get better.'

AUSTRALIA v ENGLAND (First Test)

Brisbane, December 1, 2, 3, 5, 6. England won by 7 wickets.

Australia *First Innings*

G. M. Wood c Taylor b Old	7	*Second Innings*	
G. J. Cosier run out	1	(2) lbw b Old	19
P. M. Toohey b Willis	1	(1) b Willis	0
*G. N. Yallop c Gooch b Willis	7	lbw b Botham	1
K. J. Hughes c Taylor b Botham	4	c & b Willis	102
T. J. Laughlin c sub (Lever) b Willis	2	c Edmonds b Willis	129
†J. A. Maclean not out	33	lbw b Old	5
B. Yardley c Taylor b Willis	17	lbw b Miller	15
R. M. Hogg c Taylor b Botham	36	c Brearley b Miller	16
A. G. Hurst c Taylor b Botham	0	b Botham	16
J. D. Higgs b Old	1	b Botham	0
Extras (lb1, nb6)	7	not out	0
		(b9, lb5, nb22)	36
Total	116	Total	339

Fall of Wickets
1 – 2   2 – 5   3 – 14   4 – 22   5 – 24   6 – 26   7 – 53   8 – 113   9 – 113
1 – 0   2 – 2   3 – 49   4 – 219   5 – 228   6 – 261   7 – 310   8 – 339   9 – 339

Bowling	First Innings				Second Innings			
Willis	14	2	44	4	27.6	3	69	3
Old	9.7	1	24	2	17	1	60	2
Botham	12	1	40	3	26	5	95	3
Gooch	1	0	1	0				
Edmonds	1	1	0	0	12	1	27	0
Miller					34	12	52	2

England *First Innings*

G. Boycott c Hughes b Hogg	13	*Second Innings*	
G. A. Gooch c Laughlin b Hogg	2	run out	16
D. W. Randall c Laughlin b Hurst	75	c Yardley b Hogg	2
†R. W. Taylor lbw b Hurst	20	not out	74
*J. M. Brearley c Maclean b Hogg	6		
D. I. Gower c Maclean b Hurst	44	(4) c Maclean b Yardley	13
I. T. Botham c Maclean b Hogg	49	(5) not out	48
G. Miller lbw b Hogg	27		
P. H. Edmonds c Maclean b Hogg	1		
C. M. Old not out	29		
R. G. D. Willis c Maclean b Hurst	8		
Extras (b7, lb4, nb1)	12	(b12, lb3, nb2)	17
Total	286	Total (3 wkts)	170

Fall of wickets
1 – 2   2 – 38   3 – 111   4 – 120   5 – 120   6 – 215   7 – 219   8 – 226   9 – 266
1 – 16   2 – 37   3 – 74

Bowling	First Innings				Second Innings			
Hurst	27.4	6	93	4	10	4	17	0
Hogg	28	8	74	6	12.5	2	35	1
Laughlin	22	6	54	0	3	0	6	0
Yardley	7	1	34	0	13	1	41	1
Cosier	5	1	10	0	3	0	11	0
Higgs	6	2	9	0	12	1	43	0

Umpires: M. G. O'Connell and R. French. Toss won by Australia.

Chapter Five

PERTH: ENGLAND GO TWO-UP

The dust hadn't settled at the Gabba before Australia's selectors were announcing their twelve for Perth. Jim Higgs, who might have been expected to prosper on the hard and bouncy Perth pitch, was surprisingly discarded after being given very little opportunity in the first Test, and Trevor Laughlin was also dropped, Carlson remaining in the squad. In place of Higgs, the experienced and reliable Geoff Dymock was called in rather than a bowler of greater speed like Lawson, and after Cosier's failure as an opener Rick Darling of South Australia was recalled mainly on the strength of two good innings against New South Wales in the Sheffield Shield.

There was much to discuss on matters both cricketing and political as we left Brisbane just at the time that a large gathering of demonstrators and an almost equally large collection of the city's blue-shirted policemen were assembling in the shimmering heat in King George's Square. A vast plastic Christmas tree, dressed with glistening gold and silver tinsel on every bright green branch, stood in the middle of the square, flanked by tempting fountains which played all day through the sweltering heat. I doubt if many city squares in the world have such an array of startling architectural incongruities as this one. On one side, protected by a line of stately palm trees, is the old Victorian town-hall, its classical columns built in a pleasing yellow stone and its centrepiece a graceful clock tower wherein a bell chimes out the quarter-hours in mellow tones. Across the square, huge skyscrapers, oblong masses of glass and concrete, tower above a Gothic-style Wesleyan church constructed of shiny red brick. And on either side the relentless traffic roars all day down the wide streets. That afternoon the police arrested 346 out of some 2500 demonstrators as the Queensland government stuck to its policy of making street marches illegal.

The journey from Brisbane to Perth via Melbourne, some 2500 miles, lasted seven and a half hours, a reminder once again of the immensity of Australia. One could travel from London to

Moscow in half that time. The England party arrived after the sun
had set on a day when the temperature in Perth reached 105 degrees, but mercifully they woke up to a much cooler day, one of
the few relatively free ones for a team now faced with a very heavy
programme.

A bevy of English county players – Chris Tavaré, Geoff Humpage, Keith Cooper, Jim Love and Kevin Sharp – joined the
official team at the nets on the day before the match between West
Australia and the touring team, which tends to be a mini-Test in
itself. Western Australia had won the Sheffield Shield in five out
of the last seven years and before they took on England this time
they had been undefeated for 31 matches. They were strong
enough to leave out two Test players – Sam Gannon and Craig
Serjeant – and they were soon demonstrating the confidence and
excellence of their cricket in this, the last home match played by
their popular and successful captain John Inverarity, who took up
an appointment as deputy headmaster of a large school in Adelaide early in 1979.

'Invers' was, in theory, as fortunate to lose the toss as Brearley
had been at Brisbane the week before. Partly because he was keen
that England should bat twice in the match, Brearley decided to
bat first despite a stiff breeze, a cloudy morning and a greenish
tinge to the pitch. By the fourteenth over England were in sore dis-
tress at 31 for six, and the pattern of an astounding cricket match
had been clearly set.

The conditions were the type that seam bowlers dream about,
allowing generous movement through the air and off the pitch
throughout the game. The fast bowler Terry Alderman was the
first to use them to full effect, taking three for six in his opening
spell of six overs. Clark, who finished with two for 50, and the
promising Porter, a prodigious swinger of the ball in the Western
Australian tradition of bowlers like Massie, Malone and Bray-
shaw, also bowled well. Porter took three for 37.

The West Australian fielding was excellent, with Wright, who
held five catches, sharp behind the stumps and Charlesworth
taking one memorable catch to dismiss Botham, sprinting back
from cover to hold the ball as he dived full length with his back to
the pitch.

Edmonds, who batted an hour for 18, and Emburey, who
stayed 70 minutes for 22, held the bowlers up in the afternoon but
in the morning session only Brearley, who made 11, offered any

prolonged resistance until Roger Tolchard came in at number six. It was a great opportunity, after two more failures by Gooch and Radley, for 'Tolly' to claim a Test place for himself as a batsman, and he responded to the challenge with his usual enterprise and instinctive skill. For a long time he could do no more than survive whilst more vaunted batsmen floundered, but after receiving one piece of luck when he was missed by Hughes at slip when 14 he began to score more freely, with cuts, square drives and the occasional scientific swing to leg. It was a fine piece of improvised batting which earned him 61 not out, of a total of 144.

The sun had come out when Western Australia started their reply but it did not stop the ball swinging and seaming, thus disproving an unwise criticism by Boycott of his captain's decision to bat in the morning. In a loud voice, in the hearing of several TV cameramen and members of the crowd, he claimed that the captain was stupid for batting first but that no one would criticise Brearley 'because he had been to Cambridge.' Boycott, admittedly, was under personal pressure. He made it plain that he was unhappy about being out l.b.w. and he was to hear later in the day that, despite receiving considerable support, the Reform Group seeking to unseat the Yorkshire Cricket Committee and to reinstate Boycott as captain, had failed. This, as will be related shortly, had immediate repercussions on Boycott in Australia.

After Lever had bowled Wood for two it was Botham, with a spell of three for five in 26 balls, who caused the batting collapse. Hendrick was even more dangerous when he came on first change, getting a steeper bounce than anyone else and taking three wickets with the help of two excellent slip catches by Brearley and Botham and a third behind the wicket by Tolchard to dismiss Inverarity, who had played straight and well for 72 minutes.

Tolchard, indeed, had enjoyed a memorable day. His 61 not out blazed like a bonfire on a bleak day for batsmen. Seventeen wickets had fallen on the first day and the 'Fremantle Doctor', the breeze which normally blows in from the Swan River each afternoon but which on this occasion had come on its rounds earlier, had been the villain of the piece along with a much grassier pitch than is normal for Perth.

The wind blew wildly again on the second day, the freakish swinging and seaming of the ball continued, and the mayhem resumed to such an extent that nineteen more wickets had fallen by the time that the two West Australian survivors, the aggressive

Yardley and the highly promising Marsh, had reeled back into the pavilion at six o'clock. The sun was shining gloriously then, as it had been for most of the day, but the clarity of the atmosphere – or, to put it another way, the lack of humidity – seemed to make no difference. Hendrick and Botham finished off the West Australian innings in four overs and by teatime England had been bowled out once again. It was like watching trains coming in and out of a busy station: a wicket fell once every twenty minutes in the first two days and the average score of the thirty-six batsmen who had fallen was less than ten.

England's second-innings procession, however, was not entirely the result of the conditions, or indeed of some more good bowling by Alderman, Clark and – in particular – Yardley and Porter. Additional reasons were a certain lack of English application, excellent West Australian fielding, which for once matched that of the touring team, and some astute field-placing by Inverarity, whose captaincy had an inspired and assured touch. Thoughtful and undemonstrative, his method was strikingly similar to Brearley's and one could not help feeling then that he would have been a sounder choice to lead the Test side than Yallop.

England's second-innings total of 126 was the more disappointing for the fact that Boycott and Gooch seemed to have weathered the early storm efficiently when Gooch flicked at a wide legside ball and was very well caught by Wright, who looked a likely Test wicket-keeper of the near future. Boycott had stayed for 88 minutes when he became the first of five victims for Yardley, who bowled his off-spinners fast and flat, often with three short-legs, and who ran in every ball as if expecting a wicket. Boycott was the first of three men to be caught off bat and pad by Marsh, although once again he remained at the wicket as if to suggest that he had not hit the ball. Boycott was out of form and out of luck, a hapless figure, unwilling to talk further about his future with Yorkshire and, temporarily at least, stripped of the armour which gave him his stature: runs.

Without the solid start which England needed from Boycott and without Randall for this match, no one looked like making a substantial score, although Edmonds, opening his account with a powerful 'pick-up' off his toes to despatch Yardley over mid-wicket for six, hit effectively for a time and Tolchard again dug in for the best part of an hour before a ball from Yardley spun back off a dead bat onto the stumps. Tolchard was one of the players

Above Gower sweeps Bruce Yardley past Wood on his way to the first of only two English centuries in the series. *Below* Another Australian run-out, and another promising Darling innings is nipped in the bud. Botham (not in the picture) deceives Darling with a swift pick-up and accurate throw. Miller does the rest and Toohey looks on in dismay.

Darling hooks Willis for four at Perth. A brilliant and audacious hooker, he was taught a painful lesson when he was harshly dropped by the selectors after falling into England's obvious hooking trap at Adelaide.

who found it difficult to pick up Yardley's flight, which caused
one or two of them to feel he had an unfair action. Yardley had
been called for throwing by Douglas Sang Hue in the West Indies
but from the boundary one could not discern any obvious jerk in
his action.

Any chance that Western Australia might get the 219 runs they
needed to win, with more than two days of the match still available, was soon squashed by Ian Botham, who swung the ball away
from the bat and whipped it back in off the pitch with devastating
effect. Wood, his first victim, at least reached double figures and
played two impressively quick-footed hooks, but Western Australia ended the second day at 46 for six and although Yardley hit effectively the match was all over after 35 minutes of Monday's
play, England winning by 140 runs, their fourth first-class win in
successive games. By now the weather was really hot again and it
was difficult to imagine that if the match had been *beginning* in
such conditions the bowlers would have prospered quite as much
as they actually did. Nevertheless anxious questions were being
asked of the WACA curator, Ron Abbott, with the Test match
due to start at the end of the week.

In the match before the England versus Western Australia
game the pitch had also defied definition or explanation; on the
first morning there was such bounce and movement that three
New South Wales batsmen had bones broken. Yet despite the fact
that they were thus handicapped, the depleted New South Wales
side batted on and on in their second innings and comfortably
avoided defeat on a pitch which apparently became as dull and
lifeless as the hair of the girl before she used the correct shampoo.

John Inverarity's theory was that the green pitch provided for
the international match was possibly a reaction to the criticism
which followed this drawn Sheffield Shield game. All this fuss
over the pitch was very unexpected because during its seven years
as a Test ground the lowest score by any side was Australia's 169
against the West Indies in 1975 and batsmen generally had come
to consider Perth as something of an earthly paradise. Indeed,
whereas many Test-match grounds around the world owe their
reputation to their antiquity, many to the beauty of their physical
surroundings, and many others to their unusual size or the excellence of their amenities, the fame of the WACA at Perth rested
squarely on its pitches. Good batsmen all over the world would
say that because of their unusual pace and the exceptionally even

nature of their bounce the Perth pitches were second to none. As every cricketer knows, a fast true pitch is the best type on which to play the game. A batsman quick enough to get into the line of the ball and play the orthodox strokes will prosper, whilst bowlers of exceptional pace or with an ability to get unusual spin or bounce will have their rewards because of the extra speed of the ball off the pitch.

It was no coincidence, for example, that the one match which Clive Lloyd's West Indies side won against Greg Chappell's Australians in 1975–76 was the one at Perth when Roy Fredericks led an assault on Lillee and Thomson which the free strokeplayers in that talented West Indies team were unable to repeat on other grounds where the thicker grass and less even bounce made attacking batting a more hazardous business. With such a short history – Test cricket started at the WACA in 1970 when Ian Redpath and Greg Chappell, in his first Test, scored hundreds for Australia and John Edrich and Brian Luckhurst did so for England – the ground had not yet built up that special mystique and tradition which gives an added atmosphere to the other Australian Test grounds. But the WACA has its own idiosyncrasies. The ground is open on its eastern side, which gives it less of the atmosphere of a modern stadium and more that of a friendly club ground; the seagulls gather on the large outfield in greater profusion here than almost anywhere else and, quite unique, the 'Fremantle Doctor' blows up the Swan River every evening, an ally to tired fielders and to spin bowlers alike.

The fact that the WACA seemed to have been transformed overnight from a ground batsmen dream about into one which gives them nightmares made it very difficult for England's selectors to decide on their best team as the second Test approached. One possibility was obviously to stick to a winning combination and a balanced attack with two spinners. Australia's selectors, who thought they knew Perth, had only one spinner in their twelve. Should England do likewise and leave out Edmonds, who did not bowl a ball against Western Australia, though he batted well in both innings? If so, the obvious move was to bring in Hendrick who had looked the best bowler in the match. Much would depend on the look of the pitch later in the week.

If England's attack was to consist of four fast bowlers plus Miller there was a case for bringing in Tolchard instead of Taylor on the grounds that Tolchard would be as capable as Taylor when

standing back and would not have much work to do up at the
stumps where Taylor was far his superior. Alternatively there was
a strong case for Tolchard coming in as a specialist batsman at
number five. This in turn would depend on whether Brearley felt
ready to take on the heavy duties of opening the batting as well as
captaining the side. In the event he was unwilling to do so, and the
return to form of Gooch in the one-day country match at Albany
settled the issue for the time being.

An alarming new factor entered into calculations on the
Tuesday before the Test. Bob Willis, who had bowled in pain and
discomfort throughout the Brisbane match, had resumed training
a few days after arriving in Perth, but when he tested his injured
toe in the nets he found bowling impossible. It was painful for him
even to draw on a sock, such was the soreness of an inflamed blis-
ter on the outside of the fourth toe of his left foot.

Willis had to withdraw from the team to play at Albany two
days before the Test. He was to have captained whilst Brearley
rested but Bob Taylor did so instead. Geoff Boycott might have
been the choice had his troubles not suddenly multiplied as a result of an incident during the Western Australia match. It was revealed in the umpire's report on the match that Boycott had called
umpire Don Weser a '. . . . . . . cheat' during play on Sunday after
he had turned down a confident appeal by Ian Botham against
Kim Hughes. Weser asked Boycott if he would care to repeat the
comment and he apparently did so. Boycott was reported and on
the instructions of Doug Insole he duly apologised. A statement
issued two days later said that the matter had been amicably settled, although the umpire's report still had to be considered by the
Australian Cricket Board and by the TCCB.

The rumours grew wilder now. Boycott, one journalist revealed, had broken down when signing autographs: he was on the
verge of giving up the tour and going home. Did the person who
wrote this consider *asking* Boycott if he had any intention of
returning home? Did he consider that, with his mother gone and
his fight to stay as Yorkshire captain lost, there was nothing for
Boycott to gain by returning home but plenty of lost prestige to be
regained if he could overcome his problems in Australia in the
way that he had always done in the past – namely, by returning to
form and scoring runs?

Not for the first time I found myself feeling very sorry for Boycott. It is never pleasant to see a man being kicked when he is

down. But it also remains a puzzle how someone can show such extraordinary self-discipline during an innings and yet be unable to hold back his feelings at other times. The public gaze on a man like Boycott at a time like this can be burning hot: some people crack more quickly than others in the heat. The emotional character rarely, if ever, comes unscathed through a public career. If Boycott could be more relaxed, more philosophical, more tactful, less obsessed with what others are thinking and saying about him ... but then perhaps he would not be the great batsman he has been if he were all these things.

He found some consolation and some shelter from the storm by sharing the first century opening partnership of the tour with Graham Gooch at Albany. England won their sixth successive tour match in a canter and enjoyed a pleasant, if also long and tiring, day away from the oppressive heat of Perth. Both Boycott and Gooch were run out by direct hits on the stumps from mid-off aimed with great accuracy and velocity by Greg Willy, a local farm manager who was also said to be deadly when it came to hurling stones at kangaroos.

Both Boycott and Gooch, however, had made themselves thoroughly at home on an excellent pitch, which later gave some help to England's spinners but none at all to the country eleven's bevy of medium-pacers. Boycott, slow but sound, made 29 and Gooch, after a sensible period of reconnaissance, suddenly took complete command, driving confidently on the offside, cutting crisply off the back foot whenever the ball was pitched short, and either pulling or driving four huge legside sixes. It was a perfect innings in the context of the match. Gooch needed runs to ensure his Test place and got them impressively. He also entertained the crowd and enabled England to get too big a total for the country eleven to match. Thanks to some accomplished hitting by a local farmer, Bob Miguel, and later by Ted Ditchburn, who had batted with distinction in several previous encounters with touring teams, the country side looked capable at one point of embarrassing their distinguished opponents, but Taylor wisely kept Edmonds and Miller wheeling away and there was never a dull moment as wickets fell and runs were scored at a hectic pace. Edmonds had been given so little bowling of late that it was particularly pleasing to see him take six wickets, and all in all it was a happy day both for the England team and for the local enthusiasts who had put such hard work into making the 250-mile journey south so worthwhile.

A crowd well in excess of 6000 was a remarkable demonstration of the interest shown, because Albany only has 16,500 inhabitants in all. It is an attractive town with some rugged coastal scenery nearby and was the first settlement in Western Australia. Not the least of its attractions is that in summer it remains some ten degrees cooler than Perth. A reconstruction of the tiny sailing ship, the *Amity*, in which the first settlers landed in 1826, has been built near the splendid natural harbour which helps to make Albany an important commercial port, as well as a holiday resort. Wheat, meat and wool are the main products exported from the flat hinterland. The other great local industry had been – until a month before the England team's visit – the whaling business at Chain Beach, which had finally come to an end as a result of government pressure to protect the endangered sperm whale. This lent a special value to the gift of whales' teeth mounted on teak board which Doug Insole and Bob Taylor took home with them on the Fokker Friendship aircraft which bore the team back to Perth through some turbulent weather at the end of an exhausting but memorable day.

The pace of the tour was unrelenting, however. After a comfortable night in the luxurious surroundings of the Sheraton Hotel, so handsomely placed in the centre of Perth and overlooking the wide blue sweep of the Swan River, it was back to the nets next morning. The captain announced fourteen names on the day before the match, delaying his final choice until the exact state of the pitch had been ascertained on the Friday morning.

For the first time there were also some illnesses and injuries to be considered. Willis's trouble seemed to have been overcome by protecting his injured toe with a chiropodist's foam rubber cradle, but a decision on whether he would play was left until the last moment. Miller went down with a stomach upset on the day before the game but happily recovered in time: at Perth, at least, he was considered to be ahead of Edmonds if only one spinner were to play, largely because of his greater batting ability. Lastly Old once again complained of a sore back. He had done so before the first Test and been told to play regardless. But Hendrick's form was now such that the selectors this time took Old at his word.

The first morning of the Test dawned cloudy, windy and warm. Though the pitch looked a little less green than the one on which England had beaten Western Australia, the conditions

were obviously going to favour seam bowlers. England replaced
Edmonds with Lever and Old with Hendrick, and with both sides
so equipped and the conditions as they were it would have been
almost the unorthodox decision to choose to bat first. So, after the
coin had been flown in, as at Brisbane, by parachute, and Brearley
had called 'heads' in vain, Yallop asked England to take first
knock. When, an hour after the start, England had struggled desperately to 10 for two he must have been feeling very pleased with
life.

It was the worthy Hogg who opened the England gates. He
bowled two maidens before, in a remarkable third over, he got rid
of Gooch and Randall in four balls. Neither wicket could be attributed to any great malice in the pitch. Gooch steered rather than
edged a good-length ball close to his off-stump to Maclean and
Randall then played his first ball safely before Hogg was warned
by the umpire for running down the pitch. Perhaps irritated by
this, Hogg's next delivery was a classic bouncer. Moving across
his stumps in his usual way, Randall had to rock back inside the
line at the last moment as the ball reared in and flashed past his
throat. His elastic movement had knocked his cap askew and as he
straightened it he also touched the peak in a gesture of deference
reminiscent of the moment when he had doffed his cap to Lillee
during the Centenary Test. The next ball was also short and Randall got into position to play a short-arm, flat hook shot. He
seemed half to change his mind, though, and only succeeded in
top-edging the ball, which curled up towards the square-leg umpire. Wood ran from backward short leg to clutch the falling ball
gleefully to his chest.

After five overs, therefore, England had lost two of their best
strokeplayers for three runs and the experienced grafters, Boycott
and Brearley, were brought together to stop the rot. They did so,
but it was a slow and desperately sticky process. Both players
might have been l.b.w. to Dymock and Hurst had umpires Brooks
and Bailhache, back in harness, not been feeling in a charitable
mood towards batsmen. Dymock bowled particularly well,
angling the ball across the right-handed batsman and occasionally
swinging it back in to hit the pads. Runs had to be hewn out, like
inaccessible coal.

At lunch England were 30 for two and it was sad that Brearley's
dismissal, after holding on well for 114 minutes, should have come
about because he was trying to get the scoreboard moving. He had

got away with one edge through the slips off Dymock, now operating from the Swan River end, but he was not so lucky the second time, shaping to steer the ball past gully but succeeding only in edging it to Maclean.

Whereas Brearley had been forced to work for every run, Gower immediately changed the whole tempo and atmosphere of the match. He scored a comfortable offside single from his first ball and although he had some serious early problems with Hogg, once being hit on the helmet when he ducked into a bouncer, he generally made batting look an altogether more comfortable exercise from the moment that he came in. The contrast between himself and Boycott could hardly have been more marked: the one fluent, relaxed, effortless; the other stiff, stern, often laboured, playing the same shots over and over again. Boycott's runs came almost exclusively from legside pushes, either to midwicket or to long-leg. He scored not a boundary all day, making 17 before lunch, 19 in the afternoon session and 27 in the last two hours. Yet he stuck there. That was the whole point of the exercise so far as he was concerned and no doubt his colleagues were pleased too, even though most must have felt that he should have been looking for some runs later in the day rather than concentrating solely on survival.

Gower gave Boycott two and a half hours' start and drew level with him for the first time when he had made 25. He reached his fifth 50 in eleven Test innings off 102 balls with four fours and, surviving one confident l.b.w. shout when a ball from Yardley kept low and struck him on the back pad, he moved serenely on to his second Test hundred, his driving elegant and controlled on both sides of the wicket.

He had another difficult time when Yallop took the second new ball as soon as it was due. Gower ducked and defended through two torrid overs from Hogg and Boycott twice played and missed outswingers from Hurst. But Gower suddenly got the measure of Hogg again, first square-cutting, then off-driving him for perfectly timed fours. He then off-drove Hurst for three before ondriving him for his ninth boundary and the one which took him to a delightful hundred. He had spent the previous Australian season scoring runs freely and impressively in first-grade cricket for Cottesloe, one of the suburbs of Perth, so he was especially pleased to have scored his first Test hundred in an Ashes series in Western Australia. Hurst ensured that he wouldn't try to celebrate with any rash shots by bowling him two successive bouncers, and there was time for another confident but vain appeal by Dymock for a caught-behind before the first day ended with England solidly placed at 190 for three after 72 overs of toughly fought cricket.

Gower expressed his gratitude to Boycott in the dressing-room afterwards for helping him to keep concentrating but, as he also said, the excellence of the bowling and the pressure of the occasion made it much easier for him to keep his head down in Test cricket. His record was outstandingly good and contrasted sharply with the inconsistency of his scoring in other first-class cricket. From his very first ball in Test cricket he had proved himself to be completely at home in the highest company, a man who genuinely relished the big occasion. His own batting and Hogg's magnificently hostile fast bowling had embellished the prosaic nature of the rest of the performances on the opening day.

The second day was even more enjoyable to watch. Part of the reason was the larger crowd, 8,791, as opposed to the 7,883 on the first day, which lent a greater air of excitement and animation to the cricket. The weather had also improved and we were given one of those clear blue Perth days with a cooling breeze. But best of all the play had the true cut-and-thrust of Test cricket at its best.

Gower was out in Higgs's third over of the morning having added only one to his overnight 101. His fourth-wicket stand of 158 with Boycott was the main substance of the England innings. It needed a good delivery to dismiss Gower, moving away a fraction as Gower played forward and hitting the off-stump. Hogg bowled well again in his first six-over spell, and England could add only 21 in the first hour despite the fact that Boycott looked in better form, timing the ball more solidly and showing a greater inclination to look for runs.

His seven-and-a-half-hour marathon was finally ended by Hurst who, after all his frustrations the day before, at last got Tom Brooks to raise his finger twice in the space of two overs. Botham was first to go. After a forty-minute reconnaissance he pulled Dymock through mid-wicket for four, repeated the shot for three, then off-drove Hurst for two. England, and the match, might have profited from a speedy 50 by Botham now, but Hurst trapped him in front of his stumps with a ball which came back, and then Boycott fell in the same way to a ball of rather fuller length. Whatever else the crowd might have thought of his laboured innings they also appreciated its value because they applauded him generously as he walked out, head held high. He had been aiming once again towards mid-wicket and there was no doubt at all that his blade was nowadays less straight and his attacking shots much more limited than in his halcyon days. This was not the Boycott who had blazed his way through Australia eight years before, scoring 657 runs in the series before missing the final Test.

England were six down for 242 at lunch with the Derbyshire pair of Miller and Taylor holding the fort. Taylor departed soon after the interval when, with an uncharacteristic rush of blood, he moved several paces down the pitch to Yardley but succeeded only in lofting the ball to mid-wicket. This, however, was indication of a more urgent search for runs by England and it was Miller who led the way in guiding the England tail to exactly 300 before he was ninth out. He got into top gear by straight-driving Yardley for four and when Hogg returned, bursting with aggression, Miller celebrated his survival of another confident appeal, this time for a legside catch by Maclean as the ball brushed Miller's chest on its way through, by first hooking and then square-cutting to the boundary. Lever stuck with Miller for an hour before, having made 14 out of a partnership of 42, he was well caught by Cosier at first slip off the deserving Hurst.

Hogg returned to get through Miller's defences at last after his best innings against Australia, but Willis held on for a while with some graphic demonstrations of his one-handed forward defensive before, with a huge twirl of the bat, he scooped Hogg high to mid-on. Hurst was underneath the ball but Yallop sprinted across from mid-off to hold the ball two-handed as he fell. It was a spectacular end to an England innings which on the whole had been a laboured affair, occupying the first 600 minutes of the match and 117.5 overs. One felt, though, that England had at the very least gone a long way towards insuring themselves against defeat.

With two hours to bat on a golden evening and the pitch now playing quite well, Australia had every chance to get away to a good start. Brearley had to choose two new-ball bowlers from Willis, Hendrick, Lever and Botham and decided that the last two would be likely to swing the ball more. It was Lever who achieved the first break in Australia's frail armour, swinging a ball back in to the left-handed Wood to trap him leg before in his second over.

Darling and Hughes, however, both began competently, and Lever, though he was bowling to four slips and a gully but only

one leg-slip, seemed to be bowling more inswingers than outswingers. Willis soon came on in his place and it was he who again
nipped the Australian innings in the bud. Hughes showed his local
crowd one spectacular shot, a cracking square-cut off Willis for
four, before Willis literally broke his off-stump as he pushed forward inside the line.

Once again the sheer concentration behind Willis's bowling was
impressive. Not a ball was delivered without some premeditated
purpose. Seldom if ever was one wasted. He walked back, and ran
in, and moved about in the field, as if locked in his own world. At
38 Yallop became his second victim, pushing towards mid-on as a
ball of perfect length (bowled from over the wicket) moved across
the left-hander's body and took the off-stump.

Toohey and Darling, however, kept Willis and the other England bowlers at bay, and Darling in particular, his fair head protected by a white fibre-glass helmet, began to play some handsome
strokes on the offside. Then Brearley brought on Miller for a
speculative over just before the close and disaster struck just when
it seemed Australia might end the day on a high note. Toohey
glanced Miller fine on the legside, Hendrick took the pace off the
ball and Botham ran back from forward short-leg with great
speed and opportunism to throw the ball over the top of the bails
to Miller at the non-striker's end. Darling had come up the pitch
looking for a single; he turned too late and lunged desperately but
vainly for the crease as Miller whipped off the bails.

Thus did Australia find themselves perilously placed at 60 for
four, still in danger of a possible follow-on at the start of the third
day. It was a hot and muggy Sunday, despite a continuation of the
easterly breeze blowing across the ground. Miller was able to use
it to float the ball across the right-hand batsman and he began the
day with another impressive spell of off-spin bowling from the
Swan River end.

Willis bowled from the southern end and Toohey settled in
against him competently, playing a fine leg-glance for four to start
the scoring. Toohey was to play an excellent innings but in such a
defensive vein for the greater part of its course that he did not
score another four until forty minutes after lunch. This was at
once testimony to the tightness of England's bowling and to the
determined concentration of Toohey's batting.

Alas, his partner, Cosier, is not in the same class. Looking like
Henry VIII with his red beard, his red curly hair and his bulk, he

gave no great confidence to Australian supporters before driving firm-footed at Willis and edging to Gooch at fourth slip. In the next over Maclean tried to sweep his second ball from Miller, edged it onto his pad and was caught at silly-point, again by a delighted Gooch.

England's fielding and bowling were now outstandingly good and Australia must have wondered where the next run was going to come from. Toohey was twice denied runs off Willis by dazzling stops, one by Randall at cover, another by Miller at short-leg. A second miraculous diving stop by Randall cut off a certain four by Yardley when Lever briefly took over at the grandstand end. Another resounding drive by Yardley, however, did earn him four runs and it was not until Hendrick returned to the attack that Yardley was out, touching a perfect outswinger to Taylor and not even waiting for the umpire to raise his finger. It is a pity that more batsmen did not follow Yardley's example because it was partly the excessive number of appeals, and the refusal of most batsmen to walk until they were given out, which made this such a difficult game to umpire.

It was strange that whereas in theory one of the weaker points in this Australian side was the apparent frailty of its tail, in practice England often found the later batsmen more difficult to remove than the specialists, and so it proved in this case. The main reason, of course, is the fact that the old ball bounces so much less in Australia than the new one. Toohey was by now thoroughly established, and although he did not look capable until late in his innings of taking the initiative from the formidably accurate England bowlers, he never looked in trouble. This was a crucial innings both for him and for the Australian cause generally, for much hope had been placed in Toohey when the series began. His recent form had been poor and if the selectors had found themselves forced to drop him they would have been depriving themselves of one of the few players of proven Test class still available to them.

Toohey was joined by the redoubtable Hogg who again showed himself to be a determined competitor, a batsman who did not believe in much movement of the feet against quick bowlers but who did possess a very good eye. He showed this almost at once with a crisp cut for four off Hendrick, and some more solid blows in front of the wicket took Australia past the 110 they needed to avoid the calamity of being asked to follow on. When Maclean had fallen at 79 and six wickets had already gone this had seemed a distinct possibility. As it turned out, however, England had to labour until teatime under the hot sun before the last wicket was taken. Hogg looked thoroughly affronted when he was adjudged caught-behind off the inside edge against Willis after making 18 and batting for more than an hour either side of lunch, but when he pointed to his hip as he walked past Tom Brooks that stern critic of players' tantrums turned his back and walked pointedly away from him as a father might ignore the complaints of a child when his patience has worn thin. It was the gesture of a man tired of being in a position where players, crowd, broadcasters and press could all freely criticise without having the same responsibility. Three days later he retired.

Hogg's exit, however, merely permitted the entrance of an equally resolute and in some ways better organised batsman: Geoff Dymock. He had worked hard at his batting in moving up the order to number eight for Queensland, and by playing very straight and sensibly for another hour he was able to share with Toohey a stand of 57 which gave Australia a much greater chance of saving the game. It was Dymock, indeed, who was at the other end when Toohey gave the third-day crowd of 9,802 their most exciting over of the day. Botham decided to test the little man with some short stuff and Toohey, knowing the new ball was due shortly, took up the challenge with a gusto which again invited comparison with Doug Walters. Four times Botham dug the ball in. Four times Toohey stepped back and hooked the ball off his eyebrows over mid-wicket. Three of the shots went for four and one for two. Had not the outfield, so heavily fertilised and watered as to penalise good batting throughout the match, been so thickly grassed, the fourth shot too would have reached the boundary.

The proliferation of lush green outfields has long been a worrying trend in modern cricket. They have altered the whole balance of the game. If a batsman plays a glorious cover-drive which beats the one-saving field but only gains two runs rather than four, the balance is surely wrong. If the seam bowlers are able, because of the lushness of the grass, to keep the shine on the ball all day long, the balance between fast bowlers and spinners is wrong too. This is the next most important reason, after slackening over-rates, why scoring rates have generally declined: indeed, why one no longer sees the heavy scoring which used to characterise Test matches of yore. One has only to look at the freak English summer of 1976 when, at least in county cricket, spin bowlers had unusual success and batsmen scored more heavily than normal, to see the difference that dry, fast outfields can make to cricket. The other great difference, of course, is that if the pitches themselves are over-watered or -fertilised they tend to give too much help for too long to the seam bowlers and too little too late to the spinners. The old traditional 'good cricket wicket' was a hard true one which enabled batsmen to play shots with confidence, fast bowlers to get some help with the new ball, and spinners to turn the ball as the pitch became tired and dry late in the match.

The taking of the new ball was the final turning-point in Australia's first innings. Before he discarded the old one Brearley had a long conversation with the umpires about whether or not Dymock, who had held England up for more than an hour, should be allowed to face a bouncer or two. Yallop and Brearley had arrived at a civilised solution to the bouncer problem by agreeing before the first two Test matches as to who should face bumpers and who should not. Generally speaking the last three batsmen on either side were protected, but if any should hang around for a long time they could be entitled to expect the occasional short ball. Brearley felt Dymock was well enough established; the umpires felt that he should not be attacked in such a way *with the new ball*. In the event Hendrick bowled Dymock with a good-length ball between bat and pad only two balls after unwrapping the 'new cherry' and Willis, after somehow hitting Hurst's off-stump without dislodging a bail, then had him caught behind to end the innings at 190, 119 behind England. Willis's return of 5 for 44 took his tally of Test victims in 1978 alone to 56.

Frustrated by a slow over-rate, some steady bowling, notably by Dymock, and the outfield, Boycott and Gooch could extend the lead by only 58 more runs in the final two hours. In perfect batting light both played well enough, Boycott looking much more confident, authoritative and assertive than in his first innings and Gooch hitting at least one pleasing stroke, a four to long-on off Yardley which might with a few more inches have been a six. But England would have hoped for more than a lead of 177 with only two days of the match to go. Boycott survived two more 'incidents'. Having eschewed use of the now fashionable fibre-glass helmet he ducked into a short ball from Hogg and was struck squarely on the side of the head. The ball flew down to third-man for four leg-byes with the force of a perfectly timed late cut. Yet

Boycott showed neither pain nor concern: he merely smiled cheerfully in the true Yorkshire tradition.

There was no smiling a few balls later, however, when he played at a ball from Dymock and the Australians leapt and yelled in unison for what they thought was a snick to the wicket-keeper. Boycott and umpire Brooks remained motionless as statues. Fortune was smiling on 'our Geoffrey' again. He was 23 not out at stumps, Gooch 26 not out, and England relaxed on the rest day knowing that although they were now in an impregnable position they would be unlikely to have enough time, on what seemed now to be a blameless pitch, to bowl Australia out a second time for a two-nil lead in the series.

The weather on the rest day was disappointing for those hoping to catch up on their suntans, but overcast skies and the occasional drop of rain did not stop some of the England players sailing a catamaran on the Swan River or several of the Australians from taking a boat across to Rottnest island. For officials whose responsibility was the transport of fifty-seven players and writers more than two thousand miles across Australia, however, there was little chance to relax. A strike by groundstaff at airports around Australia was playing havoc with the Christmas arrangements of the nation, and the England team made contingency plans to cancel their forthcoming three-day match in Adelaide and to travel instead by train across the Nullabor. Instead of an air journey of little more than three hours, the idea was for the team to leave Perth railway station on Wednesday night, the evening after the finish of the Test match, and to go via Adelaide to Melbourne, arriving on the Saturday morning of 23 December. For some of us this would have been an exciting opportunity to see the heart of Australia which would not otherwise have arisen, but for those players out of the Test team it might have meant no cricket for a month. In the event, however, the strike was called off.

It was hot, sticky and airless when play resumed on Tuesday morning. Perth's traditional dry heat and breezes were nowhere to be felt. The pitch seemed to have turned from grey to white. No wonder Brearley admitted before play began that he would like to have had Edmonds in the side now. As he pointed out, he was not to know that he was going to lose the toss and four specialist seamers might yet do the job for him. But the principle of fielding a balanced attack seemed likely to be vindicated again.

Australia had an encouraging start. After a friendly maiden by
Hurst to Gooch, Boycott was trapped l.b.w. by Hogg's third ball.
It was much the same story as with Boycott's many previous l.b.w.
dismissals: the ball coming back in from the off and the batsman
aiming to mid-on rather than playing with a dead straight bat. Of
Boycott's eleven dismissals on the tour so far, five had now been
leg-before.

This was the prelude to some exciting cricket. Randall began
with a sharp single to mid-off which had the ponderous Gooch
running for his life, then cover-drove Hogg for a glorious four.
Gooch was quickly infected with this spirit of aggression and he
splendidly square-cut both Hogg and Dymock for four before,
when 35, he edged a hot low chance off Hogg to Hughes at second
slip. This was not accepted, but although Gooch hooked Hogg for
another four it did not take long for the bowler to have his revenge. Twice he brought the ball back to hit Gooch's voluminous
pads and, with that certainty which inspires confidence in him,
umpire Bailhache upheld the second appeal.

Brearley himself came in at number four rather than promoting
a freer scorer, pushed tentatively at his first ball, and was caught
behind off the outside edge to give the rampaging Rodney two
wickets in two balls. Gower survived the hat-trick and if Brearley
was able to get over his own disappointment he must have realised
that from the team's point of view the combination of Randall
and Gower was likely to be rather more productive.

Randall was in marvellously uninhibited mood. A few weeks
before he had told me that his two ambitions on the tour were for
England to win the Ashes and for his own moderate Test record to
be improved. He quite genuinely put the first ambition before the
second and his play on the fourth morning was clear evidence of
this. He drove, cut, hooked, and on one occasion slogged his way
to 45 in 65 balls as if his Test record were not of the slightest concern to him. Only when Yallop turned to Yardley's off-spin did he
look like being restrained, and it was Yardley who took his wicket
when Randall moved down the pitch, swept and the ball lobbed
up to be caught by Cosier at leg-slip. Only when he was halfway
back to the pavilion did Randall realise that the ball had, in fact,
probably struck him above the right wrist and that he had walked
unnecessarily. He was on the point of turning back but decided
against it and merely smiled at the stupidity of his sacrifice.

For some recent England sides the loss of such a player batting in such a manner at such a time might have been a grave setback: in this team Randall simply made way for Botham and the attack continued to be carried to the Australians with equal belligerence and unselfishness and to equal effect. Botham swept Yardley for four second ball and in the off-spinner's next over drove him powerfully for two more boundaries between mid-off and the bowler. Botham had overtaken Gower at lunch when England were 150 for four; 92 for four represented a good morning for them.

As long as Australia continued to take wickets, however, they were able to keep England's scoring within reasonable bounds, and Hogg yet again kept them in the match with his spell after lunch. Gower looked disconcerted by one short ball before Hogg had him caught behind, trying to force off the back foot a ball which lifted and took the top edge. There was one spot at the Swan River end which Hogg had found on both occasions and which Lever was to exploit later in the day.

Botham and Miller, the last front-line batsmen, kept the scoring going at a healthy rate, adding 25 together before Botham moved down the pitch to try to hit Yardley back over his head. He did not quite get to the pitch of the ball and instead lofted a catch to Wood, running back from deep mid-off.

From this point the initiative switched to Australia as they worked their way through England's long tail and England themselves began to have second thoughts about the wisdom of losing wickets with too much gay abandon. Indeed when Miller, after two resounding hooks off Hogg, followed Lever into the pavilion at 201, lofting Yardley to wide mid-on, Willis and Taylor actually seemed more interested in using up time rather than looking for runs. Taylor was severely handicapped by a strained groin muscle and had to bat with Randall as his runner. Hogg took the new ball and soon claimed Taylor's wicket with the help of Maclean's fourth straightforward catch before the deserving Dymock finished the innings five minutes after the scheduled tea interval. Yardley, with three for 41 as a reward for a steady and intelligent spell, and Hogg, with five for 57, took the bowling honours. Hogg now had 17 wickets at an average of 13 each from his first two Tests.

The match was thus in an intriguing position when Australia began their second innings needing 328 to win with five minutes under eight hours to get the runs on what was basically an excellent pitch. There was many an optimist in Perth who believed they could get the runs given a good start on this fourth evening. But a menacing grey sky was threatening to upset the predictions both of these patriots and of the majority who felt that an England win or a draw were still, in that order, the most likely results. Willis raced in with even greater vigour than normal from the Swan River end as the breeze rose and died every few moments in the thundery atmosphere. It was rather appropriate weather for the state of the match: unpredictable, potentially explosive.

Wood, his Test place threatened by his poor form and his refusal to sign for more than one year with established cricket, unlike the rest of the Australian team, edged Willis low to Brearley in the first over and for once the England captain was not able to hold on to a devilish chance which only just carried to him. But Lever was more lucky when he took the new ball from the grandstand end. Darling had just negotiated a torrid over from Willis, in which he hooked one short ball for four but received a second straight into his most tender parts – with painful consequences, despite his abdominal protector. Now, to prove that his luck was really out, he got a ball from Lever which lifted from just short of a length to head height. He did well to fend the ball off with his glove but it carried to Boycott at mid-on and Darling departed sadly to hear that his state side South Australia had lost their match in Adelaide to Western Australia after being on top for three days. It was definitely not his day.

Now Australia were in grave danger of another early collapse but, with Willis pawing the ground in his eagerness to start his third over, Wood and Hughes appealed against the gradually fading light and the umpires came to their rescue only a few minutes before the storm, which had been threatening for most of the day, broke decisively over the ground to end play for the day an hour and a half early.

Australia therefore began the final day at eleven for one with any slim hope of victory gone and only a draw to play for. On the other hand the loss of that hour and a half had greatly improved their more realistic chances of a draw. A clear, hot sunny morning gave a much greater chance of withstanding the first few dangerous overs whilst the ball was still red and hard. Willis and Lever put all they knew into their opening stints, but Hughes and Wood looked far more comfortable than they had the night before. Hughes square-cut Willis for four and Wood twice hit Lever off

his toes for what ought to have been boundaries had not the
already slow outfield lost still more pace after the rain. All went
well until, forty minutes after the eleven o'clock start and in
Willis's fourth over, Hughes shaped to cut again. This time the
ball bounced higher than he had expected and moved in towards
his chest with the result that Hughes had to hit the ball in a tucked-
up position. He sliced it straight to Gooch at fourth slip and
Gooch held on with both hands to a hot and crucial catch. Australia were 36 for two as Yallop walked out in his white helmet to join
Wood.

Wood, so like a boyish, slightly smaller and left-handed version
of Greg Chappell in his erect bearing and in the impression he
gives of self-contained composure, continued to play with an
equal measure of confidence and competence and at the end of the
first hour Australia had added 39 more runs for one more wicket,
a rate of progress which still kept their outside hopes of an unexpected victory alive.

There was much excitement amongst a small crowd of 4,493,
basking in glorious sunshine tempered by a breeze at last blowing
up from the traditional quarter. Coming from Fremantle there
was a pleasant salty tang to it, too; it provided great relief after the
mugginess of the previous few days. 'We played in temperatures
over 100 for three days here last year,' said Bobby Simpson, rather
ruefully. There was a cheerful atmosphere amongst the press
and broadcasters too. It was Bill O'Reilly's birthday, and Ken
Casellas of the *West Australian* and Brian Williams of Reuters
had both become fathers for the first time during the previous
twenty-four hours.

But the chances of their celebrating an Australian victory as
well as the happy arrival of two new Australian citizens plum-
meted to zero soon after Hendrick and Botham had taken over
the bowling from Willis and Lever. The first chance of an England wicket was not taken. Wood, who never needs much per-
suasion to hook, despatched Botham to square-leg for four,
then tried to repeat the shot and instead lofted the ball high
into the blue firmament above Boycott's head at mid-wicket. It
was a catch Boycott would have expected to take perhaps nineteen times out of twenty in fielding practice. But this was a
Test when all eyes were gazing at the falling ball and the figure
circling uneasily beneath it. Perhaps the ball swirled a little in
the breeze and no doubt it was difficult to pick up against the

blue of the sky; at any rate Boycott misjudged its line of descent
and sprawled as the ball brushed both hands and fell to ground.

But the immediate disappointment of Wood's escape, when he
had scored 28, was forgotten by England when Hendrick broke
through again in a decisive way when the total had reached 58.
First Yallop, who had looked distinctly unhappy, flicked at a ball
on his leg-stump and Taylor caught the thinnest of deflections;
then Toohey, on whom much seemed to depend after his first-
innings 81 not out, pushed forward to the ideal late outswinger,
got another thin edge, and the Derbyshire pair had struck again.

That really seemed like the beginning of the end. In fact, it was
the start of the main Australian resistance. Boycott had a second
chance to catch Wood at mid-wicket when he miscued a legside
swing at Botham. This time Boycott was late to move and had
further to run but again got both hands to the ball before dropping the chance. Then, to add insult to his personal mortification,
Boycott promptly caught Wood off Botham – off a no-ball!
Before lunch, taken at 80 for four, Cosier was also missed, a hard,
high caught-and-bowled chance to Hendrick's left hand off his
own bowling.

Wood and Cosier batted with steadily increasing confidence
after the interval and again it seemed that a draw might be the
most likely outcome. Wood reached a fifty which eloquently
spoke both of his ability and of his inexperience, one might almost
say of his cricketing naïvety. Here were Australia desperately
needing a gutsy, backs-to-the-wall grind to deny England their
victory; if Australia had ever had any realistic chance of winning it
had long gone. Now Wood was continuing to go for his attacking
shots whenever a half-chance presented itself. He played some
handsome ones, too, but there would have been a more appropriate time and place for them. In a Test match with the Ashes at
stake it should have been surrender at no price. One small incident
was evidence of Wood's lack of strategy. He cut a ball towards
point for a single. Randall for once misfielded, the ball deflecting
off his hands no more than six or seven yards. He can cover that
ground in the blink of an eye, yet Wood went a quarter of the way
down the pitch again looking for a second run before Randall's
lightning recovery made him realise it would have been suicidal
to go on running. He made his ground just in time. The point was
not so much that he had disobeyed one of the elementary rules of
running between the wickets, but more that his outlook was

wrong. He was taking risks all the time instead of concentrating single-mindedly upon survival.

The same criticism applied even more strongly to Cosier. He played some splendid, spirited strokes. They would have looked well in a one-day match or in a chase for runs. But in this context his innings was almost schoolboyish. As someone said, if Cosier had scored a century Australia would still almost certainly have lost. The lessons of cricket are hard indeed. Cosier batted entertainingly and well. He made 47 against outstanding bowling in difficult circumstances. Yet he did not stay long enough at the crease. Australia lost and the vice-captain was to lose his place as a result.

Even so, if the attacking partnership of Wood and Cosier had lasted even half an hour longer than it did England could have so lost the initiative that a draw might have been honourably achieved. It was certainly invigorating batting for home supporters whilst it lasted. The fifty partnership came up in only 52 minutes, Cosier going through his repertoire of hearty short-arm drives, cuts and pulls with the gusto of his regal likeness tucking in to the meat course. Botham was hit for ten in one over. Miller replaced him, bowling into the south-westerly breeze, and at first got some rough treatment too. A renowned critic, a former first-class off-spinner and county captain and an unashamed patriot, muttered to me: 'We need a wicket badly. I wish Brearley would put Miller on the *other* end.' I muttered something about the breeze. 'It's the pitch which'll get him the wickets, not the breeze,' was his passionate reply. But cricket makes fools of the wisest. Within minutes Miller got a ball to drift across Cosier's body on that very breeze and the batsman's hearty sweep made no contact. Instead he was hit low between the legs in front of the stumps and Miller's appeal was upheld by umpire Bailhache.

Cosier and Wood had put on 83 but this time there was to be no arresting of the Australian decline. Cosier's dismissal began a collapse which was as inevitable and as embarrassingly one-sided as anything which England had suffered at the hands of Lillee and Thomson four years before. Wood was next to go. Lever returned, Wood played forward, Lever and the England men behind the bat appealed half-heartedly; umpire Brooks raised his hand halfway, seemed to think better of it, thought again and then lifted his finger decisively. Wood looked at the sky in disbelief, then walked slowly away, later to make his feelings about the decision even plainer.

Tom Brooks, who had told me in the Chappell/Denness series
that he had grown weary of the pressures of umpiring Test cricket,
had announced his retirement during the lunch interval. He said
this time that he had realised during the game that 'the old mental
and physical machines weren't synchronising', and that he would
rather be watching the match than earning 800 dollars (£500) for
umpiring it. Of Wood's dismissal he said afterwards: 'You do
what you have to do, what you think is right, and I have no regrets
on that score.' Brooks was retiring at the age of 58 and whatever
the controversial aspects of his final match may have been he had
always been a fair, dignified, respected and likeable umpire.

It was all over very quickly after this. Maclean edged Miller to
slip; Yardley, after one or two defiant blows, was caught by
Botham at full stretch to his left at second slip, a phenomenal
catch; and Hogg and Hurst both had their stumps hit.

It so often happens after a decisive Test win that all the attention is given to the losers instead of to the winners. It was worrying, of course, for Australia that Yallop's young side was not
getting enough runs to give itself a chance, despite the unpredictable England batting and the excellence of Rodney Hogg. But
Willis, Lever and the Derbyshire pair of Hendrick and Miller had
all bowled superbly on a pitch which had continued to do just
enough to give them a chance. England were too good, and I do
not believe that Ian Chappell's 'World Series' Australian side
would have withstood them much more effectively. Yet the
memory of the floating voters in Australian cricket was short.
Most of the Packer Australians had been discredited and soundly
defeated in England eighteen months before. But to Australians
by and large it was a perfectly natural reaction to this second successive defeat to claim that England were winning because they
were not playing against a full-strength Australian team.

AUSTRALIA v ENGLAND (Second Test)

Perth, December 15, 16, 17, 19, 20. England won by 166 runs.

England *First Innings*		*Second Innings*	
G. Boycott lbw b Hurst	77	lbw b Hogg	23
G. A. Gooch c Maclean b Hogg	1	lbw b Hogg	43
D. W. Randall c Wood b Hogg	0	c Cosier b Yardley	45
*J. M. Brearley c Maclean b Dymock	17	c Maclean b Hogg	0
D. I. Gower b Hogg	102	c Maclean b Hogg	12
I. T. Botham lbw b Hurst	11	c Wood b Yardley	30
G. Miller b Hogg	40	c Toohey b Yardley	25
†R. W. Taylor c Hurst b Yardley	12	(9) c Maclean b Hogg	2
J. K. Lever c Cosier b Hurst	14	(8) c Maclean b Hurst	10
R. G. D. Willis c Yallop b Hogg	2	not out	3
M. Hendrick not out	7	b Dymock	1
Extras (b6, lb9, w3, nb8)	26	(lb6, nb8)	14
Total	309	Total	208

Fall of Wickets
1 – 3   2 – 3   3 – 41   4 – 199   5 – 219   6 – 224   7 – 253   8 – 295   9 – 300
1 – 58   2 – 93   3 – 93   4 – 135   5 – 151   6 – 176   7 – 201   8 – 201   9 – 206

Bowling	*First Innings*				*Second Innings*			
Hogg	30.5	9	65	5	17	2	57	5
Dymock	34	4	72	1	16.3	2	53	1
Hurst	26	7	70	3	17	5	43	1
Yardley	23	1	62	1	16	1	41	3
Cosier	4	2	14	0				

Australia *First Innings*		*Second Innings*	
G. M. Wood lbw b Lever	5	(2) c Taylor b Lever	64
W. M. Darling run out	25	(1) c Boycott b Lever	5
K. J. Hughes b Willis	16	c Gooch b Willis	12
*G. N. Yallop b Willis	3	c Taylor b Hendrick	3
P. M. Toohey not out	81	c Taylor b Hendrick	0
G. J. Cosier c Gooch b Willis	4	lbw b Miller	47
†J. A. Maclean c Gooch b Miller	0	c Brearley b Miller	1
B. Yardley c Taylor b Hendrick	12	c Botham b Lever	7
R. M. Hogg c Taylor b Willis	18	b Miller	0
G. Dymock b Hendrick	11	not out	6
A. G. Hurst c Taylor b Willis	5	b Lever	5
Extras (lb7, w1, nb2)	10	(lb3, w4, nb4)	11
Total	190	Total	161

Fall of Wickets
1 – 8   2 – 34   3 – 38   4 – 60   5 – 78   6 – 79   7 – 100   8 – 128   9 – 185
1 – 8   2 – 36   3 – 58   4 – 58   5 – 141   6 – 143   7 – 143   8 – 147   9 – 151

Bowling	*First Innings*				*Second Innings*			
Lever	7	0	20	1	8.1	2	28	4
Botham	11	2	46	0	11	1	54	0
Willis	18.5	5	44	5	12	1	36	1
Hendrick	14	1	39	2	8	3	11	2
Miller	16	6	31	1	7	4	21	3

Umpires: T. F. Brooks and R. C. Bailhache.   Toss won by Australia.

Chapter Six

MELBOURNE: BREARLEY LOSES AT LAST

Whatever the effects may have been of World Series Cricket on the course of the series for the Ashes, there was no questioning the changing attitude of a substantial proportion of the Australian public towards what had once been derided as the Packer Circus. World Series Cricket was being marketed much more effectively in its second year. Its gates were rising dramatically by comparison with the first year, largely because of the increase in night matches. Simultaneously the gates for established cricket were falling. The crowds at Brisbane had been considerably lower than four years before. In the five days at Perth only 35,667 people had paid to watch – less than half the figure of four years before. On the principle of political swings one could also expect reduced crowds in the two major cities of Melbourne and Sydney. The Melbourne Test would, as usual, be the touchstone. The Australian public has never tolerated losers for long but the Ashes were not yet lost, and from one's own observations, interest in the series was still extraordinarily active.

Goodness knows how many conversations I had, in the days around Christmas, about the worth of Australia's young team, the excellence of Brearley's captaincy and Willis's bowling, and the disruption to the game caused by World Series Cricket. Before Christmas I was fortunate to rest for two days on the 7,000-acre Mount Schanck estate near to Mount Gambier close to the southern coast of South Australia. But I was able to see on television the last hours of the three-day match in Adelaide which produced an exciting finish and was played in an appropriate spirit of goodwill. England had declared their first innings at 234 for five after Boycott had made four runs in just under an hour and a half at the crease on a green pitch before he was caught behind. This followed South Australia's 241 during which Old defied a migraine and bowled particularly well. After England's sticky start Tolchard yet again compared favourably with his colleagues, hitting 72 in 59 minutes, and Radley began his rehabilitation with a sound 60. He said afterwards that he attributed his run of low scores not so much to being hit on the head as to a total lack of luck just when he most needed it. The previous twelve months, he believed, had been successful partly because his luck had been so much better.

South Australia's second innings was notable for some delightfully subtle off-spin bowling by John Emburey, whose five for 67 compared almost embarrassingly favourably with Edmonds's none for 91, although Edmonds bowled chinamen for his last six overs to hasten the declaration. Blewett left England the stiff target of 239 in two hours plus fifteen overs. Boycott was relegated to number eleven after his recent slow scoring but took the insult in good humour. 'Wilfred Rhodes started at number eleven and went to number one,' he said. 'I've done t'opposite.'

The alternative opening pair, Brearley and Randall, set off at the right pace. Randall was in his usual good spirits. He hit Bill Johnston's son David for six but soon after Johnston hit Brearley in his middle and Randall immediately summoned Bernard Thomas and a stretcher. No sooner had Thomas arrived than Brearley popped up smiling, whereupon Randall put Thomas onto the stretcher and he was borne off instead! It was Gooch, hitting some glorious cover-drives, who took England close to their target but, when he was stumped, wickets started to fall regularly and a South Australian double over England looked very possible. Miller, however, kept his head and his wicket, as well as pushing the score along, and when Boycott emerged at number eleven 16 runs were needed from 15 balls. Amidst much excitement, although before only a small Sunday crowd, the target was reduced to eight needed off the last eight-ball over. Boycott found his old style to hit the third of them firmly for four backward of cover off the back foot – his first boundary in fourteen hours and seventeen minutes at the crease – but two were still needed off the last two balls. Miller could not score off the penultimate delivery from Blewett but hit the next towards point. Although he and Boycott ran a comfortable single they could not take the second which would have brought victory. The scores were therefore level but the match officially drawn because not all the wickets had fallen.

It was a cheerful preliminary to the Christmas festivities. The team arrived in Melbourne in a violent thunderstorm a few hours later, but the weather was at least warm between the showers when the team celebrated Christmas with a lunch party at their hotel. The team's entertainment officers, Messrs Lever and Hendrick, had ordained that the chief entertainment should be a fancy dress competition; Bob Willis appeared as a faceless blind umpire with a white stick, Derek Randall as the Queen, David Gower as a cowboy, Ken Barrington in the full-dress uniform of a bandmaster, Bob Taylor as an executioner, and Doug Insole as Inspector Clouseau. It was Insole who won the first prize of a toy duck.

After the festivities the afternoon dragged for most of the players as a Christmas away from home invariably does. So far only one of the wives, Kathy Botham, who had been obliged to come early because of her pregnancy, had joined her husband; loneliness tends to bite hardest of all at Christmas, the traditional gathering-time for any family.

Journalists and broadcasters, as well as cricketers, were obliged to be in Melbourne on Christmas Day in preparation for the first of the One-Day Internationals due to be played the next day. In the two days before then my own family had a chance to see the real Australia. The Mount Schanck Station once comprised more than 100,000 acres before the Clarke family who own it sold major portions of it at bargain prices to soldiers returning after the war. The land around is now farmed in relatively small settlements, though to British eyes 7,000 acres is still a very large area and it took Reg Hayman, whose family has managed the Station for the Clarkes for three generations, most of a hot and sultry morning to drive us around the southern portion of the estate on Christmas Eve, checking on the well-being of the large holdings of cattle, horses and sheep. The hard realities of country life in Australia were very evident. Strips of land alongside each of the huge grass paddocks, already drawn of their moist spring greenness and now the colour of straw, had been optimistically ploughed to break up the bush fires which would almost certainly strike at some time during the long summer ahead. During our tour of inspection Hayman's experienced eye picked out two sheep from the masses of others (all newly sheared in a huge nineteenth-century limestone shearing-shed) which had been struck down by the dreaded blow-fly. Hundreds of these merciless insects will make their home in the soiled wool around the animal's tail and lay their eggs there; unless the sheep can be clipped, dressed and disinfected quickly it will be eaten away until all it can do is lie down and die.

For the men who work the land and care for the animals it may be a tough life but it is also a good one, set amidst miles of rolling pasture-land broken by the large belts of fir plantations and by the two isolated volcanic hills, Mount Gambier and Mount Schanck. Mount Gambier's chief attraction, apart from some old houses built from local limestone and a thriving timber industry, is the extraordinary blue lake which forms a huge natural reservoir in a volcanic crater. It retains an almost dazzling blue colour no matter what the hue of the sky, changing to a darker blue in October. Its depth has declined but the lake is still apparently bottomless and scientists have been unable to explain the reason for its unfailing blueness. Exactly two years before, I had spent Christmas Eve seeing the Taj Mahal at Agra. At times like this when the chance arises to see natural or man-made wonders at first hand, the often hectic and wearying nature of travelling the world in pursuit of a cricket team is forgotten. In the few days around Christmas I also saw, in the wild, koalas, kangaroos, emus and a variety of other birds including penguins, pelicans, parrots and, perhaps more common but still strange to English eyes, black swans.

One more brief observation before returning to cricket: the telephone rang several times whilst we were staying with the Haymans. No one rushed to his feet to answer it. Each time the conversation, even on one occasion the meal, was finished first. The caller never seemed to ring off. In the country, the real country, there is seldom any need to hurry. Soon after I got back to Melbourne I was rung by my office at three o'clock in the morning and I knew that I was back on the job.

The Boxing Day plans of many of Victoria's sports-mad public, however, were ruined by Melbourne's capricious climate. The Christmas Eve thunderstorm was followed by another of almost equal ferocity on Christmas night, and play in the first of the One-Day Internationals for the Benson and Hedges Cup was abandoned without a ball being bowled. The Australian Cricket Board was not insured, indeed they would have lost more money if they had been, for they would have had to have nominated two hours during which ten points of rain would fall before insurance money could be claimed. Not enough rain fell in the period they would have chosen, the two hours before the match was due to start. For the Board, although the match was hastily rearranged for a date later in the tour, it was a severe blow. Some $100,000, or more than £60,000, was lost, at least for the time being, and so too was the chance to hit back at World Series Cricket with an expected crowd of 40,000 or more. Boxing Day is traditionally a day when Melbourne crowds turn out in their thousands not only for the cricket but also for the start of the Open Tennis Championships at Kooyong.

The disappointment, however, did not last long – except for Gary Cosier and Phil Carlson who, despite being dropped from the Test squad, had been due to play in the Benson and Hedges match. They flew back to Brisbane disconsolate at losing an opportunity to prove the selectors wrong.

Such was the dampness of the turf at the MCG that the nets were still dangerous to play in the following day, despite fine weather for most of Boxing Day – a fact learned painfully by Mike Brearley, who decided to risk a quick net against the eager young Jonathan Agnew. The second ball delivered by Agnew from no more than a three-pace run-up lifted to hit Brearley over the right eye, even though he was wearing one of the new fibre-glass helmets. The wound required six stitches but Brearley quickly silenced rumours that he would not be fit to play in the Test, and within twenty hours was facing a combination of Willis, Old and Hendrick in the nets before announcing not only that he would play but also that he would open the batting, with Graham Gooch at last dropping down the order to number four. It was a sensible move in theory, so long as the two wise old heads at the top of the order did not let things get too bogged down. If on the other hand they could give England a reasonable start, the quartet which followed them – Randall, Gooch, Gower and Botham – would on a good day be capable of handing out an almost Caribbean-style hammering to the attack. They would need to be given, however, a faster pitch and outfield than Melbourne would provide after its rainy spring.

The other surprise in the England side was the inclusion of Emburey rather than Edmonds as the second spinner. The relative performances of the two in the match in Adelaide was the reason for the decision. Edmonds, who would have been an automatic choice at the start of the tour, had lost the marvellous rhythm and control he had enjoyed for most of the year, largely because he had been given relatively little bowling to do.

John Lever was named in England's twelve with Hendrick being preferred to a now fully fit Chris Old, but it was Lever who was named twelfth man when the vital Test began on a fine, cool morning before a crowd which grew during the day to 35,174.

Australia left Yardley out of their twelve, the inclusion of Border for his first Test giving Yallop – like Brearley – a balanced attack of three faster bowlers and two spinners.

It was Yallop who won a vital toss and with no hesitation chose to bat first on a pitch already dry and patchy in appearance. Willis began the attack from the southern end, struck Wood on the pads first ball and appealed confidently for l.b.w. It was a deceptive start although Willis proceeded to beat Wood more often than not in his first few overs. Botham shared the new ball and also appealed for a bat-and-pad catch off Wood during his first over. It hardly looked then as though Wood would still be batting at the end of the day, but he responded by driving the first four of the match square on the offside to a tremendous roar of encouragement. It was the first of many good and positive strokes – mainly cuts and hooks – played by both Wood and Darling as they took Australia past fifty in only the thirteenth over. There was little movement for the England bowlers either through the air or off the seam, and only Willis got the ball to bounce. Even he had a no-ball hooked firmly to the boundary by Darling.

For all the admirable confidence and assertiveness of this opening stand, there were three hair-raising moments in the first hour when the boyish enthusiasm of Wood and Darling might have ended in disaster. At 27, when Darling was nine, he pushed the ball straight to Randall at cover, started off on a mad single, turned in mid-pitch and would have been run out by yards if Randall's studied throw had hit the stumps. Ten minutes later Wood was 20 when he survived a second run-out opportunity to Hendrick who, following through off his own bowling, had time to take aim with his under-arm throw but still missed. Yet again Darling might have been run out when he misjudged Gower's ghost-like speed across the turf, but again the fielder's throw missed the stumps. On an unlucky day for the batsmen all three might have been wickets thrown away. Instead, such is the thin line between success and failure in cricket, Australia passed the previous best opening stand by either side in the series at 59, and before an hour and a half was passed Brearley was calling up Emburey for the first over of spin.

In a sense the change worked, for a wicket fell in Emburey's second over, but it did so through the run-out which both batsmen seemed intent on achieving. Too often one describes a run-out as suicidal but on this occasion it would be difficult to find an adjective more apt. Wood hit Emburey firmly to Boycott at mid-on and started up the pitch without calling. Darling ran down the pitch looking for the run which was never there and Boycott calmly threw the ball to Emburey, who removed the bails.

65 for one became 65 for two when Hughes was hit on the boot and was judged caught behind first ball. Poor Hughes looked, both to the naked eye and later to the eye of the merciless slow-motion replay, to have been far harder done by than anyone sent on his way by the maligned umpire Brooks in the previous game. Max O'Connell was the unfortunate umpire this time, and as Hughes walked unhappily away one wondered not for the first time whether some technical wizard might not soon produce a small television receiver which umpires could keep in their pockets and if necessary consult before making a decision.

Happily Yallop began his innings with a succession of authoritative strokes, notably several full-blooded off-drives, and at lunch Australia, from only 23 overs, had scored 88 for two. It had been an entertaining and pleasing start to the match, lightened by one moment of humour when the public address announcer requested a 'Mr Willis of England' to go to the England dressing-room. Willis junior was doing his best in the middle at the time but his loyal father had just arrived from England and answered the call instead.

The atmosphere was authentically and uniquely Melbournian during the perfect summer's afternoon with the huge crowd bellowing their good-humoured disapproval if an Englishman had the temerity to appeal and cheering every run by Wood and Yallop.

The captain must have been even more pleased about winning the toss when, just for a few overs after lunch, Hendrick began to suggest that the pitch had been underprepared. Twice he got deliveries to kick off just short of a length around middle stump at the northern end, and on another occasion a ball grubbed through low beneath the bat. Hendrick indeed was very unlucky not to take Yallop's wicket when he edged the first lifter at comfortable catching height to Brearley's right at first slip. He was then 17 but he survived to hit some more rousing strokes, including a confident lofted on-drive off Miller. But at 126 Botham, who had replaced Hendrick at the Southern Stand end, persuaded Yallop to drive and the low fast edge was superbly caught by Hendrick, diving to his right. Yallop had hit four fours in his

41 and his confidence and assertiveness must have been a tremendous help to Wood, who was having some mid-innings doubts at the other end after being hit on the glove by Hendrick and sustaining a badly bruised finger.

Against the off-spinners, alternately Miller and Emburey (the latter had the greater reputation but on this occasion the former bowled the better, with a subtler flight), Wood was more confident. It is true that Wood twice survived appeals off Emburey, one for a bat-pad catch, another for a catch behind, but he and Toohey began to score runs freely once Toohey had got his bearings. Ten runs came off one over from Botham, four of them from a crisp, wristy old-fashioned leg-glance by Toohey. When 15, however, Toohey was missed off Botham by the unfortunate Brearley. Like the first chance it was a catch Brearley would normally have 'gobbled'. After tea he left the slips for a time. His injured eye was perhaps slightly obscuring his vision. The result, in any case, was that Toohey and Wood were still together at tea, and the big crowd basked contentedly in the perfect weather, with a healthy total of 166 for three to be discussed.

Runs continued to come at a smart pace after the interval and Toohey, though his driving was impure at times, the right hand dominating and the timing accordingly not perfect, still attacked the bowling with relish. He fell to what can only be described as a conjuror's trick. He clipped Miller hard off his toes towards midwicket. Randall ran at top speed to his left and, with an elastic left hand, plucked the ball up off the ground as it flew past him. It was the Nottingham imp at his most devilish, and one almost expected a puff of smoke and a magic wand.

However Allan Border now came in to make absolutely certain that the day would end, as it began, with Australia in control. His was a most assured first innings in Test cricket. He played very straight and showed a mature judgement of the right ball to attack and the one best left alone. After he had made an initial good impression with a quiet, solid start to his innings, he seized on a rare short ball from Miller and pulled him powerfully over midwicket, one of the best shots played all day. Before long he was confronted with the new ball, taken by Brearley as soon as it became available, and he had few moments of anxiety against it. Willis, who had not bowled since lunch, could summon no dangerous bounce or movement from the pitch and the few balls which had behaved oddly after lunch were believed at this stage to be the exception to the general rule of a true, slow pitch.

Wood and Border both knew that, no matter how good the pitch might be, it would be likely to give some help to Higgs in the later stages of the match, and they set their minds on sticking together until the close. Wood's century would be an individual bonus and it came, sure enough, in the very last over of the day with a straight-driven three off Botham. On a faster outfield this, like many of Wood's other shots, would have gone to the boundary and he would have needed less than six hours to reach his first Test hundred against England in his initial first-class innings on the Melbourne Cricket Ground. For that matter Australia's 243 for four might have been worth perhaps 300 for four on many another ground. But they were in no mood to complain. Despite the risky running between the wickets, despite the one piece of ill-luck suffered by Hughes, they had built a strong position and for that Wood was largely responsible. He had hit the ball beautifully off his legs all day and his concentration and technique had stood the test of some determined and accurate bowling by all five members of the attack.

It was a welcome change of luck for Australian cricket, and the Australian Board must have slept better in the knowledge that the first-day takings of $74,034 would help their ailing finances and that England would be hard pressed now to make it three wins in a row.

They knew too that it only needed a fine day for a massive Saturday crowd to assemble at the MCG and, sure enough, a fine blue morning it was. As I came across the huge grassy park which surrounds the great arena, swarms of eager supporters in shorts and sun-hats, eskis in hand, were making their way like worker ants to the turnstiles. In amongst them I came across Bob Parish, the introverted chairman of Australia's Cricket Board, looking and sounding quietly satisfied but in no way smug. His pleasure was less for himself and his Board colleagues than for Yallop and his young team.

But a major setback awaited them. Hendrick delivered the first over of the second day to Border, who took his score to 29 with a solid cut to third-man for four. Brearley had to run back to collect the ball from the white iron railing in front of the Northern Stand but a few balls later he was holding the same ball aloft in his left hand, very relieved to have taken a low slip catch from an edged forward defensive by Border. Hendrick thoroughly deserved the wicket after his accuracy and ill-luck the previous day, but even he can hardly have expected that this wicket would be the prelude to an extraordinary subsidence by the remaining batsmen.

The crucial wicket now, of course, was that of Wood, and Miller took it before he had been able to add to his overnight score. Moving up the pitch to drive, Wood aimed to leg instead of hitting with the spin into the covers and mishit the ball to Emburey at short mid-wicket. In the same over Hogg tried to drive on the offside (against the spin again) and lofted to Randall at mid-off.

Two more wickets fell one run later at 251 with Hendrick taking over from his Derbyshire colleague. He bowled Dymock off his pads with a ball of full length, then burst through Hurst's frail defensive push like a battering ram assaulting a piece of plywood.

Maclean now found himself with only Higgs to keep the innings alive and he managed to lift the score to 258 before playing across Botham and being bowled. Australia's last six wickets had fallen for 16 runs on a pitch still, so far as one could see, as solid and predictable as a Christmas pudding.

On such a pitch, indeed, one had visions of Boycott, who had not scored a hundred at Melbourne, batting through a long afternoon to build up another winning position for England. False vision if ever there was one! Rodney Hogg had a little breeze from the south and, more important, the hot breath of the patriotic thousands in the 'outer' to blow him on his way. Not that he needed any help. He charged in at Boycott like a bull smarting from the first bite of the bandarillo, and although Boycott calmly negotiated the first over he was bowled by the third ball of Hogg's second. It was of full length and as it came back a little Boycott played outside it. The fans in the 'outer' almost lifted the roof off the Southern Stand as they roared and danced their delight. Four years before, Hogg himself had been one of the amorphous mass in that vast concrete stand, cheering on Lillee and Thomson to 'kill the Poms', and he had little dreamed of what lay ahead. At that stage, indeed, he was struggling unsuccessfully for a place in the Victorian state side, let alone the Australian one.

Randall walked out on his favourite ground, practising his strokes as usual, and glanced the first ball he received from Hogg to fine leg for one. Brearley played the next ball safely down into the gully but the following one was a beauty, cutting back sharply to strike him only half-forward on the front pad, and umpire

Melbourne (third Test). *Above* Yallop falls to the Derbyshire pair of Taylor and Miller in the second innings. *Below* Kim Hughes too often got himself out when in full flow, as he did in this innings at Melbourne. He was responsible for some of the most memorable strokes in the series, like this full-blooded pull. Taylor's positioning behind the stumps is perfect.

Graeme Wood hooks Ian Botham during his matchwinning 100 in the third Test.
He batted with stern application but marred several good innings by impetuous
running between the wickets. In manner, looks and bearing he strongly resembles
Greg Chappell, on whom he clearly modelled himself.

O'Connell quickly affirmed Hogg's triumphant appeal. England had lost two wickets for three runs after three overs, and the only mystery was why Rodney Hogg had not been knighted along with Jack Brabham in the New Year Honours list which had been published in the morning papers.

Gooch came in at number four (he might as well still have been opening) and played soundly and calmly until lunch. The fact remained, however, that Australia had got right back into the game again and that eight wickets had fallen in the first two hours for 23 runs on a blameless pitch. It made not an ounce of sense.

Gooch and Randall did their best to improve England's position after the interval. Randall hit Hurst gloriously off the back foot through the covers for four, but this was to be his only moment of complete control. He was driven back into his shell by the fire of Hogg and the accuracy of Hurst, who was embarking on an eight-over afternoon spell which was eventually to earn him Randall's wicket. Gooch was very much the senior partner for once, if only because he received considerably more of the strike. He hit one sumptuous off-drive off Hogg and at other times worked the ball away effectively on the onside.

Hogg gave way to Dymock and the left-hander caused Randall as much trouble as anyone, plugging away just outside the off-stump. When he had made eight Randall edged an intended drive low to the right of Border at second slip but the chance slipped away. As it turned out it was of little consequence, because Randall was out soon afterwards, much to his exaggerated dismay. He shaped to hit Hurst to the legside and was given out l.b.w. as the ball hit the front pad. There must have been some question in umpire French's mind about the fact that Randall was fully forward, but his clear opinion was that the ball would have hit the stumps and Randall won no new friends amongst the Melbourne thousands by staying at the crease for several seconds.

England's situation became critical when Gooch followed him into the pavilion soon afterwards. He was aiming to force the ball on the offside but it lifted a little and left the bat and Border, at second slip, held on to the fast-travelling snick at the third attempt.

Gower now brought some style and authority to the batting and after a brief period when his timing was not quite as good as usual, he began to reel off some of those gracious shots which make him such a joy to watch. Two strong sweeps and two more strokes either side of cover – one off each foot – all off Higgs, were perfect shots which gave England's total at least a semblance of respectability at tea when they were 75 for four with Gower 29 not out and Botham two not out. But the decline had only been arrested, not reversed. Gower was out early in the evening session, the first of an increasing number of batsmen during the game who could lay the blame squarely at the door of the pitch. The ball came back a little from the off and kept low to trap Gower l.b.w. and so give Dymock a second wicket. Now, at 81 for five, there was only Botham and Miller before the tail and the looks on the faces of the players in the England dressing-room were like the expressions of men resigned to their fate. The tide had turned Australia's way at last and the sweep of it was all-consuming.

Botham did his very best to play King Canute. He could only defend at first and he did so soundly enough, largely against Higgs who tied everyone down after tea to such an extent that, after conceding 17 runs, mainly against Gower, in his three overs before the interval, only three more runs came from his next eight. At last Botham began to attack, or to try to do so. He square-cut and straight-drove Dymock successfully, but Higgs was more of a problem. Botham twice opened his shoulders against him but the ball, now starting to turn quite sharply for the leg-spinner, spun out of reach. Hogg returned and Botham drove a no-ball majestically through the covers before hooking him for another four and then pulling to mid-wicket for the single which at last brought up England's 100 in 211 minutes off 41 overs. It was Botham's first and final fling, however. He drove again at Higgs in the next over and lofted the ball towards Darling, who fell forward at extra-cover to hold on gleefully to the catch. Darling's fielding in the covers had been a model of aggression and enthusiasm.

England's innings was in ruins now and there was no way back for them. Miller, who had already been missed at slip when he tried to drive Higgs – Hughes actually did well to get his left hand to a tricky chance – set his mind to defending. He played out over after over against Higgs with a resolute forward defensive. Meanwhile Hogg began the mopping-up operation at the other end. First Taylor was bowled by a ball which kept particularly low, though Taylor also played right across the line of flight and therefore gave himself little chance. Then Emburey, after some stout defence, was also bowled, the ball coming back between bat and pad and again keeping a trifle low. The pitch was now behaving so

eccentrically that one felt the match was as good as over. Miller
and Willis, however, blocked their way defiantly through to six
o'clock, by which time England had reached 107 for eight and
Miller had batted 110 minutes for three runs, thus putting himself
at the top of one of Wisden's more unusual record lists. 122 runs
had been scored in the day, fourteen wickets had fallen, and many
a wise cricketing head sought for the reason in vain. The pitch undoubtedly had begun to deteriorate alarmingly early, but it seems
to be a fact that the modern Test batsman seldom gets the better of
the modern Test bowler. Less favourable pitches, the use of fertilisers, the improvement in fielding and the greater number of
good fast bowlers are all valid reasons. (More of this later.)

For once the rest day of a Test match fell after two days, and
since it was a Sunday I was also able to take a day off myself. With
much trepidation I spent it playing in a cricket match against an
Australian Harlequin side which included amongst other famous
names Frank Tyson and Jonathan Agnew. The Harlequins are an
offshoot of the famous London rugby club and this match in aid
of the St John's Ambulance Brigade was to celebrate the birth of
the cricketing activities of the club fifty years before when Jack
Hobbs, Maurice Leyland, Tich Freeman, Percy Fender, George
Duckworth, Patsy Hendren and Phil Mead had represented the
'Quins' against a Sydney 'Bohemians' team which included
Arthur Mailey and Bill Taverner.

Fifty years before the Harlequins had won by two runs.
Whether that finish was contrived I do not know, but there was
nothing false about an exciting finish this time in which Frank
Tyson won the match for the Harlequins with a six to mid-wicket
in the last over of the game. From a personal point of view three
runs and two wickets was hardly a heady performance with which
to see out the old year, even if one of the wickets was that of the
highly promising Wayne Larkins, generously surrendered after a
fine first innings in Australia at the beginning of his Whitbread
scholarship. There was also some excellent batting by the young
Victorian left-hander Gary Watts for the Bohemians and an admirable spell of off-spin bowling by that wise old professional
Jack Simmons, who removed Roger Tolchard when he was
threatening to win the match off his own bat.

Ken Barrington, against whose enthusiastic leg-spin I meekly
succumbed, giving him his first wicket in Australia for many years
(although he claimed plenty in the nets where he liked to imitate

Jim Higgs in giving his players practice against the type of bowling they so seldom see in England), believed that the pitch at the St Kilda Oval was as good as any on which the England team had played throughout the tour. It was at St Kilda that Bill Ponsford and Bill Lawry played much of their early cricket and also here that Victoria played in the Sheffield Shield when the MCG was *hors de combat*.

Barrington and Boycott, the two with the longest memories of pitches in Australia, were convinced that they had recently undergone a serious decline throughout the country, with few of the hard dry brown strips of old, fast in pace and even of bounce. Yet pitches consistently make fools of players and pundits alike. The one on which only 122 runs had been scored for the loss of fourteen wickets on Saturday behaved itself again on the first morning of the New Year, perhaps pacified by the roller. Whatever the reason Willis, Miller and Hendrick between them added 36 more runs in fifty minutes. Willis played in his usual honest brave fashion, undemonstrative but grimly determined. Hogg bowled Miller with a well-pitched delivery after Miller had stayed at the crease for a further 15 minutes and doubled his score with one shot. His seven occupied, in all, 125 minutes. Hogg's final figures of five for 30 gave him 22 wickets from his first two and a half Tests, and one could not recall an innings completed by England in the series when Hogg had *not* led his side off the field.

He had to wait to do so on this occasion until Willis had spooned a catch to Darling to give the worthy and reliable Dymock his third wicket and to set the seal on a fine fielding performance by Darling. The most significant over, however, was one on which only 122 runs had been scored for the loss of fourmore bounce and turn than he had from the other, and one felt that if Australia could get 200 in their second innings England's fourth-innings task would be beyond them.

The first-innings lead, in fact, was 115 and Wood and Darling built on that comfortable cushion with both competence and confidence in the hour before lunch. It was very hot, and the sky was a deep and flawless blue. Whilst Melbourne temperatures approached the nineties, England was awaking to a wintry New Year. There were floods in the West Country and four inches of snow in the centre of London. Early-morning listeners heard also of a spate of bombs in Northern Ireland. They would be looking for better news from the Antipodes, but Wood and Darling were in no mood to oblige. Wood looked especially safe and assured, making 15 of the 31 scored by the two young openers before lunch.

Perhaps because it was so hot, perhaps because of a general hangover, the crowd was not as big as had been expected. Nor was World Series Cricket suffering by contrast. In the second game ever played at the Gabba by the wandering mercenaries, a crowd of just under 18,000 packed the ground to see the Australians beat the West Indians. No doubt, as with all the World Series games, many of them had been given complimentary tickets, but the fact that a crowd of only 5,000 had watched the West Indies versus the World encounter the day before suggested again that the Packer publicity was working. The public were going to support the Packer Australians as if they *were* Australia. The battle to give Chappell's men a national identity had been won.

No one was unaware of the challenge. The biggest of the many slogans slung from the railings of the Melbourne stands said simply: FAIR DINKUM CRICKET. Brearley surprised many people after lunch when he persisted with a fast or medium-pace attack from the southern end, where Higgs had delivered such a dangerous over in the morning. Apart from the occasional ball keeping low the pitch again behaved itself quite well and England worked away assiduously through the hot afternoon, eventually taking three wickets. Darling and Wood took their opening stand past fifty for the second time in the match. Darling survived yet another probable run-out when Wood called for a dangerous single and Gower intercepted from mid-wicket but just missed the stumps with his under-arm throw. But he did not last a great deal longer, cutting against Miller's spin to be beautifully caught again, low down, by Randall.

Hughes quickly eradicated memories of his first-innings ill-fortune, tucking in with relish to Botham when he replaced Hendrick from the southern end. He began with a crisp straight-drive down the ground, then glanced Botham for four more before turning to attack Miller at the other end with a whip off his toes and a cover-drive. Each brought Hughes three, though on most grounds the ball would have reached the boundary.

Botham plugged away manfully, resisting his natural instinct to fire the ball in full blast and concentrating on line and length. He had his reward at last when Wood, who had shown an increasing penchant for sweeping the ball off his stumps, tried to do so to the slower ball, missed, and was bowled. Botham now was at the end of his tether after six steady overs and Willis took over to force Hughes and Yallop back on the defensive. Australia, however, were in the happy position of knowing that plenty of time was on their side and that they were not far off a total which they could feel was a safe one.

Yallop looked less certain than he had in his first innings and snicked Willis just in front of Hendrick at second slip to earn four of his sixteen runs. The next break came when at last, in the final over before tea, Brearley brought on a spinner at the popular end. Emburey was by now operating steadily from the northern end, so it was Miller who got the chance and dismissed Yallop as he cut and top-edged a catch to Taylor.

Miller had been described by a distinguished fellow-member of his union, Ian Johnson, as the best off-spinner he had seen from England, which was high praise indeed when one considers that Laker, Appleyard, Tattersall, McConnon, Titmus, Allen and Mortimore had all been to Australia since the war. Excessive praise indeed, but there was no questioning Miller's striking improvement since he had straightened his approach to the stumps and trusted himself to give the ball air and yet to control it.

Hughes showed him only limited respect, however, moving down the pitch soon after tea to hit him majestically for six into the seething crowd in the 'outer'. Toohey joined in the fun for a while, hitting one drive past mid-off – again off Miller – with really murderous power. Lindsay Hassett said that it was the first time he had seen Toohey truly time a drive in the whole series; against India the previous year Toohey's power had reminded him of Stan McCabe. It was clear that England had still not seen the best of the little man from the New South Welsh country and his innings was quickly nipped in the bud when he launched himself into a lofted on-drive against Emburey and saw Botham flop forward at wide mid-on to take a good catch.

The character of the cricket now changed completely. Emburey from the Members' end and Hendrick from the popular one suddenly shackled Hughes and Border to such an extent that seven overs and nearly forty minutes went by without a run scored. It was mean, accurate, testing bowling and before long it had its reward. Border, who had been crowded by four men as Emburey tormented him with his immaculate off-spin, tried a sweep in desperation and overbalanced as he brushed the ball to Hendrick at backward short-leg. With a speed that bewildered, Hendrick scooped the ball up and flicked it at the stumps in a single movement and Border was run out. An infuriating way to go, but a piece of shining brilliance by Hendrick who had already wiped from the memory that moment of humiliation in the equivalent Test four years ago when his hamstring had snapped as he ran up to bowl and his captain had been left with only four bowlers early in the game.

Border's unusual demise was followed quite soon by the more important wicket of Hughes, who got going again with two more boundaries before giving himself up to the first ball delivered by Botham when he took over again from Hendrick. He jumped down the pitch intending to drive over the top, as he had successfully driven the spinners, but merely mishit to Gower in the covers.

Rodney Hogg now joined that sturdy fighter Maclean, and most of the 30,038 spectators applauded every time he put bat to ball. Such encouragement no doubt made all the difference to his bowling but may not have aided his concentration with the willow, and as soon as he aimed an attacking blow at Botham he lost his off-stump.

Australia ended the third day 278 runs ahead, at 163 for seven, with the new ball due and a few optimistic England supporters believing that their task was no longer impossible. The pitch had not deteriorated any further, contrary to most expectations, and those batsmen who had put their trust in forward play and a straight bat had, given patience, managed to survive for long periods.

Brearley withheld the new ball for a time on the fourth morning, a cool grey day although the high clouds held no apparent threat of rain. Hendrick opened the hostilities to Dymock from the southern end with Emburey continuing from the other. It was the off-spinner who struck first when in his second over Maclean once again tried the sweep which had cost him his wicket a few times already. The ball struck the glove and was caught at backward short-leg. Maclean waited for the umpire's decision.

Dymock went in the next over, mishitting a drive to Brearley at square-leg, and then Higgs overbalanced, Taylor stumped him and England were through their initial work in 25 minutes with only four runs added.

To win, still against all odds, England had to get off to a solid start. Boycott safely felt his way through the first over from Hogg, a relatively gentle one, but Hogg likes to work up to full pace and he seldom if ever drew blood in the first over of a spell. For once it was not Hogg who took the first wicket this time. Dymock bowled into the wind from the north and had Brearley caught behind, the fifth time the captain had been dismissed in this way in six Test innings. It was a shot which must have given Brearley nightmares for some time. He stretched to drive a wide delivery on the up but merely deflected the ball low into Maclean's gloves and set out on that long and miserable return to the pavilion, no doubt wondering if he was ever again going to play a major innings in a Test match.

The crisis grew deeper in the following over after Randall had been denied a four by the sprawling Darling in the covers, then had taken two to mid-wicket. He went back instead of forward to a good-length ball from Hogg which, because of the angle of delivery, must have been close to the leg-stump. Umpire French was in no doubt that it would have hit and Randall could really only blame himself for going back on a pitch which demanded a forward stroke to virtually everything.

For the second time in the match, therefore, Gooch found that there was very little difference between opening the batting for England and going in fourth. In fact he had come in during the third over in both innings and as in the first he now proceeded to bat with an admirable composure and command. He drove Dymock handsomely past cover for four, and but for Darling's speed would have had similar reward from an equally well struck drive off Hogg. Boycott was also looking quite at home: a solid push-drive through mid-off took him into double figures and not long afterwards he leg-glanced Hogg for his first four in a Test since Brisbane. Hurst replaced Hogg in the ninth over and caused Boycott more difficulty, five times rapping him on the front pad and appealing to umpire French, who might as well have been stone. Boycott was still there at lunch, 15 not out; Gooch had moved confidently on to 26; England were 50 for two and their ship was still afloat.

Gooch continued in the same handsome vein after the interval, driving Dymock on the offside for a two, a three and an imperious four in the first two overs of the afternoon. Yallop turned once again to the faithful Hogg from the southern end. His first over, as ever, was mild and Gooch looked entirely at ease. But Hogg worked up considerably greater pace in the second over, so much so that he began to stray down the legside as he strained for a bit of bounce from the lifeless and motley-looking turf. Ironically it was the very lack of bounce which helped to end Gooch's gem of an innings at 40, during Hogg's next over. He came well forward; the ball kept low, came back and hit the pad, so far as one could tell, a little outside the line of the off-stump. There was little doubt that the ball would have hit the stumps. Whether it was out under the l.b.w. law, Gooch having played a shot, was more questionable. At any rate, umpire French affirmed Hogg's appeal and Gooch's outstanding knock was over.

Gower came in to replace him at 71 for three and very soon he was facing Higgs, bowling in Hogg's place from the southern end where all the bowlers had got more help from the pitch. It was the sternest possible test of technique for both Gower and Boycott, who was clearly relishing the challenge. Higgs was joined just before three o'clock by Allan Border, whose first over of left-arm orthodox spin received only minimal respect from Boycott. He was looking to attack him at once and soon hit the ball away square on the offside off the back foot with something of his old authority. It was developing into a tense and exciting tussle in what was now bright sunshine.

Border, pitching the ball into the rough outside the left-hander's off-stump, caused Gower rather more problems and one ball beat the outside edge and Maclean too to go through for four byes. The runs were coming alarmingly fast and easily for Australian comfort, and awful doubts were starting to enter the minds of their supporters. Yallop was looking a little lost out in the middle and his detractors amongst the press and the old Australian players were saying that he was too defensive and devoid of imagination. There was, no doubt, more than a grain of truth in both assertions, but the odds in a match like this so greatly favour the fielding side in the fourth innings that one felt another break would come. It did so at last when Boycott and Gower had added 51 and tea was already brewing in the pot. Hurst was the successful bowler; Boycott, after a very laudable innings, went as he aimed to hit though mid-wicket and was struck in line with middle and leg stumps. There was the world of difference between England's tea score of 123 for four and the 123 for three it might have been. Instead of a well-established Boycott and a Gower not quite into his stride but able to take his time with Boycott looking so good, England resumed instead with Gower as the senior partner and Botham to accompany him.

Hogg inevitably returned for his customary post-prandial burst. Roars of encouragement went up again from the double tiers of the Southern Stand as that curly-haired enthusiast gathered speed again with his crouching run and launched himself into each ball with the early scent of victory in his nostrils. For once, though, he was out of luck. Gower edged him casually to Maclean when he had made 32 but the low chance evaded Maclean's gloves as he sprawled to his left. All day Maclean had given an impression of untidiness, but a pitch like this one really sorts the wheat from the chaff and it was a hellishly difficult one for wicket-keepers.

Gower celebrated his escape by square-cutting Hurst for four and with Botham settling down to play a restrained defensive innings and Gower always capable of anything, tension again began to build up. In ones and twos the last pair capable of upsetting the odds calmly took the score along to the 160s, and a target of 120 with six men left began to look a genuine possibility again. Hogg and Hurst gave way to Dymock and Higgs, who knew that, with Hourn breathing down his neck, he must not fail his side or himself.

At last Higgs did manage to pitch a perfect looping leg-spinner, after deceiving Botham with a googly the previous delivery. Botham for once allowed himself the luxury of a drive; without getting to the pitch he edged a catch to a much-relieved Maclean. Australia's joy was summed up by Darling flinging his baggy green cap in the air before embracing the tubby Maclean like a child hugging his teddy bear. It was the final break for Australia and at last Yallop went fully onto the attack. The tide swept in much faster now with two more England wickets washed away in the last forty minutes as the day ended in a crescendo of Australian appeals. Perhaps it was not surprising, such was the pressure on two umpires who had done their best on a difficult day, that Taylor was adjudged caught behind when the camera suggested he had not touched the ball – Hogg's 25th wicket of the series – and that Miller succumbed to a bat-pad catch off Higgs. England ended the day still 112 runs away from their target of 283 and the Australian celebrations had already begun, with only two more wickets now needed. Below the surface of the cheers which rang out at the end of the day one could almost hear the deep sigh of relief from all those people in Australia who knew that their cricket was alive again.

Wednesday 3 January dawned sunny and calm. It was a working day. The game might be over in two minutes or two balls. Yet some 7,000 people bustled through the turnstiles free of charge to salute the coming triumph. One man brought a trumpet with him and marked the arrival of Willis and Emburey at the crease with a resonant rendering of the Last Post.

If Willis, Emburey and Hendrick had been statistically minded they might have taken comfort from the fact that they could in theory win the match without disturbing England's ninth- and tenth-wicket record partnerships against Australia: 151 by W.W. Read and W.H. Scotton at the Oval in 1884 and the famous 130 by R.E. Foster and Wilfred Rhodes at Sydney in 1903–4. But in these circumstances on this pitch such tailend heroics were out of the question and it took just 25 minutes for Australia to capture the last two wickets. Emburey held out resolutely but Hogg was too good first for Willis, who fell to a high right-handed catch by Yallop, and then for Hendrick, who was bowled by a ball which came back a long way.

Hogg had taken five for 36 in the innings, ten for 66 in the match, and 27 wickets in three Test matches. This time the pitch had given him neither bounce nor pace, but like Michael Holding at the Oval in 1976 he had continued to take wickets by bowling straight and fast on an unresponsive wicket. Bob Willis had not taken a single wicket, in itself a remarkable fact.

Graeme Wood won the Man-of-the-Match award for his disciplined batting in both innings, especially his first-innings 100 which had formed the basis of Australia's 103-run victory.

Australian cricket could breathe again. The crowd gathered round the two teams in front of the pavilion for the presentations, a reminder that Test matches are also played for money these days although no one, I believe, had given that matter a single thought during the first four absorbing days of the match. If it had been a World Series match we would have been reminded of the money at stake at least once an over. You played for Australia but you *worked* for Mr Packer. The ashes of the bail presented to the Hon. Ivo Bligh nearly a hundred years before still meant so much more than dollars in the bank: the Ashes were valueless, yet priceless. 'We can do it now,' said Graham Yallop to the crowd gathered round him on the outfield, and patriotic hearts were stirred.

It was certain that Australia would now be a much harder side to beat. There was a new confidence about them and a new spirit which one had noticed even before the match had begun, in the practice sessions on the MCG the day before. The backbiting had stopped and though Yallop had revealed no special qualities as a leader, his side now believed more both in him and in themselves.

For Mike Brearley it was a time of personal crisis and for his team a time to show their true worth. The captain remained calm and charming in defeat as the media, with whom he had established a relationship of trust, crowded round and asked whether he would still be leading England three days later at Sydney. Brearley, though his batting record in the series so far was dismal – 37 runs in six innings and only one run in the last three – replied that he would, but that he had not yet decided whether to open the batting. Four years previously Denness had dropped himself as captain for the fourth Test at Sydney after having made only 65 Test runs till then. But England were already two Tests down then and Australia duly won at Sydney to regain the Ashes. One felt it was much more likely that this time England would pick themselves up and take the Ashes themselves at Sydney. But for the moment they were on the back foot, and Brearley's run of fifteen Tests without defeat (ten wins and five draws since June 1977) had come to an end. Though the official overall gate of 128,758 (the crowds watching on the last day were not counted) was little more than half the attendance of the equivalent Test in Melbourne four years before, established cricket could sleep more easily.

One final thought about Melbourne before moving on to Australia's most exciting city: the best cricket pitch, as everyone knows, is a hard, fast 'belter', but such a pitch does not guarantee a good cricket match. The Melbourne pitch has never in recent years been anything other than slow and low, yet within four years three classic Test matches had been played there by England and Australia. Perhaps, to be honest, this match needed a more sustained effort by England in the fourth innings for the word classic to be fairly applied. But they did reach 163 for four, needing only 120 more, and I spoke later to one Australian who said that he had simply not been able to go on watching: 'I thought we had thrown the game away. I could not bear it any longer. But Botham was out soon after I left and everything changed.' This had been the true stuff of cricket: unbearable tension and the sudden change of fortune.

AUSTRALIA v ENGLAND (Third Test)

Melbourne, December 29, 30, January 1, 2, 3. Australia won by 103 runs.

Australia *First Innings*			Second Innings	
G. M. Wood c Emburey b Miller	100		b Botham	34
W. M. Darling run out	33		c Randall b Miller	21
K. J. Hughes c Taylor b Botham	0		c Gower b Botham	48
*G. N. Yallop c Hendrick b Botham	41		c Taylor b Miller	16
P. M. Toohey c Randall b Miller	32		c Botham b Emburey	20
A. R. Border c Brearley b Hendrick	29		run out	0
†J. A. Maclean b Botham	8		c Hendrick b Emburey	10
R. M. Hogg c Randall b Miller	0		b Botham	1
G. Dymock b Hendrick	0		c Brearley b Hendrick	6
J. D. Higgs not out	1		st Taylor b Emburey	0
A. G. Hurst b Hendrick	0		not out	0
Extras (lb8, nb6)	14		(b4, lb6, nb1)	11
Total	258		Total	167

Fall of Wickets
1 – 65   2 – 65   3 – 126   4 – 189   5 – 247   6 – 250   7 – 250   8 – 251   9 – 252
1 – 55   2 – 81   3 – 101   4 – 136   5 – 136   6 – 152   7 – 157   8 – 167   9 – 167

Bowling	First Innings				Second Innings			
Willis	13	2	47	0	7	0	21	0
Botham	20.1	4	68	3	15	4	41	3
Hendrick	23	3	50	3	14	4	25	1
Emburey	14	1	44	0	21.2	12	30	3
Miller	19	5	35	3	14	5	39	2

England *First Innings*		Second Innings	
G. Boycott b Hogg	1	lbw b Hurst	38
*J. M. Brearley lbw b Hogg	1	c Maclean b Dymock	0
D. W. Randall lbw b Hurst	13	lbw b Hogg	2
G. A. Gooch c Border b Dymock	25	lbw b Hogg	40
D. I. Gower lbw b Dymock	29	lbw b Dymock	49
I. T. Botham c Darling b Higgs	22	c Maclean b Higgs	10
G. Miller b Hogg	7	c Hughes b Higgs	1
†R. W. Taylor b Hogg	1	c Maclean b Hogg	5
J. E. Emburey b Hogg	0	not out	7
R. G. D. Willis c Darling b Dymock	19	c Yallop b Hogg	3
M. Hendrick not out	6	b Hogg	0
Extras (b6, lb4, nb9)	19	(b10, lb7, w1, nb6)	24
Total	143	Total	179

Fall of Wickets
1 – 2   2 – 3   3 – 40   4 – 52   5 – 81   6 – 100   7 – 101   8 – 101   9 – 120
1 – 1   2 – 6   3 – 71   4 – 122   5 – 163   6 – 163   7 – 167   8 – 171   9 – 179

Bowling	First Innings				Second Innings			
Hogg	17	7	30	5	17	5	36	5
Hurst	12	2	24	1	11	1	39	1
Dymock	15.6	4	38	3	18	4	37	2
Higgs	19	9	32	1	16	2	29	2
Border					5	0	14	0

Umpires—M. G. O'Connell and R. French.   Toss won by Australia.

Chapter Seven

PHOENIX FROM THE ASHES

There was hardly time to catch breath between Melbourne and Sydney. The short journey was made on the same day that Australia won the third Test, but there were still only two clear days before battle began again.

Perhaps it was because the tour was now at a crisis point or perhaps because summer had made a sudden and late appearance there that Sydney seemed more alive on our second visit. At the hotel where I stayed, the Chateau Commodore at Potts Point, the mouth of the great harbour is almost within touching distance as one looks across a sparkling blue stretch of water, studded with small sailing boats, to the scores of bays and inlets which lead out to the open sea. It is as if half the coves of Cornwall have been packed together in a small area on the hottest day of summer. There are even grey slate roofs atop whitewashed houses and an old stone church or two. But the analogy ends with the palm trees and the skyscrapers which rise up on the shores near the centre of the city; inland the streets have all the worldliness, glamour and squalor of any big city. Behind the hotel, King's Cross is like the Soho of a few years ago, in the London of the swinging sixties. In amongst the shops, restaurants and massage parlours the air is thick with corruption. The invitation to vice is brazen, not furtive. It is lighthearted, almost tongue-in-cheek, but there are enough visible examples of humanity sunk low for one to return with some relief to a hotel balcony open to the fresh sea breezes.

Whilst the players practised on the morning after their arrival the media men of Australia and England did battle for the Benson and Hedges 'Ash' at the Raleigh Park Oval. One is bound to record that Australia were successful in a limited-overs match by eight wickets with three overs to spare and this despite a fine 87 by England's guest artist Ken Barrington. He was out to the ABC cricket commentator Peter Meares, a former Sydney first-grader, who so exploited a hard and very green pitch that he took seven for 18 in his permitted eight overs. The BBC correspondent salvaged some tiny honour by bowling Bobby Simpson for 78 when he was hitting at everything. He played so well, indeed, with such marvellous footwork and immense power that one wondered whether Australia might not have been better placed in the series if he had stayed on another season to lead them again.

However, under Yallop there was now a new confidence, though this received a setback when John Maclean, the vice-captain, was struck above the left eye by a ball from Alan Hurst whilst practising on net wickets which both captains described as thoroughly inadequate. Maclean's injury was similar to the one suffered by Brearley before the third Test, and again a helmet failed to prevent a severe cut requiring six stitches. This time, however, there was also serious swelling, and a replacement was called up for Maclean in the person of 27-year-old Ian Maddocks from Victoria. By strange coincidence his father Len had gained his first Test cap as Australia's wicket-keeper in 1954 when Gil Langley cut an eye in a Sheffield Shield match.

In the event, Maclean passed himself fit to play an hour and a half before the match began in torrid heat and extreme humidity. England had named an unchanged eleven and Australia did likewise, with Yardley again their twelfth man. Their decision had been easy; Hourn would still have to await his chance, and Lawson, the other New South Welshman in contention, had taken very few wickets in the Sheffield Shield. It was only justice that Higgs and Hurst, the two who were threatened, should retain their places in the winning Melbourne side.

England pondered various ways of strengthening the batting – Brearley dropping down the order again; Tolchard coming in for Taylor or one of the bowlers; Old replacing Hendrick; Edmonds replacing Emburey. Each was in turn rejected by the four selectors, Messrs Insole, Barrington, Brearley and Willis.

As at Melbourne it was sure to be a good toss to win, and at last Brearley had some luck, winning only his second one of the tour whilst Yallop lost his first in eleven games. So, at eleven o'clock, Brearley and Boycott walked out into the broiling heat which had already driven the members in the pavilion enclosure and the Noble Stand into the bars as much for shelter as for sustenance. Elsewhere there was less shelter and the few patches of green still visible on the Hill were quickly filled by hardy young Aussies stripped to the waist with only their 'eskies' for solace. The best place to be seemed in the shadow of one of the floodlight chimneys, and there is little doubt that the threat of 100° temperatures kept the crowd down to the official 20,824.

If it was going to be hard for spectators in the sun it should have been harder still for bowlers. But Hogg's first over, delivered from the Members' end, brought out some early life and movement in the well and evenly grassed strip. Hogg began the match with two wides which tested Maclean's agility and his ability to see the ball clearly through his half-closed left eye. It also suggested that in the high humidity the ball would swing and, sure enough, Brearley was twice hit on the pads by Dymock in the latter's first over, both times surviving appeals to umpire Dick French, whose colleague this time was Robin Bailhache.

Brearley was hit on his chest by a ball from Hogg in the next over which lifted from not very short of a length, but after bowling three overs Hogg had to leave the field, temporarily overcome by the heat and his asthma. There had been times at Melbourne when Hogg had appeared close to exhaustion and had needed some urgent words of encouragement by Yallop to keep going, and it was a reminder of how brave a performer Hogg was. Strangely enough, his absence, far from slackening the pressure on England, suddenly increased it.

Hurst came into the attack in his place and, just when Boycott and Brearley seemed to be getting over the worst, broke through in his third over, the eleventh of the innings. Boycott was forced to make a late adjustment to his half-cock defensive stroke as the ball lifted and left the bat and was edged high to the left of Border at second slip. Border dived to hold the ball safely in both hands, although it would have carried more comfortably to Hughes at first slip.

Hard on the heels of Boycott's demise came the most decisive incident of the day, because two balls later Randall hooked at a shortish delivery pitched outside his off-stump, overbalanced, yet hit the ball hard in the middle of the bat only for Wood, fielding perhaps twelve yards from the bat at backward short-leg, to cling on to the ball as it rocketed towards his midriff. One can imagine the chagrin which Randall must have felt as he walked back, and what thoughts lay behind Brearley's look of despair as he turned away and glanced up at the sky. If the ball had gone for four one would have been applauding Randall's audacity. The fact remains that it was an over-ambitious shot for so early in the innings. No wonder Wood flung the ball high in the air in exultation before being swamped by his colleagues. Randall would have revelled in

Above A rare moment of Australian triumph as Hogg bowls Hendrick to wrap up the third Test. *Below* Boycott c Border b Hurst in the fourth Test at Sydney. Hurst took over from Hogg as Boycott's chief tormentor, concentrating on his off-stump and finding the great Yorkshireman far more fallible in that area than he used to be.

Above Randall hooks Hurst for four during his patient vigil at Sydney. His innings of 150 was the decisive one of the series. Without it England might have lost a second successive Test. *Below* Botham's hooking was always a risky business and Hogg (hit for four on this occasion at Sydney) was happy to see him taking a chance.

Perhaps the decisive wicket on the exciting final day of the fourth Test. Yallop is caught and bowled by Hendrick during the most important of this bowler's many fine spells on the tour.

The end nears for Australia: Maclean is caught by Botham within arm's reach of the batsman in the second innings of the fourth Test. Miller is the bowler.

these conditions if he had only built his innings with some early care. After he had gone little went right for England.

All this occurred whilst Hogg was in the pavilion, and although he soon returned he was obliged to stay out of the attack for the length of time he had been away: 24 minutes. Brearley and Gooch dealt with the bouncing ball well enough for a time, although with yet another lushly grassed outfield runs came only fitfully, in ones and twos.

Hogg returned in place of Hurst and there was a suggestion of fatigue about some of his deliveries. But the seventh ball of his second over was fast and of full length and it ripped out Brearley's off-stump as he played forward inside the line. England were now 35 for three and already in the mire. If they were to drag themselves out, Gooch and Gower must stick together until lunch. With twenty minutes to go before the interval, Yallop brought on Higgs for an early bowl. It was a sensible piece of captaincy, for England were in no mood to attack him and Higgs would be likely to get more bounce now than later in the match. He bowled well enough but Gooch received one legside long-hop which he despatched with an almost audible sigh of relief to the square-leg boundary, the first four of the morning after 114 minutes. But Australia refused to stop their forward march. Off the last ball before lunch Gower was caught behind the wicket by the courageous Maclean as Hurst, bowling from round the wicket to the left-hander, got the ball to lift and come back, thinly brushing the glove on its way through as Gower tried to pull the bat under the ball. England therefore ended an extraordinary first morning of the fourth Test with four wickets down for 51 and the advantage of winning the toss virtually squandered. There had been plenty of life in the pitch but not enough, surely, to explain this sorry position.

Gooch and Botham proceeded after the interval with the utmost caution. Higgs continued from the Randwick End and started to reel off accurate maidens as he had done at Melbourne. Hogg bowled three overs from the Noble Stand End but with rather less control than usual and with a tendency to stray down the legside. But though he was flagging and Higgs was not turning the ball more than an inch or two, England made no attempt to take the initiative.

At last Higgs bowled a bad ball, a rank long-hop, and Gooch seized on it with all his might and pulled it towards deep mid-wicket. Peter Toohey was on the boundary not far from the huge banner proclaiming, in large red lettering, THE PETER TOOHEY STAND. Either side of Toohey there were open spaces as big as a sheep station. But as if directed by remote control the ball curved out towards Toohey who, running in fast, clung on to a magnificent low catch. So often the spinner's bad ball gets him a wicket, but one could not help feeling sorry, once again, for Gooch.

Miller, such a diffident starter of an innings, never looked in the right sort of mood to stop the slide. He edged England's second four of the innings past gully off Hurst, then went forward and edged an outswinger to the wicket-keeper. Maclean took the catch low down with his usual competence, but a few minutes later he walked sadly off the field, head cast down, complaining that his hands had lost all feeling. The drugs which he had been taking to reduce the swelling around his eye had combined with nervous tension to make his hands completely numb. Yallop, who even during Australia's darkest moments in the first two Tests had never lacked confidence in himself, took over the gloves with some relish. He had kept wicket a little before, in Melbourne district cricket, and he did so now with obvious enjoyment and no little skill.

Meanwhile Maclean was in such a state in the dressing-room that he lost his balance as he came out of the shower and was forced to lie down. The extreme heat in the middle had worsened his plight because such breeze as there was, blowing the flags on the elegant green roofs of the old Victorian stands, was not getting to the players. If England had been able to get their innings going it would have been hellish for bowlers: as it was, they were having the time of their lives.

Only Botham stood as a serious obstacle in their path now, but for a while he could score only slowly. Taylor, after hitting Higgs for four wide of mid-on, fell to the leg-spinner when a ball bounced more than he had expected and he was well caught low in the gully by Border. Emburey departed meekly two overs later, pushing forward submissively to Higgs and virtually placing the ball into the hands of Wood at short-leg.

At last, in Willis, Botham found a partner resolute enough for him to launch the offensive which was now England's only hope of a respectable score. He began to reel off spectacular shots in the manner which the planeloads of England supporters, who had come out from the cruel English winter, expected. Before tea he square-cut and off-drove Dymock for majestic fours before turning the next ball to mid-wicket for two more. At the interval England were 119 for eight, and afterwards Botham reached his fifty with a hook for four off Hogg followed by another glorious off-driven boundary. His driving, however, was much more convincing than his hooking and it was no real surprise when, after hooking one more four very fine to the legside boundary, he perished to a catch behind as he tried the stroke again. Yallop thus took his first wicket-keeping catch in Test cricket.

The ninth-wicket stand of 43 was by a long way the highest of the innings. Willis and Hendrick managed eleven more runs but at twenty minutes to five it was all over. Hendrick made a quick 10 before Hurst bowled him to finish with five for 28, by far the best analysis of a chequered Test career. Before this innings he had taken only 13 wickets in five Test matches. He had not let Australia down at any stage of the series, but this was the first time that he had played a starring role. For once it was Hurst, not Hogg, who led his side off the field. But Higgs, who had bowled 18 overs without change at the Randwick End, was equally deserving of the honour. If England had only been able to score at a reasonable rate off him, Yallop would never have been able to keep his faster bowlers going for long periods in such heat. It was an opportunity tragically wasted as far as England were concerned, and the Australians who had bowled and fielded so well could hardly believe their good fortune after losing the toss. With Hogg not at his best and Maclean, as they say in Australia, 'crook', they might have had a day's grilling in the sun whilst the strokeplayers in England's middle order made hay. That it did not happen was due in great part to Australia's good cricket but also to some bad and characterless batting by England. They were at one and the same time short both of enterprise and of application. They did not look for quick singles – Brearley even turned down a second run on two occasions which could easily have been taken, and there was a general lack of zest. In contrast Randall had sacrificed his wicket by being too ambitious before getting a sight of the ball.

Just for a moment England had an opportunity to strike back and salvage some honour from the worst day of their tour. Willis's fourth ball lifted a bit higher than Wood expected, he played the ball onto his wicket from outside the off-stump, and Australia were one for one. It was a good, hostile first over from Willis, but it was totally deceptive. Willis was not feeling well, suffering from headache and nausea due to a virus and to dehydration. He could find no real rhythm in his bowling subsequently. Darling began to play him with complete confidence and Willis erred when he continued to pitch the ball short after Darling had been caught behind the wicket hooking at a no-ball. Every time Willis pitched short again, Darling hooked him fiercely to the boundary and Hughes soon joined in, cover-driving Botham for four and then hooking the hapless Willis past mid-on. Soon afterwards Willis, who had bowled six no-balls, walked off to the sanctuary of the dressing-room. Darling, hooking and cutting joyously, all style and enterprise beneath his white helmet, got too many short deliveries from Botham as well as Willis, and even when Miller came on for a couple of exploratory overs before the close he was able to pull another short ball through mid-wicket for his sixth four. Australia ended the day only 96 in arrears and England's tired and deflated, though not yet dispirited, side, made their way back from Paddington to King's Cross desperate for the cool beer and the air-conditioning. Brearley called a team meeting in the manager's suite that evening. Unconsciously, perhaps, his team had become a trifle complacent and slipshod. The tough professionalism of their work earlier in the tour had temporarily gone. It was a critical moment in the tour.

Australia had made 56 in only 67 minutes on the first evening, but although the tide of the match continued to flow strongly in their direction for the first part of Sunday's play, it was not until well into the second session, after four hours, that they passed England's paltry total. England bowled far better than they had done before and Australia, knowing that time was on their side, approached the task with the proper discipline required in Test cricket. The weather again was fiercely hot and humid.

Willis took the field at the start of the day but was still unwell, and it was Hendrick and Botham who began the attack. Darling and Hughes were content at first to 'get 'em in singles', running with speed and understanding as if to show up the sluggishness of some of England's running between wickets the day before. Hughes hit the first four of the morning after twenty minutes, an off-drive off Botham. He then edged Hendrick, who had beaten both batsmen outside the off-stump, for a four to third-man, the ball bouncing just in front of Gooch at third slip. In the same over Darling got an inside edge but the ball bounced into the pads rather than the stumps.

The luck, certainly, was going Australia's way. Willis came on and bowled an excellent three-over spell during which he three times rapped Hughes on the pads, twice appealing in vain, and then came within an inch of forcing Hughes to play onto his stumps off another inside edge. In the same spell Darling was beaten outside his off-stump and Willis must have wondered if he was ever going to take another wicket.

Hendrick replaced him and for a time Darling and Hughes were forced to defend as Hendrick from the Members' end and Emburey from the Randwick wheeled through a succession of flawless overs. But both batsmen had grown up fast during the series. They were prepared to wait for scoring opportunities without being prepared to hand the initiative entirely to the bowlers. When Botham returned to take over from Hendrick, Hughes survived an l.b.w. shout that was more a prayer than an appeal before Darling pulled Botham through mid-wicket to reach his first fifty against England, to tumultuous applause. He had been much more restrained in this second phase of his innings but it was not long before he was adding to the six boundaries he had scored the previous evening, twice throwing himself at balls pitched outside the leg-stump by Emburey and hitting them on the half-volley to the custard-coloured picket-fence. For much of its circumference the fence was covered with advertisements but there was room elsewhere for spectators to drape their banners and a wide selection included 'Pommy Power', 'Come see the red ball fly', 'Hoggy', 'Boycott the Boss', 'Toohey's so great they named a brewery after him', 'Sir Rodney Hogg' and, at the foot of one of the floodlights, 'The bespectacled Henry Blowfly Stand'.

The pattern continued until lunch. Hughes smeared an intended square-cut over the heads of the slips for four, Darling twice cut very late to third-man off Hendrick, confident, almost cocky shots, and at the interval the second-wicket pair were still together. Australia had added 70 runs and consolidated their position against some tight bowling.

England at last had a change of luck, however, and in the afternoon they fought back exceptionally well. Willis's first ball after the interval was just short of a length outside the off-stump and Hughes, almost as if the shot had been premeditated, launched himself into an intended drive on the up which finished by being virtually a forehand drive. He carved the ball hard to mid-off where Emburey took a good two-handed catch, stretching to his right.

Yallop thus joined Darling at 126 for two and settled down to play a solid and sensible innings. He was helped by the fact that Willis, after bowling only two overs after lunch, had to go off the field again with headache and sickness. He returned to the hotel and to bed for the rest of the day.

Yallop hit Botham to mid-wicket to level the scores an hour into the afternoon session and Darling then hooked Botham for four to take the lead. It was an appropriate shot because Darling had continued to score most of his runs with the hook or pull. A maiden Test century was now beckoning. His defence had looked suspect at times during this innings and his habit of getting square-on in defence might cause him greater problems on greener wickets, notably in England, but he is a talented stroke-player and a hundred now would have been no more than he deserved. His dismissal came as a surprise, at a time when England were at their lowest ebb with Australia in complete control at 178 for two and Hendrick, like Willis, off the field with nausea and exhaustion.

It was Miller who took the vital wicket, not without a trace of welcome good fortune. He bowled a ball of full length just outside Darling's leg-stump and Darling leg-glanced firmly but straight into the hands of Botham at leg-slip. The chance came fast and low and it was the first of three excellent catches by the Somerset all-rounder, who showed again during this tough afternoon that he is not just a fair weather cricketer. No one tried harder than he did as England fought back into the game, and he showed too that he was learning from his mistakes. A few weeks before he might have tried to experiment too much or to dig the ball in short to hustle the batsmen, but the England plan was to keep things tight without going wholly onto the defensive.

Botham had just finished a four-over spell (which on this day was a long one) when Darling was out, but Brearley at once brought him back again to greet Toohey and, much to the dismay of the Hill spectators who had given Toohey the kind of welcome they used to give Doug Walters, Toohey proved as fallible in the early part of his innings as Walters, now languishing in the Packer Australian Second Eleven, always did in England. Botham, relishing bowling (as he had relished batting) on a pitch with some life in it, got a ball to bounce just outside the off-stump and Toohey, trying to force off the back foot, sliced it to Gooch at third slip.

Border, the chunky left-hander, now joined Yallop, the tall one. Yallop, hitting some fine shots off the back foot against the faster bowlers and two confident whacks over mid-on against Miller's slight off-spin, prospered whilst Border played himself in sensibly and these two took Australia into tea at 199 for four. The weather hereabouts had suddenly changed for the cooler, and for a time grey skies threatened rain. Several of the players came out after tea with sleeveless sweaters on and amongst them was Hendrick who had rejoined his colleagues shortly before, after eleven overs in the pavilion looking pale and feeling sick.

After two overs the new ball became due and Brearley summoned it at once, calling on the weary Botham and Hendrick in the absence of Willis. The latter, fit and firing, would have been invaluable now, but no one deserved a wicket more than Hendrick and at last he got one, when Yallop failed to move his feet to get over a ball lifting around his off-stump and Botham dived left to take the edge at second slip in both hands.

Border and Maclean held the fort solidly for a while after the captain's departure but they could score only slowly. Maclean, batting in a helmet for the first time to protect the cut eye which still gave him the look of a heavyweight fighter or a prop forward, seemed less likely than Border to perish against the new ball, but Brearley, no doubt aware that the off-spinners had given him the greatest trouble throughout the series, brought Emburey back into the attack and he deservedly took his first wicket at 235 when Maclean went right back onto his stumps and was trapped in front. The slow graft by Maclean and Border had made the crowd restive, and Boycott, fielding in front of the Hill, suddenly found himself joined by a bearded gentleman who looked at least six foot six and eighteen stone and who insisted on placing a green cap on top of Boycott's England one. Boycott reacted sensibly and with good humour considering he had been bombarded from time to time by tomatoes, oranges, eggs, and the inevitable beer cans.

Hogg looked in little trouble when he joined the resolute Border and hit Emburey boldly over mid-wicket for four, but fifteen minutes from the close England had another reward for an excellent day's work when Border played a ball away to the onside and called Hogg for a single. Hogg hesitated, and then as Border kept on coming returned to his crease. Gower picked the ball up at mid-wicket and threw it underarm to the wrong end, but Miller,

catching the ball by the stumps, threw it accurately to Taylor at
the other end and Hogg was run out.

So Australia ended the second day, which they had begun 96
runs in arrears, exactly 96 to the good at 248 for seven. There was
no doubt that they were still in a position of strength but they still
had to bat last on a pitch expected to take increasing spin and
England's four bowlers (with some steady support at one point
late in the day from Gooch) had given their side an outside chance
again. All would depend on the batsmen redeeming themselves in
the second innings.

For a while the bowlers could relax and feel thoroughly satisfied. Cleverly used by Brearley, they had kept their side in the
match and Bill O'Reilly, watching with experienced eyes from the
press box, said that he had found himself 'grudgingly admiring
one of the greatest Test bowling performances'. Hendrick was his
particular hero and certainly the figures confirmed that impression: after eighteen overs of hard labour he had taken one for
39 and bowled not a single bad ball.

The gates on the first two days, 20,824 and 20,485, had been
lower than might have been expected from the position of the
series and were still following the heavy downward trend, which is
not to say that interest in the match was lacking. But the Monday
crowd was genuinely disappointing. The official attendance was
13,659. It was another hot and sunny day with intense humidity
and Willis was still not well enough to take the field again for England as the two left-handers, Border and Dymock, resumed their
eighth-wicket partnership.

Border began with some confident strokes. A hook to fine-leg
off Botham took the lead to a hundred and in Botham's next over
Border hit a cracking square-cut towards the Paddington Hill, the
little grassy mound some sixty yards beyond the Hill itself.
Dymock propped up the other end capably and Hendrick, though
he bowled well again, could get close to a wicket only once in his
opening four-over spell when Border edged just past Gooch's left
hand at third slip. Hendrick's overs cost only eight runs but when
Botham relieved him after a short rest Border hooked him to the
boundary and on-drove for two. The slenderness of Brearley's re-
sources became apparent again.

Border's first Test fifty came with a leg-glance off Emburey
after three hours and ten minutes of impressive batting. He had
looked a Test cricketer from the moment he had gained his first

cap and this had been just the solid and determined innings which Australia needed to make sure that their advantage was not squandered.

Dymock had been batting in all for 66 minutes when Botham bowled him a legside bouncer, which Dymock hooked at and missed. Umpire Bailhache immediately told Botham not to bowl short to Dymock and Brearley discussed the issue at length with the umpire, obviously feeling that Dymock had looked capable enough for long enough. Brearley's leadership as always was impressive. Absolutely refusing to hurry or to be worried by the cat-calling of the crowd he resolved the matter with Bailhache before walking over to tell Botham the outcome. The latter, no doubt doubly determined, as so often happens in these circumstances knocked out Dymock's off-stump two balls later. Perhaps, too, Dymock's concentration was affected. At any rate, he drove inside the line.

This was not the end of the tailend resistance. Jim Higgs had a highest Test score to date of four not out, but he now batted for forty minutes and made eleven before Hendrick at last got a ball to leave him and the reliable Botham took a straightforward catch at second slip. Border had time to drive Miller through the covers for his fourth four before calling Hurst for an impossible run as he tried to steal the bowling, Miller following through to run Hurst out with an underarm throw.

The Australian lead in the end was 142. England now desperately needed a major stand between two of the first three batsmen. One had come to feel that Randall was now a more important member of the batting line-up than Boycott, who no longer seemed capable of playing a dominating innings. But that he would prove hard to dig out in these circumstances, no one had any doubts. Everyone, therefore, was totally unprepared for what happened at the start of the innings. England had ten minutes batting they would rather not have had. Hogg opened the bowling from the Randwick End. Normally his whole body sways as he charges up to the crease like a jumbo-jet gathering speed for take-off. But this time he ran in languidly, no more than threequarters of his normal distance, and turned his arm over at much less than normal velocity. It was an obvious loosener and Boycott shuffled across to play defensively. The ball cut back, hit the back pad, Maclean and Hogg appealed and umpire Bailhache lifted his finger high above his right shoulder. It was one of the most astonishing moments one has witnessed on a cricket field: Boycott out first ball to a gentle opening delivery. Bill Frindall buried his beard in his book of Test cricket and pronounced that he did not believe it had happened before. It was the first time in 67 Test innings that Boycott had been out for a duck. It was only his seventh Test duck and Hogg followed only three other bowlers in dismissing him without scoring in a Test. The others were Gary Sobers, who did it three times, often deceiving Boycott with the late inswinger; the big New Zealander Dick Motz, who did it twice; and Peter Pollock of South Africa, who had certain similarities with Hogg, not least in that he generally put his faith in bowling straight and fast.

Boycott again expressed his feelings about Australian umpires when he walked into the pavilion, but on this occasion he had been given no time to cool down before a Federal MP, who had already shown his hostility to Boycott, tackled him with a comment which may or may not have been provocative. Boycott could hardly be blamed this time for a brief, heated comment with a familiar ring to it. The same MP had sent a telegram during the Perth Test saying that Boycott's innings had 'done more harm to cricket than the Boston strangler did to door-to-door salesmen'. One's impression was that this politician was not doing any good to cricket himself.

With Boycott gone, it really was Randall or bust for England now. Both Randall and Brearley survived loud l.b.w. shouts before lunch but the former perhaps was overdue a decision in his favour and he warmed the hearts of despairing England supporters with a perfect off-drive off Dymock, truly a stroke not a hit. A great and decisive innings had been launched.

The early overs of the afternoon made fascinating watching. Brearley and Randall looked for runs through the gaps and approached their burdensome task with a refreshingly positive attitude. Hogg bowled very fast and very straight, as well as to a full length, operating first from the Randwick End, then from the Members'. Once he hit Brearley on the chest with a shorter delivery but the ball seldom got past the bat and confidence gradually grew. Randall, with the occasional controlled straight drive and one well-played hook for four, and Brearley, pushing the ball off his legs or steering it down to third-man, kept the scoreboard working just fast enough to maintain the initiative. After an hour of the hot and sultry afternoon the deficit had been cut back to less than a hundred. The fifty came up after 86 minutes with Randall the senior partner and Brearley defending dourly and safely.

Yallop switched his bowlers around and the fielding remained keen and sharp, but the break would not come for Australia. The one bad over of the afternoon was bowled by Hurst, who, with three slips and a gully to operate with, allowed England ten runs down the legside. Higgs, in contrast, was accuracy itself and was treated with respect which amounted almost to suspicion as he bowled six overs before tea for only two runs.

Brearley was 33, Randall 37 when England took tea, in much better heart, at 74 for one. A famous recovery had begun, and Brearley left his blue fibre-glass helmet and his gloves out in the middle, a visible demonstration of the fact that his job was not yet fully done. Before tea he had played staunchly. Afterwards it was possible to say that he had played fluently too. He pulled a rare short ball from Higgs decisively for four and took the full fury of a determined assault by Hogg, who put heart and soul into every ball of a three-over spell, striving to get underneath Brearley's defence. But Brearley resisted with some comfort, once hitting a half-volley off his toes with a force which surprised those who believed he was a strokeless wonder. It is nearer the truth to say that he has the strokes but seldom trusts himself to use them.

For a while in the evening session Randall suffered by comparison, Higgs causing him the greatest concern although he drove him past mid-on to the Hill with perfect timing. When the hundred was finally reached in the fortieth over both players were 47 not out. Drinks were taken soon after and it was significant that the players and umpires rested in the shadow of one of the chimneys. It was still excessively hot.

Brearley got to his fifty first, hitting a full-toss away to mid-wicket off Border. It was his only substantial Test score in Australia since the second innings of the Centenary Test and it had been timely indeed. Randall followed him to fifty in the following over. . He had hit four fours, two more than his captain, and faced nineteen fewer balls (163 in all) but there had been little to choose between the two innings. It would now be interesting to see whether they could increase the scoring rate against a tiring attack. But far from doing so they allowed the two spinners, Higgs and Border, to dictate affairs again and with 35 minutes' play left the left-armer, rated as a very ordinary orthodox spinner in Shield cricket, got the wicket which Australia so badly needed. Brearley pushed forward to him as he had done so often but played inside the line of the ball, which turned a fraction to hit the off-stump. Brearley and Randall had added 111 and the dreaded 'Nelson', England's unlucky number, had struck again.

Remarkable to relate, Border might well have had two wickets in one over had Maclean been able to hold on to a tricky low edge off Gooch's bat as soon as he came in. But after this Gooch played solidly enough whilst Randall became so desperate about keeping his wicket intact that he missed several full-tosses which he would normally have despatched to the boundary. In between each ball, Randall went for a walk around his crease, muttered to himself, fidgeted at each piece of his equipment with more than his usual fury and generally gave an impression quite the opposite of a batsman who had the bowlers at his mercy after a long innings. More than once he walked out to the square-leg umpire to have his face sprayed with a fly-protector. One way and another the cricket had become slow and disjointed but Randall succeeded in staying in and at the close was 65 not out with England now just nine runs in arrears.

The players went their separate ways on the rest day, which was as mercilessly hot as all the others. Some went to the golf-course, some to the beach, some to the hotel pool, Boycott and Miller to the nets and Willis, now recovered, to the hypnotherapist, Dr Jackson, who had helped England's prime fast bowler develop the right mental attitude for big matches after a meeting during the Centenary Test. The visit this time was a social one, but Willis was aware that he had some lost time to make up for and that, if England could set Australia a big enough target, he would be responsible for making an early breakthrough before the spinners came on.

Would the target be big enough? The weather was still so hot that just to sit still in the sun was an exhausting business. Indeed, within five minutes of sitting at a typewriter clad only in bathing trunks rivulets of sweat were channelling down my chest like rain on the outside of a window. For the players conditions were as bad as anything any of them had known.

The position at the start of the fourth day was remarkably similar to that at the same stage of the Brisbane Test, with roles reversed, so perhaps it was not surprising that Yallop still professed himself to be more confident of victory than Brearley. At the Gabba, Australia were just behind England with seven (as

opposed to eight) wickets in hand. Although their revival continued on the fourth day, the 170 which they eventually set England was not enough. The pitch at Sydney, however, was likely to
take sharper spin and the England plan was first to try to make the
game safe and then, if possible, to set Australia a target of around
230. If they could do this, the Ashes might be theirs within two
days. If not and if the batsmen were to fail, it would be two-all and
the series might still go either way.

Hogg and Higgs began the bowling before another rather
sparse crowd, kept down in numbers again by the sweltering heat.
Hogg at first was given only two slips but despite the oppressive
weather he struck Gooch on the shoulder with one ball and in
his third over got another to rise past the off-stump and send
Maclean rocking back as he took the ball in front of his chest. But
he was played with four-square assurance by Gooch which bode
well for England, and when Hurst replaced Hogg, Randall drove
him through extra-cover for three before Gooch, with a handsome cover-drive which Toohey saved brilliantly, got the run
which wiped off England's deficit.

It was Higgs, not the quicker men, who really needed watching
and Gooch was severely taxed by the problems he caused after
failing to hit a rare full-toss where it deserved to go. Pushing forward, Gooch was within an inch of being caught by Wood at silly
mid-off and in Higgs's next over he danced down the pitch to
drive, edged and was dropped by Hughes at slip, the ball brushing
through his fingers on its way to the third-man boundary. It was
hard on Higgs but Gooch had received less than his share of luck
earlier in the series.

The temperature at noon was 38° Centigrade, more than 100°
Fahrenheit, and drinks were being taken every forty minutes.
Without them everyone would have wilted. There was a delay
when Randall drew back as Hurst ran in to bowl because a man
was being taken away on a stretcher close to the sightscreen. An
ABC cameraman had fainted in the heat and fallen over the edge
of a stand more than twenty feet to the concrete below, fracturing
his skull.

Yallop, unaware of the reason, made an exhibition of himself
by gesturing angrily towards Randall as if he were trying to waste
time. But he was clearly wise to withhold the taking of the second
new ball which had now become due, and he had his reward when
he switched Higgs to the Members' end after eight overs for 21

runs at the other. Gooch pushed forward to a leg-spinner and was given out caught off bat and pad as the ball bounced up and was taken by Wood diving forward and to his left. Gooch left no one in any doubt by his facial expression that he thought the ball had come off his pad. That Higgs deserved his wicket, however, nobody could deny. England at this stage were 169 for three, just 27 runs ahead.

Gower, suffering from a temperature, at once imprinted his genius, making all others, Randall included, seem laboured by comparison. He drove his first ball from Higgs through mid-off for three, off-drove still more commandingly to the boundary in the same over and then in Higgs's next over turned his mind to the onside, sweeping for four and then on-driving for two. In the space of a few balls he had gone through half the repertoire of attacking shots. A straight drive followed, this time off Border, and at lunch he had made 18, Randall was still in residence with 87 and England were 49 ahead at 191 for three.

Yallop persisted with the old ball and the spinners after the interval, and Gower continued to play more fluently than Randall, who looked unwilling or unable at this stage to move into a higher gear. Higgs bowled round the wicket to Gower with only three men on the legside, a strange field for a leg-spinner bowling to a left-hander. It did not prevent Gower from piercing the off-side field with another glorious drive and, 25 minutes after lunch, after 84 overs, Yallop took the new ball. As often happens the result was a sudden injection of pace into the scoring rate. Randall loves to have the ball coming fast onto the bat and almost as soon as Dymock took the ball it was driven square on the off-side for only the second four the Nottingham Imp had managed all day.

Hogg walked in to take the ball from the Members' end and the small crowd summoned up enough energy in the steamy heat to cheer him on. His second ball was short and Randall hooked it, with a confident swivel, firmly to square-leg for four, to move to 99. Hogg pitched short again, Randall pivoted a second time and the ball flashed off the middle of the bat in front of square to the fence in front of the Ladies' Pavilion. After six hours and 51 minutes and having faced 355 balls, Randall's ninth four had taken him at last to his second Test hundred. He celebrated with yet a third hooked four in the same over and one could only guess at his feelings as he looked up at the big scoreboard on the Hill at the end of the over. His ignominious second-ball dismissal in the first innings and the long barren tour of India and Pakistan the previous winter were in the past now. It had been an innings of monumental determination and he was now in a position to guide England beyond their present hopes of a draw towards a possible victory and the Ashes.

Gower and Randall between them had added 50 in an hour, but Gower had little of the strike for a while and just when Australia were starting to despair the magic of Hogg worked again. Gower moved his back foot not quite far enough across to square-cut and Maclean held on to a low catch to the relief of every Australian in the ground.

Gower had played remarkably well for a sick man and Randall could not keep the impetus going when he left. Indeed England added only ten runs in the next fifty minutes before tea. Hogg managed another over before retiring from the attack after taking one for four in five overs. Hurst replaced him, but it was Higgs who should have ended Randall's innings half an hour from tea when Randall tried to force off the back foot and edged through the hands of Hughes at slip. Randall was then 113 and he could add only four more before surviving another chance to Maclean, off the inside edge against Hurst. Botham, as usual ill at ease against Higgs, had made only two in fifty minutes and the lead at tea, with six wickets left, was just 105.

To win Australia had to hold their catches, and the luckless Higgs saw yet another chance go to grass in his second over after tea when Randall prodded out and edged to the left hand of Yallop, who had taken over from Hughes at slip. Randall was then 124 and Higgs's figures read one for 90, a gross injustice.

Border now joined Higgs again and continued to be treated with exaggerated respect, especially by Botham, who patted forward to half-volley after half-volley when he would normally have driven violently. He had batted against his nature for 6 runs in 92 minutes when he played tentatively forward to Higgs and the ball popped up for Wood to take a simple catch at silly mid-on. It was a relief to me, and no doubt an immense one to the umpires, to see Botham walking without waiting for a decision. Australia's frustration had been increasingly evident, but some frivolous appealing and ham acting by Maclean did them no credit. The excessive appealing and over-reaction of players to umpiring decisions was one of the more unfortunate aspects of the series, and both sides were equally guilty.

If occupation of the crease was Botham's sole intention, or the sole intention of his captain, it could be accounted a successful innings, but he would have had a much greater chance of playing a major role if he had not concentrated solely on survival. Brearley explained later that he had laid down an overall strategy and then left it to each batsman to decide how to apply it when he got to the middle.

Randall, too, had decided that remorseless defence was the answer and now that Botham had gone he was again obliged to shoulder the main responsibility for the saving of the match. England were, in effect, 125 for five. Miller was the last man before the long and vulnerable England tail. He has many detractors and it is true that he is an unpredictable player who often seems not to be in the mood. But he has seldom failed when there is an urgent need for a staunch innings, and he now played through the last hour and twenty minutes for sixteen not out with a sensible blend of all-out defence mixed with a willingness to hit the bad ball. In other words, on this occasion at least, he applied a more intelligent method than Botham.

Randall, weary but willing, struggled on towards six o'clock with careful strokes towards mid-wicket or extra-cover, and the occasional firm pull, taking him to 150. It was interesting that, for a man known primarily as a strokeplayer and an entertainer, both his Test hundreds should have come when England were fighting a rearguard action and that both times he should have had the determination to keep going after getting to three figures. A small invasion of bare-backed youths and children sprinted across the outfield to salute his achievement; it was cooler now and a southerly wind had blown up to give everyone a little more energy, but a few minutes later Randall played wearily outside a straight ball from Hogg, was hit on the pad and given out l.b.w. After nine hours and 49 minutes at the crease (more than five and a half hours during the second phase of his innings) the cold beer awaiting him in the dressing-room must have beckoned like the original apple to Eve.

Taylor stayed with Miller for the last, tense twenty minutes of the day and when stumps were drawn England were 162 runs ahead with four wickets left. The match was still so poised that each of three possible results seemed likely. If Australia had not missed five catches, four of them off Higgs, who finished the day with two for 123 from fifty overs, their position would have been much stronger. England, for their part, had achieved their primary objective of batting through the day. They had scored only 171 in three remarkably even sessions of 58, 56 and 57, and with a little more enterprise they too would have been more favourably placed than they were. But no doubt Brearley was right in believing that there could be no half-measures in such a situation. At least everyone was kept guessing, and it was a brave person who put money on the outcome.

Whatever happened it seemed certain that 11 January would be the decisive day in the series. The weather was cooler but it was still fine and warm when Higgs moved in to bowl the first over before the small crowd one had now sadly almost come to expect. (It grew to 8,755 later as the match approached its exciting climax.) Higgs immediately got a ball to turn sharply past both Miller and Maclean for byes but it was Hogg who took the first wicket after twenty minutes. The first ball of his third over cut back off the seam to beat Miller as he pushed forward and was struck on the front pad. After a moment's thought umpire French lifted his finger and England were 307 for seven, 165 runs ahead. Miller had added only one run to his overnight 16 and now only the tail remained to hold up Australia.

The news from the England dressing-room was that Gower was in bed with a temperature and would take no part on the final day but that Willis and Botham were better, if not at peak fitness. Hogg now joined the casualty list, going off with a strained side, but this was less a blow than it might have been at another time because Higgs was the man England feared most.

For the best part of fifty minutes Emburey and Taylor kept the fight going with some sensible cricket, most of the runs coming off Hurst, who got two balls to rise up to Emburey's chest, both of them fended off close to legside fielders, but otherwise he posed no great problem.

At the end of the first hour England were 327 for seven, but at 334, with the lead 192, Jim Higgs at last had the kind of success he had threatened throughout his marathon stint. Emburey aimed to drive to leg against the spin and spooned the ball towards Darling, who ran in from cover to take a good catch. Willis now came in, lunged forward in his familiar way to the first ball and edged it to Toohey at second slip. 58th over lucky for Higgs!

England were 192 ahead when these two wickets fell but Taylor pulled a ball from Border for four and Hendrick, sensibly attacking, snicked Higgs for three and authentically square-cut him for four before he too pushed forward and was caught by Toohey. Higgs was clapped off the field by his colleagues after recording his best figures in a Test, five for 148 from 59.6 eight-ball overs. England had added 46 more runs on the fifth morning and all the elements of a classic finish to a Test were now there: both sides in with an almost equal chance and time very much a part of the equation.

When Australia began their innings 26 minutes before lunch, their task was to score 205 in 266 minutes (206 plus the mandatory 15 overs in the last hour). They made a positive and confident start before lunch, scoring 15 from five overs. Eight came off two overs bowled by Willis before the big man walked sadly off to the pavilion, still feeling weak and dizzy from the 'flu bug which had struck the England camp. Hendrick looked more dangerous and must have been close to having Darling l.b.w. before lunch was taken. He appealed twice against Wood in his first over after the break – both times the batsman shuffling across and aiming to leg – but at the other end Wood hit some fine shots off Emburey, who had come on whilst the ball was still new and shiny.

Emburey pitched a little short at first and both batsmen pulled fours off him before Darling hooked again, with tremendous power, straight into the head of Botham fielding at forward short-leg. He was wearing a helmet, but was still knocked over and stunned by the force of the ball. Since he already had a headache the blow cannot have done him any good. Emburey was taken off after bowling three overs for 19 runs and Miller came on to bowl more tightly in his place.

All was going smoothly for Australia at 38 for no wicket, but Hendrick had been plodding in with that pigeon-toed run and banging the ball down on a length with his usual formidable accuracy. Twenty-five minutes after lunch he got a ball to leave Darling, who was playing forward in the direction of extra-cover, and he edged the ball low to the right of Gooch at second slip. That big man of Essex flopped forward to hold a brilliant catch in both hands. England were on their way.

Hughes, however, started confidently enough and there was no cause for Australian alarm as yet, even though Wood miscued a wild drive over the top of Botham at extra-cover. In Miller's next over he drove hard and straight to Botham, now at cover-point, called 'yes' and ran. Hughes would have had a better than even chance of making the run if he had answered the call at once but instead he desperately replied 'No, no!' Wood kept on running, Hughes stayed in his crease and Botham coolly picked the ball up and threw it to Taylor's gloves at the top of the bails. Wood run out 27: Australia 44 for two. Fifteen balls and one run later Yallop played forward to Hendrick, the ball cut in, took the edge of Yallop's defensive bat and bounced back off his pads into Hendrick's waiting hands.

Hendrick was bowling superbly and when Toohey came in, knowing that his Test career was probably at stake, he needed luck to survive a first over in which Hendrick beat him with an outswinger, appealed confidently for l.b.w., and twice found the edge of the bat.

Hughes continued to move his feet to Miller but there was an air of desperation about his dart down the pitch to hit him for four over the top of mid-on. Brearley moved two men out deep to the legside boundary with a ring of three in the middle line and two short-legs. As always the Australians hated to see only two men on the offside, a tactic totally alien to their game but common enough on a turning pitch in England. This pitch *was* turning, as Higgs had shown for so long, and soon Hughes fell in Miller's leg trap, Emburey taking the simple catch off his off-spinning partner.

It was three o'clock, with two hours and forty minutes left and the slide was now really on. Brearley closed in for the kill. The Ashes, and a permanent place of honour in *Wisden*, were now just six wickets away. Hendrick came off after a splendid spell of ten overs in which he had taken two for 17, and for a time Toohey and Border held back the tide. Border looked much the most assured player since the openers had gone, pulling both Miller and Emburey (who had come back in Hendrick's place) for authoritative fours and also off-driving Emburey gloriously for a third four. But Toohey's confidence and touch were at a low ebb and he never gave a suggestion of permanence. Miller ended his fifty-minute struggle when he went down the pitch to drive; the ball turned between bat and pad and hit the stumps. If it had not done so Taylor would probably have stumped him anyway.

Maclean came in to face his recurring nightmare: he tended to be at sea against the off-spinners at the best of times. Now, with the ball turning, it looked positively unfair. He defended stoutly with his pads for a while but in the last over before tea he played forward with the bat almost parallel to the ground, the ball hit his gloves, bounced onto his pads and into Botham's hands at silly-point. At tea Australia were 76 for six and Miller had taken three for 21.

There could only be one result now, for all Border's excellence. Dymock was unlucky when he became the first to go in the evening session, dragging the ball onto his stumps from outside the off-stump. Hogg followed in Emburey's over, caught off bat and pad.

But Higgs, who might so easily have been by now one of the heroes of a famous Australian victory, was not giving in easily and he played the two off-spinners better than some of his colleagues, lasting for 25 minutes whilst Border continued to show what might have been with some ferocious pulls and commanding drives. Amidst the mayhem all around his innings was extra-ordinarily good. He never once looked in the slightest trouble. Australia had found in Allan Border a very promising cricketer who would in years to come perhaps be a member of a side which would avenge the indignities the present Australians were suffering. Higgs eventually went back to Emburey and was trapped in front of his stumps, but it was a salutary thought for Australians that if all the other batsmen had lasted as long as this man whose batting had for some time been a national joke Australia would have been able to save the match.

The moment of victory for England seemed to have come when Border drove Emburey high over the head of Lever, fielding along with Edmonds as the substitutes for Willis and Gower. Lever ran back from mid-off and, to universal surprise, dropped the ball as it came down over his shoulder. There are few safer catchers than Lever, but he cannot have been too worried that his rare error would cost his side the game. Hurst did keep England waiting for twenty minutes before he lost patience, heaved at Emburey and was bowled middle and leg. The Ashes were safe in England's hands again. It was four minutes after five by the pavilion clock and one of the most remarkable recoveries in Test cricket history was complete.

England, 98 for 8 at one point on the first day on an excellent wicket, cannot have dreamed of the final result in that dark hour; nor again when Australia were 126 for one at lunch on the second day; nor indeed when England were 142 behind with nine wickets left in the second innings.

One was sorry to read in the majority of Australian press reports the following morning about the 'pitiful', 'spineless', 'apathetic', 'miserable', 'disgraceful' performance by Australia. More words were written in this vein than about the England recovery. Of course Australia had lost a match they ought to have won, due as much to fielding lapses as to poor batting on a difficult pitch against good bowling at the end, but that England should have pressed them to the extent they did was to me the more remarkable feature. England had indeed risen like a phoenix from the ashes. With Willis effectively a passenger after his important innings on the first day and Botham, Hendrick and Gower under the weather at other times during the match, they had nevertheless shown the depth of spirit which had been fostered by Brearley since he had assumed command in 1977. After the desperately poor performance on the first day, he had warned them that the tour which had started so well might be in danger of completely falling apart. With no need for Churchillian oratory he had impressed upon his team the seriousness of their crisis. Each day for the rest of the game they had assembled in the manager's room at their hotel and discussed the situation. Brearley told his men 'We all have to realise our responsibilities,' and Bob Taylor advised them all to forget what had happened on the first day and play each day as if it were the first of a series.

Insole and Brearley had steered a careful course throughout the tour between insisting on strict professional conduct and a policy of *laissez-faire*. There seemed to me at Perth, as the second victory neared completion, Christmas approached and pretty girls, sunny weather, beautiful beaches and good food all beckoned temptingly, that there was a danger that all the rigorous work at the start of the tour might be wasted. The balance between enjoying a tour to the full and making sure that the best is given at all times on the field is a delicate one, and some of the players may have relaxed a little, perhaps without realising it. The Australian recovery at Melbourne had been an illustration of how quickly the tide could change or, as someone remarked to me, of 'how dangerous it is to feel sorry for Australian cricketers'. But thanks to Brearley's calm control and shrewd tactical brain in the field, to his own determined innings, to the lion-hearted bowling by Botham in the first innings, to the sheer excellence of Hendrick, and above all to the patient, almost bloody-minded matchwinning century by Randall, all had ended well.

As Brearley was quick to remark when he spoke after the match to the media (an aspect of his job which he disliked but which he also had the judgement to appreciate was essential), only the Ashes were won. The series was still alive. But it was estimated that the price of Australia's defeat would be a loss of potential revenue of more than $250,000 which would have come from increased gates at Adelaide, Sydney and the three one-day internationals which remained to be played. It was money sorely needed by the Australian Board for feeding back into the junior cricket which nourished the established game in Australia. The tour profits would be small after England had received their guaranteed sum of $500,000. On the other hand, since an absorbing Sydney Test – a match for the purist, not the newly wooed spectator – had attracted an aggregate crowd of only 72,813 compared with the massive 178,027 which had attended the Sydney Test on the Denness tour, there had been no certainty of vast crowds for the last two Tests even in the event of a second Australian win. As I mentioned at the beginning of this book, the malaise of Australian establishment cricket had deep-seated social reasons as well as purely cricketing ones.

Again, one is too inclined to dwell upon the problems of the losers rather than the joy of the winners. Brearley's team deserved every drop of champagne, and it was good to see Old, Tolchard, Lever, Edmonds and Radley, who had all played a part in the camaraderie of the tour, sharing the happiness. 'I am deeply pleased and deeply satisfied,' said Brearley. 'I just cannot believe it,' said Randall, officially the Man of the Match. 'Honestly,' he repeated, 'even now it's happened I just cannot believe it.' The broad smile on that freckled, impish, little-boy face epitomised the whole team's pleasure.

AUSTRALIA v. ENGLAND (Fourth Test)

Sydney, January 6, 7, 8, 10, 11. England won by 93 runs.

England *First Innings*		*Second Innings*	
G. Boycott c Border b Hurst	8	lbw b Hogg	0
*J. M. Brearley b Hogg	17	b Border	53
D. W. Randall c Wood b Hurst	0	lbw b Hogg	150
G. A. Gooch c Toohey b Higgs	18	c Wood b Higgs	22
D. I. Gower c Maclean b Hurst	7	c Maclean b Hogg	34
I. T. Botham c Yallop b Hogg	59	c Wood b Higgs	6
G. Miller c Maclean b Hurst	4	lbw b Hogg	17
†R. W. Taylor c Border b Higgs	10	not out	21
J. E. Emburey c Wood b Higgs	0	c Darling b Higgs	14
R. G. D. Willis not out	7	c Toohey b Higgs	0
M. Hendrick b Hurst	10	c Toohey b Higgs	7
Extras (b1, lb1, w2, nb8)	12	(b5, lb3, nb14)	22
Total	152	Total	346

Fall of Wickets
1 – 18 2 – 18 3 – 35 4 – 51 5 – 66 6 – 70 7 – 94 8 – 98 9 – 141
1 – 0 2 – 111 3 – 169 4 – 237 5 – 267 6 – 292 7 – 307 8 – 334 9 – 334

Bowling	*First Innings*				*Second Innings*			
Hogg	11	3	36	2	28	10	67	4
Dymock	13	1	34	0	17	4	35	0
Hurst	10.6	2	28	5	19	3	43	0
Higgs	18	4	42	3	59.6	15	148	5
Border					23	11	31	1

Australia *First Innings*		*Second Innings*	
G. M. Wood bWillis	0	(2) run out	27
W. M. Darling c Botham b Miller	91	(1) c Gooch b Hendrick	13
K. J. Hughes c Emburey b Willis	48	c Emburey b Miller	15
*G. N. Yallop c Botham b Hendrick	1	c & b Hendrick	1
P. M. Toohey c Gooch b Botham	60	b Miller	5
A. R. Border not out	0	not out	45
†J. A. Maclean lbw b Emburey	12	c Botham b Miller	0
R. M. Hogg run out	6	(9) c Botham b Emburey	0
G. Dymock b Botham	5	(8) b Emburey	0
J. D. Higgs c Botham b Hendrick	11	lbw b Emburey	3
A. G. Hurst run out	0	b Emburey	0
Extras (b 2, lb 3, nb 11)	16	(lb 1, nb 1)	2
Total	294	Total	111

Fall of Wickets
1 – 1 2 – 126 3 – 178 4 – 179 5 – 210 6 – 235 7 – 245 8 – 276 9 – 290
1 – 38 2 – 44 3 – 45 4 –59 5 – 74 6 – 76 7 – 85 8 – 85 9 – 105

Bowling	*First Innings*				*Second Inninngs*			
Willis	9	2	33	2	2	0	8	0
Botham	28	3	87	2				
Hendrick	24	4	50	2	10	3	17	2
Miller	13	2	37	1	20	7	38	3
Emburey	29	10	57	1	17.2	7	46	4
Gooch	5	1	14	0				

Umpires: R. Bailhache and R. French. Toss won by England.

Chapter Eight
ADELAIDE: DERBYSHIRE TRIUMPHANT

With more than a fortnight to go before the fifth Test, Australian cricket now had a brief opportunity to take stock. Yallop's team was robbed of an early chance to recover from its disappointment. The first of the One-Day Internationals for the Benson and Hedges Cup began at the Sydney Cricket Ground within 36 hours of the finish of the Test match. But the morning was grey and humid from the start and Brearley, whose side included Old, Lever, Tolchard and Edmonds for Willis, Emburey, Taylor and Miller, asked Australia to bat first. Wood was missed behind the wicket off the first ball of the match bowled by Lever but at 17 in the sixth over Tolchard made amends by taking a fine catch in front of slip off Old to dismiss Wood for six. The ball had swung a good deal from the outset and one was settling down to the familiar sight of batsmen struggling when a steady drizzle set in and put a slow and miserable end to the proceedings.

So the Australian selectors were given no new guidance. Carlson and Cosier had come back into the side for the one-day game in place of Higgs and Hogg (who was unwell and whose name was already being speculatively linked with WSC). Carlson had now been named twelfth man in two Tests and rain had stolen his chance of playing in both internationals: he must have wondered if he would ever take the field for his country.

The Australian Board once more found itself under extreme pressure with the victory at Melbourne forgotten by some of the press and the official team again being written off. It was under fire also for making another attempt to alter the tour itinerary to accommodate the second ill-fated Benson and Hedges match, and for so failing to promote its own events that the sixth Test match did not even appear on a widely publicised diary of forthcoming sporting events. There was no doubt that the Board was still losing its public relations battle with WSC, but this sort of thing, which ignored the fact that anyone interested knew perfectly well by now when the sixth Test was due, gave ample fodder to columnists and editorial writers who sought to perpetuate the myth that everything about established cricket was old and boring, and everything about World Series Cricket was new, glamorous and spectacular. I continued to watch the latter, when I had a chance, on television. I was pleased to see Lawrence Rowe, once such a great batsman who had lost all consistency because of trouble with a growth on his left eye and a rare astigmatism, re-establishing his position in the West Indies World Series team with an innings of 175 in a four-day match at VFL Park in Melbourne. But I could maintain little genuine interest in a bewildering mixture of matches between the same group of players. The constant and distracting advertising, the strange clothes and footwear, the odd look of the white ball, the tendency of the television commentators to exaggerate flattery and to withhold criticism, and the incessant references to the money at stake, all went against the grain. Innings like Rowe's were all too rare in any case. The growing imbalance between bat and ball in top cricket seemed to be even more exaggerated in World Series. It was commonplace to see sides bowled out for less than a hundred. In the main, the bang, crash and blood of the game were given a higher premium than the subtle, thoughtful, chivalrous and graceful aspects of traditional cricket. That game, indeed, was being turned on its head.

The final act of the revolution occurred on 17 January in Sydney when a sport became unabashed show-business with no concessions to the old game of cricket except the use of bats, wickets and ball. Massive advance publicity for the first experiment in 'co-ordinated colour clothing' attracted another huge crowd, officially given as 45,233 (such crowds, it should be reiterated, were attending the one-day games, not the four-day ones, and many were getting into the ground free). The match ball was white, the sightscreens were black; the West Indies side wore strawberry-pink shirts and trousers, the Australians wore wattle-yellow from head to toe (pads included). They looked more like pyjamas than cricket clothes. (In the West Indies pink is the colour 'gay' people wear. For the players it was one big joke, no doubt, but not for their paymasters.) Dennis Lillee worked up fierce glances as of old; two gold ornaments bounced against his hairy chest as he ran in – not quite as of old. Children and well-paid commentators yelled themselves hoarse, their excitement part of a drummed-up mass hysteria. The atmosphere was much more like a World Series baseball match than a cricket match.

Indeed it had little to do with the tense, muted excitement of a Test match and nothing at all to do with the folksy rivalry of village cricket. Both on television and in the flesh it was spectacular – brilliantly attractive to the uncommitted, the fringe audience to whom cricket's deeper subtleties are a bore.

Brearley received a personal invitation from Packer to match his victorious side against the World Series Australians at a venue of England's choice before the tour was over. The suggestion was that the sides would meet for $50,000 with the winners taking the lot. Packer's letter was splashed in a Sydney evening newspaper before it got to Brearley. It was a blatant publicity stunt which was quickly rejected as such by Brearley and Insole. There was never any possibility of fitting the proposed five-day match into the crowded tour schedule. Mr Packer was obviously keenly aware of the isolation of his 'superstars'. He had perhaps also forgotten that most of them had been part of Greg Chappell's team soundly thrashed in England in 1977. There was no need for any challenge.

Still, the attempts to promote the Chappell team continued to succeed and the disc 'C'mon Aussie C'mon' continued to climb the record charts. The tune was instantly catchy and the words produced by a Sydney advertising company, got the message across well. The lyrics, broken by choruses of 'C'mon, Aussie, C'mon,' were:

'You've been training all the winter, and there's not a team that's fitter, and that's the way it's got to be; 'cos you're up against the best you know, this is supertests you know, you're up against the best the world has seen.

'Lillee's pounding down like a machine, Pascoe's making divots in the green; Marsh is taking wickets, Hooksie's clearing pickets, and the Chappells' eyes have got that killer gleam.

'Mr Walker's playing havoc with the bats, Redpath it's good to see you back; Laird is making runs, Dougie's chewing gum and Gilmour's wielding willow like an axe.' Not great poetry perhaps, but highly effective propaganda.

There had been renewed talks during the Sydney Test between WSC, represented by Caro and Lynton Taylor, and the ICC, represented by their new president Charles Palmer, his immediate predecessor David Clark, and the secretary, Jack Bailey. These were a part of the dialogue which both sides had promised to maintain.

The disappointment of the rained-off Sydney match was assuaged somewhat by the chance to get to Newcastle two hours earlier than planned after a forty-minute flight north along the New South Wales coast. After the stifling humidity of Sydney the fresh sea breezes were doubly welcome. Newcastle's fame is built, like that of its mother city on the Tyne, upon coal. The postwar depression has passed and coal is now being exported to countries like Japan almost as fast as it can be mined, shipped through the biggest and busiest seaport in Australia. Steel is the other great heavy industry in the area, but beyond the polluted air of the factory areas the broad and beautiful Hunter River flows down to the Great Dividing Range and helps to irrigate some of the finest and most fertile vineyards in Australia. Again, just round the headland from the mouth of the port of Newcastle a rocky shoreline and some formidable surf have made the town a holiday resort: ideal for a break after two demanding Test matches.

True to the formula of matches held in relatively unsophisticated places on this England tour, thoroughly enthusiastic crowds watched the three-day game against Northern New South Wales: not least on the first day when more than five thousand saw three local batsmen, John Gardiner, Chris Beatty, a tall and hard-hitting right-hander who had just got into the state side at the age of 27, and John Hill distinguish themselves on a good pitch. Beatty's 62 included six fours, a five and a big six, the latter stroke off Edmonds who took three wickets in a good long spell.

Beatty, however, was out to neither of these Test bowlers nor to any of the other four cricketers playing in the match who had bowled for England in the current series: he fell instead to a catch at deepish mid-off by Mike Brearley off Geoffrey Boycott who, bowling his medium pace with his cap still on his head à la Grimmett or Jenkins, dropped at once onto a length and followed with another wicket in his second over gained by dint of a subtle slower ball. Had he not been obliged to look after his still slightly gammy left knee, Boycott might have bowled the New South Wales side out rather quickly. Certainly he was like a cat with nine tails after taking his wickets. His Yorkshire colleague Chris Old fell pole-axed to the turf in mock amazement.

Boycott's day, however, was hardly one of joy unalloyed. He had a pair of batting gloves stolen from in front of the pavilion after leaving them there to dry in hot sunshine, and, late in the day, he was well caught down the legside by the former state wicket-keeper Kerry Thompson after making 15 in a manner which suggested a century. His opening partner Brearley took his score to 66 the next day, but the other batsmen played too casually and had it not been for a last-wicket stand of 50 by Emburey and Lever the touring team might have been seriously embarrassed. As it was the two spinners, 'Dutchy' Holland (leg-spin) and Mike Hill (off-spin), a veteran of nine contests against various overseas touring teams, both returned good figures and deserved to do so.

But one incident had been unfortunate, when Roger Tolchard vainly attempted to hook the New Zealand-born fast bowler Glyn Davis. The ball flicked his gloves but hit his cheekbone just under the right eye, fracturing the bone. Such injuries had been two a penny on the previous MCC tour of Australia; this time there had been no important injury until now, which was one good reason for the continued success of the venture. Poor Tolchard was hurried to hospital. The early prognostications were gloomy and after a telephone conference a quick decision was made by Insole and Willis (who had stayed behind in Sydney) and Barrington and Brearley (in Newcastle) to send for another wicket-keeper.

There were only five weeks of the tour to go and a mere eight matches left: had it been any player other than a wicket-keeper such drastic action would have been unnecessary. But Bob Taylor was still not convinced that his groin injury had completely healed and it would have been foolish to risk even the remote possibility of being stranded without a wicket-keeper before a Test match. Accordingly, a year exactly after Clive Radley had been called to Pakistan to replace Brearley who had broken his arm, David Bairstow was summoned to Australia from the bitter cold of the Yorkshire winter. He had been one of the official reserves, contracted and paid to keep himself fit, and it was therefore fair that he should have got the vote ahead of Geoff Humpage of Warwickshire, who had been doing well in grade cricket in Perth and who would have taken less time to acclimatise. In the event, Tolchard made a good but unusually slow recovery. There was no damage, happily, to his eye, but an operation was required on the 'architecture' of the cheekbone.

Bairstow arrived in Tasmania within three days of the accident, having heard about his 'call-up' on his car radio. An ebullient extrovert, he quickly fitted into the party and pronounced himself delighted to be given a chance at last and to get away from all that 'snow and slush in Cleckheaton'.

England stirred themselves when they needed to in the New-castle match, winning what had been an entertaining game played in a good spirit on an excellent pitch by nine wickets with Geoff Boycott ending his run of low scores by making an authoritative century. It was only his second of the tour and like the first it was not made in a first-class match, although since this was a three-day game and three of the Northern New South Wales team had first-class experience there was a good case for the game being accorded a higher status. Boycott would obviously have liked to have recorded his 110th first-class hundred but he was probably more concerned about finding his batting rhythm again, and this he did, punching the ball past mid-on and backward of point with much of the old certainty.

Brearley also batted excellently for the second time in the match in making fifty, and Radley, in his first match since Christmas, enjoyed himself too, scoring 55 not out and batting with steadily increasing confidence and fluency.

In Tasmania, where the team arrived after a trying and tiring late-night journey, John Hampshire was the more famous of the two Yorkshiremen who had fought so tenaciously for the honour of captaining their county. But both were virtual nonentities compared to the red-faced, red-headed Lancastrian Jack Simmons whose patient work as North Tasmania's coach for the past seven years and inspirational captaincy during the island's first two years in the Sheffield Shield competition had deservedly made him a public hero. There had been doubts about Simmons returning to Tasmania the previous year, but the necessary funds had been raised by the Launceston Savings Bank and a Devonport housewife, Mrs Dell Luck, who organised a public subscription. 'Flat Jack' responded by leading Tasmania to the Gillette Cup Final. He went one better in 1979, using all the expertise he had gained in Lancashire's many winning battles to inspire his side to a thrilling victory in the final at Hobart against the more highly rated Western Australians. Simmons virtually did it by himself in the final, taking four for 17 after he had rescued a struggling batting side by hitting 55 not out. So the England versus Tasmania one-day match acquired a new status.

It took place at Launceston on a beautiful summer day before a crowd of around 8,000. The measure of what Simmons and others had achieved was clearly evident. Four years before the MCC fast bowlers had been obliged to operate at half-pace because the pitch

was dangerous: now it looked easy-paced and true. The outfield
was lush and well cared-for. There was a smart new club-house
and, nestling behind it, an excellent new indoor cricket hall with
four matting pitches and long run-ups for the bowlers. All this
suggested that the boom would be no temporary affair. There was
a snap and sparkle about the Tasmanian cricket after Willis had
won the toss and batted, but England were treating the match as
seriously as the opposition had expected they would and they won
the match eventually with almost embarrassing ease. Radley with
an inventive 44, Randall a glorious 60 and Botham a boisterous
and muscular 61 were the main contributors to an England total
which was altogether too good. Without Hampshire, who had
withdrawn the evening before the game because his six-year-old
son Paul was in hospital after being hit on the head by a cricket
ball, an all-too-familiar complaint, none of the batsmen could get
on top of a typically parsimonious England attack. The 18-year-
old David Boon, a thickly built right-hander, showed the promise
of a possible future Test player in making 15 attractive runs, but
not even the magic of Simmons could prevent the England sledge-
hammer from crushing the Tasmanian nut.

The brief flight that evening from Launceston to Hobart was a
delight. This far south the evening light dies only slowly and lasts
until nine o'clock. The greater abundance of hedgerows in Tasmania immediately makes the landscape more familiar to British
eyes and the hills have an unmistakably Scottish flavour. Hobart
itself can take on an atmosphere more Mediterranean than Cale-
donian. On the first day of the three-day match the temperature
was more than 90 degrees, unusually high for Hobart, and with
the pine-clad hills dropping sheer down into the vivid blue of the
Derwent waterway and the dry and pungent smell of pines in the
air, one might have been in the south of France, or in Greece. On
such a day, with the harbour shimmering on one side and the steep
wooded peak of Mount Wellington rising up on the other, the
Tasmanian Cricket Association ground at Hobart can have few
peers amongst all the grounds of the world where first-class
cricket is played.

One man who clearly revelled in the conditions was Chris Old,
although his particular ally on this occasion was not the clear dry
atmosphere but a pitch covered in a lush growth of grass. Bob
Willis duly bowled first on it and it was Old, with a succession of
perfect outswingers, pitching on the off-stump, then lifting and

leaving the bat, who took the first five wickets for sixteen runs before lunch. Four of his victims were caught behind by Taylor, one of them being Hampshire who was good enough to get a touch to his second ball. In another age, perhaps, the Yorkshire fast bowler might have given his new captain one to get off the mark. There was no sign of any friendly gesture from Old, however, and certainly none either from Boycott to Hampshire or *vice versa*. It would have cost little for the two men to have shaken hands in public but it is dangerous for those outside the Ridings to enter into the mysteries of civil wars therein, and it was clear that the rivalry was too intense for any reconciliation. It remained at this stage a secret within Boycott's own breast as to whether or not he would continue to play for his county under Hampshire's captaincy. He was certainly determined to show that he was still the better batsman, however, and once Old, Willis, Emburey and Miller had taken the last five wickets – despite stern resistance for a time from Docking – he settled down to play an innings of technical perfection.

The Tasmanians bowled well – notably the aggressive Cowmeadow, who had bowled the Indians out cheaply the year before and who, if the pun may be forgiven, was talking of seeking pastures new in South Australia the following season. The possibility of an opening partnership of Cowmeadow and Hogg was intriguing.

Gower briefly sparkled in the clear light of the evening, hitting Scholes, a tidy medium-pacer, for four fours in an over, but a leg-spinner named Gatenby bowled him as he tried to sweep with but a few minutes to go before stumps were drawn. Boycott was 41 not out at the close and still in residence the following morning when a thick drizzle blew down from Mount Wellington and stopped the cricket after an hour and a half. This untimely weather virtually ruined the match. When play began again at one o'clock on the third and final day there was never much prospect that England would be able to finish their job. Willis gave his batsmen an hour and a half longer, which was not quite long enough for Boycott to reach his initial first-class hundred of the tour. Miller, however, hit some good shots before being the second man out attempting to sweep Gatenby's leg-spin. On a pleasant sunny Sunday afternoon Tasmania batted more comfortably than they had in the first innings, with Hampshire making batting look a pleasure and scoring 46 not out. Whether he makes runs or not he always seems to give an impression of comfort and composure at the crease, and with his immensely solid build he can hit the ball murderously hard.

Our stay on the delightful island of Tasmania was all too brief and no sooner had the match finished than we were hastening to the airport for another trip to Melbourne. The weather there was once again sunny and hot, a welcome and overdue change of fortune for Benson and Hedges, sponsors of the one-day competition which until then had been so ill-fated. The one-day international started auspiciously for Australia when Yallop won the toss and the new opening combination of Wood and Hilditch put on 27 for the first wicket. Hilditch had won his chance when Darling withdrew from the match after cutting his hand on a boundary fence. He was unlucky, though, to play his first match on a pitch which had been used for a Sheffield Shield game. Its pace was slow and its bounce more uneven than usual, the opposite of the hard true pitch which is best for one-day cricket.

Willis, nevertheless, managed to work considerable pace out of it as he ran in with greater purpose, rhythm and self-belief than for some time. Hilditch had survived two appeals from Lever, one for an l.b.w., one for a catch behind, when he gave David Bairstow his first victim on Australian soil as he nibbled at an outswinger in Botham's first over. Hilditch had looked quite solid, and certainly very calm and determined in his first innings for Australia.

The two left-handers, Wood, going for his shots as usual although England bowled mainly at his legs, and Border, who began with a magnificent on-driven four off Botham, added 25 in five overs, and at 52 for one in the fifteenth over Australia were strongly placed. Then a melancholy decline set in and 19 overs later the Australian building had crumbled to nothing. Border's was the crucial wicket. He had looked so good in his brief stay that he had no need to press extra hard for runs, but in trying to on-drive Hendrick without getting to the pitch of the ball he lofted a catch to Willis. Two runs and one over later, Wood swept Edmonds off the middle of the bat well to Gower's left at mid-wicket. The ball before Edmonds had suggested that Gower and Brearley might swap places at extra-cover and mid-wicket, and Gower now took off like a cat to hold an unbelievable catch in both hands. One sometimes sees a top-class soccer goalkeeper arch his back like this and fasten onto the ball in the split second before it is past him and into the net. But the speed of Gower's reflexes at that moment would have done credit to a cheetah, let alone a Gordon Banks.

In the seventeenth over Hendrick had Hughes l.b.w. as he shuffled across and shaped to play to leg – a replica of many similar dismissals of English batsmen in other matches – and Australia had lost three wickets in eighteen balls for seven runs. Carlson and Yallop did, however, hold the fort until lunch, Carlson hitting two cracking legside fours off Edmonds to give his team some heart.

The brilliance of England in the field put a smart end to the brief recovery after lunch. Yallop hit a ball towards mid-off and like many a good man before him fatally underestimated the amazing speed and agility of Randall, who skipped in from extra-cover, scooped the ball up in his left hand and hit the stumps underarm from close range. Carlson soon followed Yallop to the pavilion, trying to hit Willis on the up – a dangerous business on this desperately unsuitable pitch. The result was a lofted catch to mid-wicket. Three of the last four batsmen fell in much the same way, trying to drive the ball through or over Brearley's strangulating one-saving field. Hogg, by way of contrast, steered a catch to slip. Hendrick with four for 25 and Botham with three for 16 shared the bowling honours.

England made heavy weather of getting the 102 runs they needed to win. The valiant Hogg duly produced an early wicket, yorking Brearley in his second over, but Boycott, refreshed and given new confidence by his innings in Newcastle and Hobart, made sure that the major portion of the $4,000 prize-money went to England. Early in his innings an off-driven four off Dymock was the stroke of a player in prime form again.

Australia bowled well in the circumstances, although Yallop eschewed what was probably their only hope of winning – namely, to attack and try to put the skids under England. He settled instead for a policy of nagging away to defensive fields and eventually both Randall and Gooch, the latter after hitting some handsome offside strokes, lost patience and perished. But Boycott battled resolutely on towards the not too distant goal, taking no great risks but nevertheless attempting many more attacking shots than he had earlier in the tour. It must have been a close decision between Boycott and Hendrick as to who was the Man of the Match, but it was Hendrick who smilingly collected the $400 award.

One had rather expected only limited interest in the Adelaide

Test, but in the two days which preceded the game the place was alive with cricket gossip and speculation. The Australian Board held their annual meeting there and took some far-reaching decisions which included the abandonment of eight-ball overs and a return to six balls from 1979, this for the first time since the bodyline series of 1932–33, and the possibility of some radical changes in Sheffield Shield cricket. They were also considering playing a new limited-over competition between the states, some of which would be played at night at the Sydney Cricket Ground. The Board's chairman, Bob Parish, again made it clear that only cricketers who had played in the Sheffield Shield would be considered for the national team, thus squashing further attempts to bring back WSC players in time for the forthcoming World Cup in England, but he also repeated that the official team would play against any other official ICC team whether or not other countries included WSC players. On the burning issue of the television rights he said that the Board would consider offering exclusive rights to one company or non-exclusive rights to several when the ABC contract expired at the end of March 1979.

Another of the Board's decisions was to answer assertions by some of the Australian players that a manager was needed to guide them during Tests by appointing a liaison officer during each Test to smooth the path of the captain and also of the local state secretary who had in the past 'managed' the team during Tests. There was clearly a strong feeling amongst the young Australian players that the wisdom of an experienced cricketer was needed, an Australian equivalent to Ken Barrington who could help players with their technique if necessary and generally give advice and encouragement. Graham Yallop went further on the eve of the Test, bowing to the current fashion of having sportsmen properly 'motivated' by calling in a rules football coach, Bob Hammond, to talk to his team. It was a novel idea, and no doubt the 'pep-talk' helped to concentrate the minds of the players on the task ahead. But in the past the occasion of a Test match had of itself been quite enough motivation for cricketers. Was it not the captain's own job to inspire his men?

Yallop's team was to show three changes when it took the field from the one defeated at Sydney, with Carlson and Yardley replacing Dymock and Toohey and Maclean dropped in favour of the neat and energetic West Australian wicket-keeper Kevin Wright, who had been considered unlucky not to have been called

up as Maclean's reserve in the previous game instead of Ian Maddocks. It had been Maclean's misfortune to be given his chance
for Australia too late in his career when much of his early slickness
had gone. There had been as little to choose between Maclean and
Rodney Marsh at one stage as there was now between Wright,
Maddocks and Rixon, who had only just begun to play again after
breaking his hand in a Shield match. Wright thus had a great opportunity to make himself Australia's wicket-keeper for many
years.

England, after a brief meeting of the selectors, named an
unchanged twelve. It was not considered that Edmonds had done
enough since the Sydney Test to win back his place from
Emburey. Very few people would have betted, before the tour
began, against Edmonds playing in all six Tests and it was sad to
see such a talented all-round cricketer on the sidelines. Edmonds,
possibly because he comes from a similar background, did not
have the empathy with Brearley that most of the other members of
the team did. This may have been one reason why he was not
bowling as well as he had in the previous year. He took his disappointment well, however. When I asked him after the first day
of the Test what he thought about it all he grinned and said: 'I
really don't know. Test cricket has changed so much since I used
to play it.'

The players of both teams joined in the Australia Day celebrations the morning before the match, somewhat selfcon-
sciously taking part in a 'motorcade' of vintage cars through the
Adelaide city centre. Some of the players also had to appear at a
large department store to sign autographs. This was the kind of
promotion which had stimulated bigger crowds for WSC
matches, and although the players clearly did not enjoy it all these
public appearances had their effect on the crowds at Adelaide.
This may well be something that the £20,000-a-year cricketer has
to accept as part of his job in the years to come.

The atmosphere at Adelaide has a country-town flavour; it is a
fresh, natural enthusiasm. The weather was quite perfect: a deep
cloudless blue sky, but with a gentle breeze too. The Oval (in Adelaide a genuine oval shape) was an even, vivid green, and between
the white picket fence and the backcloth of trees in the botanical
gardens was a mass of chattering shirt-sleeved spectators. There
were 25,000 of them and they were to see a memorable day's
cricket.

The most striking feature of the pitch was that it was barely distinguishable, except by the placement of the stumps, from the rest of the square and outfield, so very green and thickly grassed was it. Brearley called tails and for the fourth time in five in the series his call was the wrong one. The toss was televised and Brearley, much to his obvious distaste, was obliged, in the modern fashion for good public relations stimulated by the advent of WSC, to make an immediate comment about the pitch. The crowd heard him mumbling something about the likelihood of it being pretty awkward for the first few hours. Brearley himself had narrowly decided against taking the same decision as Yallop, namely to put the opposition in, partly because of the risk of spinners enjoying themselves in drier conditions towards the end of the game.

Both teams had settled for a balanced bowling attack, Australia leaving the sadly out-of-form Toohey from their twelve and giving Carlson the task which neither Laughlin nor Cosier had managed satisfactorily. But Yardley and Higgs were both in the eleven for the first time since Brisbane. In other words, Australia, who needed to win to keep the series alive, played the extra bowler, which was surely the right course despite their dangerously long tail. England were unchanged and, although aware of the danger of complacency and a subconscious feeling of anti-climax, quietly confident of another win if they could get through the difficult first session without losing more than a couple of wickets.

Some hope! For twenty minutes all proceeded in a peaceful and orderly fashion. Hogg, near to his record for the series and bowling before his home crowd, worked up to full pace rather quicker than normal and, watching for a time from square-on, one had that glorious cricketing sight of a fast bowler moving in at full pace against a master batsman. Twice in succession Hogg moved in with his crouching approach, arched his back, hurled the ball in short and the view from the fence was of the side of Boycott's body, perfectly positioned with the left elbow high and the head precisely over the line of the ball.

There was little chance, however, to make a closer study of Boycott's technique. When he had made six of England's opening partnership of ten – it is tempting to be cynical and observe that this was one of their better opening stands – Boycott touched an outswinger to Australia's new wicket-keeper and the events of a most exciting day's cricket began to happen at a dizzy rate.

Hurst having for once beaten Hogg to the draw, the sharpest shooter in Australia was not long overshadowed. He bowled a ball to Brearley which, in the cricketer's parlance, 'grew big on him'. Brearley, going back to play the ball in front of his face, was hit, so the television camera seemed to suggest, on the upper arm. The unfortunate umpire O'Connell, with no camera at *his* disposal, hesitated a moment, then sent Brearley on his way.

England were now twelve for two and it was already apparent that for a good while to come the pitch was going to allow generous amounts of cut and bounce for the seam bowlers. Perhaps less predictably, considering the clarity of the atmosphere and the brightness of the sun, the ball also swung a good deal through the air. Hurst, if anything, bowled better than Hogg, pitching the ball further up to the batsman and frequently beating the bat with late outswing. But it was Hogg who took the next wicket, in his fourth over, with a ball which rose from not very far short of a length to have Gooch caught off his glove by first slip running back as the batsman fended the ball away from his face. Not for the first time one was reminded of Dennis Amiss in similar difficulty against the short rising ball: there were many similarities between the methods of Gooch and Amiss both in attack and in defence. Gooch, however, had not yet proved himself to be possessed of equal depths of concentration and determination. Like Brearley, he had now been out to Hogg six times in five Tests. The time for Gooch to play a major Test innings was running short if he was not to disappear from the Test scene. The ability was undoubtedly there, but the know-how, or the instinctive will to survive, was missing.

Randall is a man who perhaps feels more deeply when he is out than he shows and he must certainly have been depressed at the manner of his dismissal this time as he drove without getting to the pitch of a wide outswinger from Hurst and edged the ball a long way wide of fourth slip. The tall Carlson dived to hold a superb catch at full stretch in his right hand. Perhaps a decade ago the ball would have gone through for four to third-man and Randall would have gone on to make a hundred. But the catch was safely held, and England were reeling at 18 for four when Ian Botham walked out to play one of the few really memorable innings of the series. First, however, at 27 Gower was l.b.w. as he played half-forward to Hurst and after exactly an hour it was safe to say that, no matter what happened later, Yallop's brave decision had been justified. Hurst's first spell of five overs had earned him three wickets for 11, and Hogg, who managed an unusually long spell of six overs, had taken two for 15.

England's plight should have been more serious still. Before he had scored a run Miller played a half-hearted hook to a bouncer in Carlson's second over and Hurst, at long-leg, so misjudged the flight of the ball that he barely laid his fingers on a straightforward chance. The Test match was less than two hours old but this undoubtedly was one of its turning-points. Miller abandoned the policy of total defence with which he had begun his innings and now started to play shots, some streaky, some good, notably one crisp pull to the mid-wicket boundary off Carlson.

England were 71 for five at lunch, Miller 25 not out, Botham, as yet subdued, 14 not out, and it was only when Miller became Hogg's tenth l.b.w. victim of the series that Botham took control of events. He began by tucking into Carlson's medium pace. A force off the back foot for two, a pull over square-leg for four and a majestic square-cut for four reeled off his bat in successive balls. Yallop said 'thank you' to Carlson and instead of bringing on Higgs, who had troubled Botham so often, turned instead to Yardley. Botham greeted him with a volley of brilliant strokes, a six to the short mid-wicket boundary picked up off his toes with almost arrogant assurance, then a four lofted over mid-on, then a punch off the back foot backward of point for two. Soon after reaching his fifty Botham hooked Yardley to deep square-leg and Hogg dropped the catch in front of his chest: only a second later did one notice that the umpire's arm was extended to signal a no-ball.

Botham continued his assault with a hook for four off Hurst and then, off the same bowler, a dazzling carve to the point boundary best described as a rackets shot. At last Yallop turned to Higgs and although Botham had some small revenge for the constraint which Higgs had applied on him hitherto, swinging another six high into the crowd in the long George Giffen stand, he was out when he tried to push a single to the offside to retain the strike. He was, in fact, both caught behind and stumped off the same ball. Whilst Botham had been blazing away so gloriously England had also lost Taylor, run out by a throw from Hogg and also by some quick thinking by Wright as Botham went for a fourth run, and Emburey, bowled by Higgs as he hit across a leg-break.

Willis and Hendrick came together when Botham, for the second Test in succession, was ninth out after saving the innings from total disaster. This time, however, the entertainment was not over. Willis decided to swing his bat in the manner of the old-fashioned tailenders and in one farcical over from Hurst he took 18 runs by stepping away to leg, swinging the bat towards mid-on yet somehow despatching the ball time and again over the top of the offside field with a corkscrew turn of the bat at the last moment. One of these extraordinary efforts actually sent the ball over the cover-point boundary for six. Poor Hurst, who had on this occasion bowled rather better than Hogg, had his figures badly damaged. Hogg himself was hit once over extra-cover for four but then took his 37th wicket of the series as Willis skied the ball again and Darling came racing in from cover, fair hair flying behind him, to hold the falling ball at full tilt. It was a suitably spectacular end to one of the most remarkable innings by a Test side one could remember, and yet again the heroic figure of Hogg led his team off the field having broken Arthur Mailey's record of 36 wickets in an Ashes series in Australia. Mailey had taken his wickets in four of the five Tests of 1920–21, having not bowled in the second match of the series. It was as inevitable that it should have been a leg-spinner who broke the record in the 1920s as it was that it should have been a fast bowler in the 1970s. Jeff Thomson had appeared to be on the point of surpassing Mailey in 1975 at Adelaide when he had injured himself on the rest day of the match. With 37 wickets for 426 runs off 171.6 overs (47 maidens) Hogg now had a realistic chance of surpassing Jim Laker's 46 wickets in the 1956 series in England.

Australia's reply to England's 169 began after an early tea with a most frightening incident. The fifth ball of Willis's first over lifted and cut back sharply from the off, hitting 21-year-old Rick Darling just below the heart. He doubled up instantly, then subsided onto the ground. The England players realised at once that he had been seriously hurt and a terrible atmosphere of silent fear crept across the huge crowd as the players huddled about the fallen figure and began taking off his boots and equipment, signalling frantically to the dressing-room for assistance. Umpire Max O'Connell said suddenly: 'He's not breathing.' John Emburey, who had learned about resuscitation and heart massage during a lecture to Middlesex players in England the previous season designed to help players deal with exactly this sort of crisis, then took the initiative and gave Darling a sharp blow above the heart, known technically as the pre-cordial thump. It caused Darling to cry out and gasp for air. The South Australian Cricket Association physiotherapist, Michael Mason, who had sprinted to the centre of the square, then turned Darling on to his side in the coma position, pulled his tongue back to the front of his mouth and removed the gum which the batsman had been chewing and which had also obstructed the passage of air. For some time Darling lay breathing irregularly and in a state of semi-consciousness, but a doctor who had also run to the pitch decided after a few minutes that the batsman should be carried by St John ambulance men on a stretcher to the dressing-room. There he was given oxygen and rested for an hour beore going to hospital for an X-ray, which revealed only a severe bruise on the chest. Darling, who could remember nothing of all this from the moment that he had doubled up as the ball cut into him, was able to resume his innings the following day with a thigh-pad strapped across the bruising, but otherwise perfectly fit. Indeed, by the evening of the incident itself, Darling's team-mates were already able to find some humour in the situation. His close friend Graeme Wood visited him in hospital that night and greeted him with the words: 'I know cricket's serious, mate, but for God's sake don't stop breathing for it again whilst I'm batting with you.'

Wood, who must have been especially shaken by what had happened, batted through the rest of the day's play with commendable concentration, but it was a disconcerting way for a team to start an innings and by the close of play England had taken four wickets for 69 runs and had virtually balanced the match.

Hughes, that attractive and flamboyant strokemaker who takes such a delight in the stylishness of his batting and gives spectators equal delight when he succeeds, hit one glorious square-cut off Willis almost as soon as he came in to bring everyone's mind back to the cricket again. But he was brilliantly caught in the gully in the next over when Emburey flopped forward to hold, at full stretch in front of him, a slowly travelling edge off bat and pad.

With Old out of the side and Willis still struggling to co-ordinate his run-up and delivery, Mike Hendrick was now England's most dangerous weapon, and having thus disposed of Australia's new vice-captain (Hughes had succeeded Thomson, Cosier and Maclean in what was rapidly coming to be considered an unlucky job) he also got rid of the captain. Yallop was nonplussed by a ball which came back a little off the seam to squeeze between his bat and pads and his dismissal meant that at ten for two, with Darling still receiving oxygen in the dressing-room, the plight of his side was worse even than England's had been at a similar stage.

The two left-handers, Wood and Border, steadied the ship. The secretary of the South Australian Cricket Association, Neil Blundell, had the good sense to announce that Darling was recovering well in the dressing-room, and this helped no doubt to calm the nerves of the players of both sides as well as of the crowd. It was particularly unfortunate that Willis, who was having such problems with his bowling, should have delivered the near-fatal ball because his opening deliveries had been good ones and he needed a couple of wickets to give him confidence again. Instead the injury to Darling upset him and it was not until the belligerent Botham replaced him in the attack that more wickets fell. Hendrick had been rested after a marvellous opening spell of seven overs in which he took two for twelve.

Botham's first victim was Border, edging an outswinger to Taylor as he essayed a full-blooded drive. Then, after waiting so long for his chance, Carlson was given out fifth ball as he played and missed at Botham's stock delivery, the outswinger to the right-hander pitched on the off-stump. The television replay once again suggested – as, plainly, did Carlson's expression – that umpire O'Connell had erred. But if the latter was getting tired of reading criticism of his decisions he did not show it off the field, where his relations with the players of both teams were clearly excellent. During the rest-day revels later in the match O'Connell was seized by a group of players from both sides and dumped, fully clothed, into the swimming-pool. He took the decision without a murmur of complaint! My impression was that although he made errors he was a fearless umpire who enjoyed the liking and the respect of both teams.

Australia were four wickets down for 24 now, but Wood, concentrating grimly, was still there when the lean and hungry figure of Yardley loped out to join him. For the last 75 minutes of an extraordinary day's cricket these two restored some sanity and survived by sensible batting. The pitch was already looking less green but from time to time the ball still moved and both players were dropped at second slip, Wood off the luckless Willis and Yardley off Hendrick. It was not the least remarkable fact of a remarkable first day that the culprit on both occasions was Ian Botham. Australia finished with 69 for four. Had the grounds-man done his watering and mowing a day earlier the match might have started very differently and batsmen might for once have prospered.

The second day was to be altogether quieter. Perhaps because it was hotter on the Sunday morning the crowd was smaller (17,357), but there was still that authentic Test-match animated buzz as Botham ran in from the Cathedral End and saw his first ball of the morning, a juicy half-volley, stylishly driven past mid-off for three by Graeme Wood. No doubt, however, Botham was not too disappointed to have an early crack at Yardley, and with the seventh ball of his over he duly took his wicket as Yardley deflected the ball onto his stumps off his body. He had not added to his overnight score of 28.

So, to a warm-hearted cheer from his local crowd, Rick Darling walked out, white helmet in hand, to resume the innings so fright-eningly cut short the previous evening. The two Australian openers were together again now, and it was imperative for their side that they should make a substantial stand. Darling cut his first ball to third-man to get off the mark and then when Hen-drick, given the ball in preference to Willis, pitched short for the first time, Darling hooked resoundingly to the mid-wicket bound-ary, scattering the sea-gulls in front of the Victor Richardson gates.

The hook had been, and will no doubt continue to be, both a bounty and a bane for Darling. When Botham, having placed two men on the legside boundary, threw down the gauntlet for the first time, Darling got underneath the ball and hooked it comfortably over square-leg for six. Adelaide, as Botham had already shown, is a good place to hit sixes square of the wicket. The total width of the ground is 138 yards, and with the wickets set on this oc-casion slightly to the pavilion side of the square the carry may have been no more than 65 yards. But Botham's second bouncer was pitched on the off-stump and Darling was not so well placed as he skied the ball to Willis on the long-leg boundary. What a waste of a good pitch and a perfect day, Darling must have reflected as he walked out! At least he had played the fast bowlers without a flinch and was clearly none the worse for his ac-cident.

Wood was showing the application which Darling had failed

to do, and in Wright he found a sensible and effective partner. The red-headed West Australian made a calm and assured start, not afraid to play an attacking stroke if the ball merited it but otherwise relying on a sound-looking defence. He survived an early appeal for a catch off the inside edge off Botham, the ball appearing to hit the pad and not the bat, but if anything he otherwise looked as solid as Wood despite the pressure of close fieldsmen. Hendrick and Botham gave way to Willis and Emburey, and it was the off-spinner, naggingly accurate as usual, who gave Wood more trouble – eventually having him caught at square-leg as he swept against the spin and without getting to the pitch of the ball.

Willis was still unable to find any pace or rhythm but he did at last take a wicket when Hogg lost his bearings to the first ball he received, pulling the bat inside the line of a ball which cut away a little and finding to his dismay that it was still in line with the off-stump. Only Higgs and Hurst were left now, yet the last two wickets were to add a further 48 useful runs. Wright, with some wristy cuts and one whole-hearted pull off Willis, took his score to 29 before he was l.b.w. hitting across Emburey.

Higgs and Hurst were together at lunch and few people expected much resistance from them afterwards: in the event they lasted for forty more minutes and added thirty more runs, Higgs batting presentably and with reasonable orthodoxy, Hurst stepping away towards square-leg and swinging the bat with as much gusto as Willis and only slightly less effect.

So it was not until half-past two that England began their second innings with a lead of five and in what were now ideal batting conditions. The light and atmosphere were clear, the pitch now noticeably browner in colour, and for all one's experience of collapsing batting sides in the previous few seasons it really seemed a safe bet that both sides would improve on their first-innings efforts. England now had a clear advantage, for they were bound to have the best of the batting conditions.

They were obviously not in any hurry and Boycott, at last getting a pitch to suit him, settled in calmly and carefully. The cricket assumed a more familiar Test-match tempo. Hogg and Hurst could get nothing much from the now blameless pitch and for once one really felt that Boycott was their master, skilfully thrusting his chest back inside the line of anything pitched short and picking up runs every now and then with studious pushes and

deflections into the gaps in the field. Later he hit two crisp fours to
the offside boundary as his confidence grew. Alas, Brearley could
contribute little except a dead bat. This was useful in itself so long
as the shine remained on the ball, but it never looked as though he
would be able to move on from his period of reconnaissance.

Carlson came nearest to taking a wicket before tea, appealing
without success for a catch behind off Boycott's thigh-pad and for
l.b.w. against Brearley. England had made 26 without loss at tea
in 70 minutes, and ten minutes into the evening session Carlson's
second l.b.w. appeal against Brearley was upheld.

The pattern of patient grafting continued with Randall's arrival. The bowling was steady, the over-rate slow, the fielding good.
Randall was just getting into his stride, having hooked Hurst for
four and cover-driven Hogg for another, when, attempting
another hook off the deserving Hurst, who has seldom bowled
faster or with better sustained hostility, he was caught off a skier
to mid-wicket. Boycott and Gooch batted comfortably until the
close when Boycott, after more than three hours of devoted and
disciplined batting, had scored 38. England, at 82 for two, were
strongly placed.

If anyone still believed that cricket is a game which follows logical courses to predictable ends they were surely disillusioned by
the events of the third day of the fifth Test. It was an extremely hot
day, humid too, and with very little breeze. The sky, such a vivid
blue on the first two days, was lighter in colour now with streaks
of white around the horizon. Although it was a public holiday to
celebrate Australia Day (officially 26 January) both the heat and
the apparent likelihood of a Boycott century may have kept the
floating voters away from the Adelaide Oval. But those who came
saw Australia have success in the morning which must have exceeded their dreams before an equally surprising and meritorious
recovery later by the Derbyshire pair of Miller and Taylor.

Hogg began the day by bowling four overs at no more than
three-quarters of his full pace before retiring to the dressing-room
seeking treatment for stiffness in his legs and a slightly strained
groin muscle. Hogg defied his captain to leave the field and soon
afterwards Yallop ran off the field himself to remonstrate with
Hogg in the dressing-room. There they had a heated exchange and
it was an hour before Hogg returned to the field after treatment.
The captain and his main fast bowler had disagreed once or twice
before during the series. If Yallop had been a selector, like

England's captain, he would have been more strongly placed to crack the whip.

At the other end Yallop employed Carlson, and the tall Queenslander responded with an excellent spell of steady seam bowling very reminiscent in pace and style to similar spells delivered for England by Basil D'Oliveira.

Gooch played just one shot to save him from total despair – a perfectly executed hook off Hogg – but after he and Boycott had added 15 runs in a quiet opening forty minutes Carlson bowled him between bat and pad. This was a blow for England but the seeds of their real trouble were sewn in the next half-hour by some disciplined bowling by Carlson and Hurst and some excellent fielding.

Hurst was altogether fiercer than Hogg and more than once he had Boycott rocking back inside the line as the ball reared up towards his chest. Carlson meanwhile bowled gentle floating outswingers to a well-protected cover field, two slips and a gully. Both he and Hurst succeeded in strangling Gower's normal free scoring, and a succession of cuts and drives were smartly stopped in the covers, Yallop and Darling making particularly outstanding saves.

Something had to give, but nobody expected it would be Boycott's patience. After being stuck on 49 for what seemed an eternity he followed a wide short ball from Hurst which lifted, failed to get on top of an intended steer towards third-man, and was well caught by Hughes high to his right at third slip. England's fortune was now in the youthful hands of Gower and Botham. One longed for them to produce a piece of batting to make all Australia sit up and take notice. One day they will surely rouse a Test crowd to ecstasy, but this was not to be the time. Botham drove firm-footed at Hurst, and Yardley, that exuberant, hyper-tensive character, hurled the ball so high when he pouched the catch at third slip that it might have been the catch which won the match.

Yallop had brought on Higgs before lunch in the hope that the leg-spinner would continue to embarrass Botham. Instead it was Gower, having played two glorious strokes through the covers off Hurst, who fell to the spinner as he pulled towards mid-wicket and was struck on the pads. At such a juncture it was not a very responsible shot, for the ball was not short enough for the stroke to have been played without risk. The leg-break turned quite sharply as it hurried into Gower and up went O'Connell's finger again as Higgs spun round in appeal. Thus it was that a few minutes before lunch Derbyshire's Bob Taylor joined together with Geoff Miller in a heart-warming partnership. The score as they came together was 132 for six.

No one anticipated any batting heroics at lunchtime, although all were agreed that the pitch was now a beauty. The sun was still beating down and it was difficult to account for the failure of England's batsmen, four of whom had been out for a mere 52 runs. Their own shortcomings had been partially responsible but so too had some sound captaincy by Yallop, some brilliant fielding, and some determined bowling by Hurst, Carlson and Higgs.

So hot was the afternoon that Carol Miller and Kathy Taylor, not yet used to the sun after the rigours of the English winter, returned to their hotel rather than stay on to watch their husbands. At teatime Kathy switched on her television to see what England had totalled. The doughty Derbyshire pair, to her surprise and everyone else's, were still together. They had batted remarkably freely and comfortably from the start. Taylor twice moved nimbly down the pitch to hit Higgs straight down the ground and Miller pulled successive balls from Hurst to the mid-wicket boundary. For the first forty minutes after lunch they scored at a run a minute, a rare feat in this Test series. It was sensible, positive batting, with no excesses but also no exaggerated caution. They played as they might have done in similar circumstances in a county championship match at Chesterfield. Perhaps the fabulous variety of trees in the botanical gardens and the mellow stone of Adelaide Cathedral sounded subconscious echoes of stands together on a sunny day at Chesterfield with its own beautiful parkland setting and its church with the crooked spire.

The new ball, taken at 161 as soon as it became due, could not dislodge the pair, and although Hogg did his best the extra nip and bounce he normally achieved were missing. The fifty partnership came in 70 minutes and at tea England at least knew that Australia would be set more than two hundred to win. Taylor, still timing the ball sweetly, was 46 and Miller, content to play second fiddle, was 31. They had added 79 between lunch and tea after watching four of the specialist batsmen go for 52 in the same time before lunch.

Taylor's first Test fifty came twenty minutes after tea when he moved quickly down the pitch to play a decisively struck on-drive off Yardley which brought him four, all run. For a time after he had reached this milestone Taylor played less well. Yardley and Higgs bowled four maiden overs until Miller broke the spell by hitting Yardley over mid-wicket. His fifty came after three hours' batting with a pull off Yardley, but when Taylor had made 53 he pushed forward without the firmness which had characterised his earlier batting and edged Higgs to Border's right at first slip. The chance went down.

Miller gave Taylor a sharp talking-to at this point and Taylor returned the compliment later when Hurst came on and Miller played a couple of loose strokes outside the off-stump. It began to look, however, as though the pair would still be together at close of play when, ten minutes from the end, Miller got a thin tickle to a ball from Hurst on his leg-stump. Wright moved across quickly and claimed a low catch. Umpire Bailhache consulted his colleague at square-leg, O'Connell nodded and Bailhache lifted his finger. Both batsmen were sure that the ball had bounced before it reached Wright's gloves. Wright, presumably, was sure that the catch was a fair one. Miller was out, at any rate, and he and Taylor had fallen only eight short of England's record seventh-wicket partnership against Australia.

England were 272 for eight at the close of play, 277 runs ahead and strongly placed. They were able to enjoy their visit to the Yalumba winery at Angaston in the Barossa Valley on the rest day much more than had seemed likely. The hospitality lavished on both teams and sundry other guests by 'Windy' Hill-Smith and his wife was delightful, and those who could drag themselves away from the wine, an opulent swimming-pool and an immaculate grass tennis court were able to see round the Lindsay Park Stud and the racing stables of one of the country's outstanding trainers, Colin Hayes. Amongst the attractions at the former were some of the offspring of the stallion Without Fear, one of which was to be presented to the Queen as Australia's Jubilee gift.

The talk turned from the Test match from time to time because Kerry Packer's Channel Nine Company had announced their intention to bid along with the ABC and the other commercial stations for the rights to televise first-class cricket the following season. The hope was growing that now the dust had settled on the original disagreement, some sort of deal would be reached in April.

This would be all the more likely if Australia were to go under again at Adelaide, although rather surprisingly it was the West Indians and not the WSC Australians who picked up the $35,000 prize-money for the finals of the one-day competition when they defeated Ian Chappell's side 3–1 in the best-of-five finals at VFL Park in Melbourne. Those who saw the games believed that they were played with genuine competitiveness and that they produced some good cricket. Certainly they again attracted good crowds. Just under 20,000 watched Clive Lloyd bat the West Indians to their win on the fourth night. Once again the match ended in chaos. Mr Packer ordered that the game should be extended by fifteen minutes so as to obtain a result, although the regulations stated that play should stop at 10.30 p.m. According to a report in *The Australian*, the Rupert Murdoch-owned newspaper which gave wide publicity to all WSC activities, Packer conveyed the decision to the WSC managing director, Andrew Caro, who asked Wayne Prior, one of the Australian playing squad, to inform the umpires and the players of both sides. Prior ran on to the field at about 9.35 p.m. to tell Ian Chappell, but the umpires were not told of the change and the match ended at 10.30 with the West Indies leading on run-rate.

A week later Caro resigned as WSC managing director, saying that 'emotionally, Kerry Packer couldn't keep out . . . I felt my authority and control were not sufficient to do the job I wanted to do.' Both Tony Greig and Richie Benaud seemed to have been opposed to Caro, believing that his understanding of cricket was not deep enough for the job. Yet it seems clear that the organisation of players, grounds, accommodation and other practical matters had been highly efficiently run by Caro.

At Adelaide England's tail-end resistance continued well into the fourth day. It was very hot indeed with a merciless sun and little breeze, and Taylor, accompanied this time by Emburey, continued to make life hard for all the bowlers. Emburey was missed at slip by Border off Yardley when he had made 17 but he hit some powerful strokes to leg and generally showed a sound judgement of which ball to hit, as well as a solid defence. Taylor, meanwhile, reached the nervous nineties for the second time in his 19-year career. He had made 97 against a South African Invitation XI in 1975–76, playing for the International Wanderers. Now, as lunch approached, he reached 97 in a Test match. Emburey took a single off the penultimate ball of Hogg's final over before lunch and

Geoff Boycott took his setbacks well and the younger members of the England side refused to allow him to take himself too seriously, constantly pulling his leg. Boycott was able to relax more in the minor games. At Newcastle (against Northern New South Wales) he took two wickets in two overs and patiently saw to the needs of some younger members of his worldwide fan club.

Above All the power and confidence of Ian Botham's cricket are captured in this picture of him lofting Yardley to the pavilion during his spectacular innings which rescued England in the first innings at Adelaide. *Below* Darling is struck on the heart by a break-back from Willis early in Australia's first innings at Adelaide. For a time he lost consciousness.

Hogg, still looking for his first wicket in the game, delivered the last ball from a shorter run-up, using the full width of the crease. The ball was angled across Taylor, who flicked at it as it passed down the leg-side, and in a split-second of anguish knew that it was bound straight for Wright's gloves. It was one of the saddest moments one has seen in cricket. No one in Australia would have begrudged Bob Taylor those last three runs after six hours of virtually flawless batting. The chance to score a Test century against Australia would never come again. Perhaps he would never get a first-class hundred now. No one in modern cricket has been so universally liked and respected as this friendly little man from Stoke-on-Trent, whose standards of integrity, natural modesty, loyalty and dedication have always been an example for other professional cricketers to follow.

John Emburey has some of the same qualities and he became the major partner after lunch, when he took his highest Test score to 42 before Hogg pierced his defences. Then Willis, using the Duncan Fearnley 'reaper' bat, which has small holes drilled into it and which had come under the threat of a ban by the TCCB in England because the captain of a minor county team had complained that it tended to cut small pieces of leather out of the ball, harvested twelve more unorthodox runs before Hogg took his third wicket of the day and his fortieth of the series. The lion-hearted Hurst (who had once been mistaken in Australia for a quitter and a hypochondriac) finished with four for 97 from 37 overs in which he had bowled outstandingly well and with un-remitting effort.

Australia needed 366 to win on a good wicket. This, in theory, was a more realistic target for them than the 205 they had needed on the last day at Sydney. Then the wicket had started to crumble. Now, at Adelaide, conditions were perfect for batsmen, as the fact that England's last four wickets had added 228 runs surely proved. It would be a test of the true quality of England's bowling and Australia's batting, and also of the tactical skills of Yallop and Brearley.

Clearly Australia's first priority was to get a good start. In Wood and Darling they had a talented but naive opening pair. This time they played sensibly, helped somewhat by the fact that Willis, who had offered to withdraw from the team before the match, was again going through mental agony as he strove in vain to find his normal whip. Brearley, unlike many captains, is seldom

seen at mid-off or mid-on but this time he went there specially to
encourage and cajole his key bowler. Willis listened in his usual
expressionless way, but hard as he tried he could not find his
rhythm and after he had bowled three no-balls in his third over
Brearley gave him one more over before calling up Botham.
Wood and Darling were now playing with some confidence, Darling hooking and cutting with panache, Wood deflecting off his
legs and occasionally driving strongly.

Botham's advent swung the game again. With the total 31 Darling moved too far across to the offside in trying to play the ball
away through mid-wicket off his hip and was bowled leg-stump.
Hughes edged the next ball through the slips and Gooch hurled
the ball in from third-man so strongly that the three became five
from the overthrow. It was an encouraging way to start an
innings. Wood played a leg-glance at the next ball and Taylor
dived to catch the ball at full stretch in his right glove. There was a
very wide deflection but umpire Bailhache made no response as
the England fielders rose as one to acclaim the 'catch'. Botham
made his frustration abundantly clear, and every ball he delivered
thereafter had all his considerable strength and determination behind it.

The inventive Brearley rested Hendrick now and brought on
Miller for his first over of the match. Hughes pushed forward to
his second ball and survived another vociferous England appeal,
this time for an alleged catch by Gooch at slip off an inside edge
onto the pad. Hughes stayed to play some glorious strokes, but
Wood's reprieve was short-lived. He drove a ball in Botham's next
over towards mid-on and called for a sharp single as Boycott, with
marvellous balance and control, ran across from mid-wicket,
picked the ball up in both hands and threw it with his right
towards the one stump in his vision. The aim was perfect and
Wood, who had been obliged to swerve to his left to avoid Botham
on his follow-through, sprawled in vain past the back-pedalling
umpire Bailhache, who lifted his finger as he himself fell. Wood
protested that he had been unintentionally impeded by the
bowler, but the decision stood and Australia were 36 for two.

Yallop and Hughes, captain and vice-captain, now dug in with
the necessary discipline and determination. At tea Australia were
44 for two; at the close, despite one or two near-shaves against
Botham and Hendrick, they were 82 for two after 130 minutes of
staunch defence punctuated by the occasional handsome drive,

hook or square-cut from Hughes.

On the final morning, burning hot and cloudless blue, Australia had their final chance to salvage some respect and honour. They needed 284 to win in six hours, but if that were to prove beyond their capabilities they still had a fair chance of saving the game on a benign pitch. Sadly, after a promising start the contest became as one-sided as if a tiger were taking on an antelope.

A sudden change of tactics by Brearley, a typically decisive piece of captaincy, changed the course of the game. In the first twenty minutes the smallest crowd of the match (4,000, bringing the overall total to 70,936) had the rare pleasure of seeing two of Australia's young batsmen playing the England bowlers with some comfort and confidence. Yallop's priority still ought to have been that of building up steadily and then, if all went well, mounting an assault late in the day. Instead he and Hughes attacked Emburey and Miller from the start. Eleven runs off one over from Emburey were enough to persuade Brearley to apply the brakes. His double change brought back Botham and Hendrick and quickly had its effect.

After six runs had come from Hendrick's first over (he was to concede only 19 in 14 overs overall) the free flow of runs dried suddenly to a barely audible drip. At drinks, after 40 minutes, Australia had reached 114 for two, a satisfactory start. One run later Hendrick, bowling over the wicket to the left-hander, got a ball to pitch on the off-stump and then straighten enough to hit it as Yallop lifted his bat out of the way.

The collapse which followed was at once an example of Australia's inexperience and England's professional excellence. The speed with which Brearley's team now seized the match and the series was bewildering. Hughes tried a flamboyant force off the back foot and was breathtakingly caught by Gower diving to his left at deep gully. Willis came back on from the River Torrens end as if he had never lost form at all, bowled Border between bat and pad with his first ball, had Yardley caught at slip driving two balls later and for the rest of his spell was once again the fast, fearsome, mercilessly hostile fast bowler who had first undermined Australia's batting at Brisbane.

When Botham tired after one of his steadiest spells of the tour, Brearley brought back Miller and in two overs he had Wright caught at short leg and bowled Hogg for 2. The battle had been won by lunchtime. Carslon hit some powerful strokes afterwards before he too fell to a brilliant catch by Gower, this time at mid-wicket. Then Hurst went down with all guns blazing. In an hour and a half Australia had lost their last eight wickets for 45 runs. It was, without question, a feeble performance, but England had been superlative in every respect on this final day.

AUSTRALIA v ENGLAND (Fifth Test)

Adelaide, January 27, 28, 29, 31, February 1. England won by 205 runs.

England *First Innings*

G. Boycott c Wright b Hurst	6		c Hughes b Hurst	49
*J. M. Brearley c Wright b Hogg	2		lbw b Carlson	9
D. W. Randall c Carlson b Hurst	4		c Yardley b Hurst	15
G. A. Gooch c Hughes b Hogg	1		b Carlson	18
D. I. Gower lbw b Hurst	9		lbw b Higgs	21
I. T. Botham c Wright b Higgs	74		c Yardley b Hurst	7
G. Miller lbw b Hogg	31		c Wright b Hurst	64
†R. W. Taylor run out	4		c Wright b Hogg	97
J. E. Emburey b Higgs	4		b Hogg	42
R. G. D. Willis c Darling b Hogg	24		c Wright b Hogg	12
M. Hendrick not out	0		not out	3
Extras (b1, lb4, w3, nb2)	10		(b1, lb16, nb 4, w2)	23
Total	169		Total	360

Fall of Wickets
1 – 10   2 – 12   3 – 16   4 – 18   5 – 27   6 – 80   7 – 113   8 – 136   9 – 147
1 – 31   2 – 57   3 – 97   4 – 106   5 – 130   6 – 132   7 – 267   8 – 336   9 – 347

Bowling	First Innings				Second Innings			
Hogg	10.4	1	26	4	27.6	7	59	3
Hurst	14	1	65	3	37	9	97	4
Carlson	9	1	34	0	27	8	41	2
Yardley	4	0	25	0	20	6	60	0
Higgs	3	1	9	2	28	4	75	1
Border					3	2	5	0

Australia *First Innings*

W. M. Darling c Willis b Botham	15		(2) b Botham	18
G. M. Wood c Randall b Emburey	35		(1) run out	9
K. J. Hughes c Emburey b Hendrick	4		c Gower b Hendrick	46
*G. N. Yallop b Hendrick	0		b Hendrick	36
A. R. Border c Taylor b Botham	11		b Willis	1
P. H. Carlson c Taylor b Botham	0		c Gower b Hendrick	21
B. Yardley b Botham	28		c Brearley b Willis	0
†K. J. Wright lbw b Emburey	29		c Emburey b Miller	0
R. M. Hogg b Willis	0		b Miller	2
J. D. Higgs run out	16		not out	3
A. R. Hurst not out	17		b Willis	13
Extras (b1, lb3, nb5)	9		(lb1, nb10)	11
Total	164		Total	160

Fall of Wickets
1 – 5   2 – 10   3 – 22   4 – 24   5 – 72   6 – 94   7 – 114   8 – 116   9 – 133
1 – 31   2 – 36   3 – 115   4 – 120   5 – 121   6 – 121   7 – 124   8 – 130   9 – 147

Bowling	First Innings				Second Innings			
Willis	11	1	55	1	12	3	41	3
Hendrick	19	1	45	2	14	6	19	3
Botham	11.4	0	42	4	14	4	37	1
Emburey	12	7	13	2	9	5	16	0
Miller					18	3	36	2

Umpires: M. G. O'Connell and R. C. Bailhache. Toss won by Australia.

Chapter Nine
OH DEAR, AUSSIES, OH DEAR

It would have been better if the tour had ended at this point. One felt after the previous England tour that six Test matches was one too many, no matter what the financial arguments were in favour of playing an extra Test at Melbourne or Sydney, and the 1978-79 series merely confirmed this view. Five Tests have always been the traditional number for a Test rubber between England and Australia – and the logical number too. It is arguable, certainly as far as Sydney is concerned, that if people know their city is only going to stage one Test a season they will attend because it is one of *the* social and sporting events of the summer. If there are two Tests many will be inclined to wait for the second. Now that the series was decided many chose not to go at all. In any case, the thorough nature of the Australian defeat had made it more likely that when the question of television rights had been settled the Australian Board would decide upon some radical changes to its first-class cricket programme, at both Test and state levels. There was a clear need for the tour to be shortened a little further and for more one-day cricket to be played, some of it at night, but the Tests had to retain their overriding importance. One viewed with scepticism the Board's plan to invite both India and England to Australia in 1979–80 – to play primarily in limited-over matches – when each country had visited in the previous two years.

One can enjoy limited-over cricket for a while – like a rich and inviting cake – but one can easily become sick of it. Cricket authorities everywhere need to strive not just for the essential income which will finance their players of the future but also for the balance and variety which will keep the game interesting to as wide a public as possible. Misconceptions arise when people who do not appreciate the game believe that speed and excitement are one and the same. On the contrary it is the very agonising slowness of a good cricket match which often makes it more exciting than other games: this, its sudden changes of fortune, and its dependence upon human nerve, courage and mental enterprise, as well as on raw skill. These deep qualities are more abundantly in evidence in Test cricket than in shorter games, and the five-day match remains also the supreme test of a cricketer's spirit and ability.

Anti-climactic as it undoubtedly was, the cricket which followed the fifth Test match certainly had its moments. After the temperature had reached 41·3° C in Melbourne the day after our arrival from Adelaide, the wind blowing all day like the hot blast from an oven door, the weather turned sour for the challenge match between the Gillette champions, Tasmania, and the touring team. Played in Tasmania this game might have meant something. As it was, there was no atmosphere at all as England beat their friends from across the Bass Strait by three wickets before a crowd of no more than two thousand on a miserable day. The best that can be said about the game is that the players served the public well by continuing to play through more or less continuous drizzle and that John Hampshire and Geoff Boycott had a brief conversation in public. Boycott had finally put everyone in Yorkshire out of their agonised suspense by announcing on the fourth day of the Adelaide Test that he would continue to play for the county. His telegram accepting a two-year contract was sent at the eleventh hour on 31 January, the deadline for his decision, which had been made, one suspects, some time before. He had decided to stay, he said, because of the loyalty shown to him by the Yorkshire public. One hoped very much now that he would settle down happily in the role of senior professional.

The rescheduled Boxing Day limited-over international followed the match against Tasmania on 4 February, and happily a crowd of more than 11,000 saw a game to remember. It began with England put in to bat on a lively pitch and Boycott playing an innings of the highest skill in very difficult conditions. But there was much less pressure on the batsmen from Carlson (though he bowled well), Laughlin and Cosier than there was from the openers Dymock and Hurst (Hogg was being rested for the Test), and by the time that Gower came to the wicket at 50 for three in the 17th over the pitch had eased. Gower proceeded to play an innings befitting his genius, driving, cutting, pulling and glancing his way to 101 not out in 100 balls. Botham with 31 off 24 balls helped him in the main assault and England, with Gower reaching his century off the last ball of the innings with a superb square-cut four, totalled 212 for six.

The crowd stood to applaud him with heartfelt warmth, and few amongst them can have given the young Australian side a chance against England's experienced bowling attack. But it transpired that England had erred fatally in leaving all their spinners out of the side, and Australia paced their effort well amidst excitement which grew to delirium towards the end.

Hughes made their final assault possible. His cultured 50 included a number of attractive strokes played with the full face of the bat. Yallop could not keep pace with him, but when Toohey replaced Hughes the little man, after so many disappointments, timed the ball from the start and with a series of neat strokes kept his side up with the required rate. At the halfway mark of twenty overs Australia were 71 for two as against England's 70 for three, and for all the brilliance of Gower's batting earlier in the day Australia were seldom behind the clock thereafter.

Yallop accelerated with some sharply taken singles and one or two old-fashioned lofted drives before Cosier returned to Australian colours to play the decisive innings. Actually, to say that he returned to the colours is not quite true, because he batted with neither cap nor helmet, giving us all the full benefit of an 'Afro' perm to his mop of curly ginger hair. This time he looked rather less like Henry VIII, rather more like a boisterous Airedale terrier. To understand the delight his innings of 28 in 14 balls created, one must remember how the England bowlers had tormented and tied down the Australian batsmen all summer. One must remember also that the crowds had become so used to losing that an ABC announcer stated the following morning: 'Australia revived an ancient tradition yesterday – beating England at cricket.'

Cosier began by hitting Botham yards over extra-cover for what was almost a six and then mowing Lever yards further over mid-on for what was easily a six. With Toohey hitting nearly as effectively but keeping the ball along the ground Australia added 40 in three overs, and from this point it was merely a question of keeping calm and coasting home. England's five seamers, Willis excepted, bowled less consistently than usual and, as Cosier rather unwisely made public later, there was a point when Brearley argued heatedly with Botham and Lever. Brearley described it as a healthy airing of views. Perhaps it was as well, with the World Cup due to be played in England a few months later, that the team should realise they were not invincible and indeed that it seldom if ever pays to leave out good slow bowlers if you have them available. A slow bowler or two would also have allowed a rather shorter match than this one, which, with brief intervals for lunch and tea, extended from 11 a.m. to 7.25 p.m.

The end was hastened by two powerful straight-drives by the strapping Laughlin, one of which bounced just in front of the sightscreen, the second of which cleared it by a distance. Australia had twelve balls to spare when Toohey drove Willis crisply down the ground and the ball was lost in a sea of invading youth. It was a wholly unexpected day of triumph not only for Yallop's team but also for Australian establishment cricket.

The match at Melbourne compared more than favourably with the third and, as it transpired, last day of the bitterly contested final of the World Series Cricket four-day competition. This featured a row between Lillee and Pascoe on the one hand and Procter and Le Roux on the other, and then, when the World team had collected the 61,000 dollars, a slanging match between Ian Chappell and Tony Greig. Chappell bowled four wides at the end to give the World side their victory (assured by a brilliant not-out hundred by Barry Richards). Chappell made a sarcastic comment to Greig (the World XI captain) as he left the field, implying, not for the first time, that he was not worth his place in the team. Both players accused each other in press statements after the match. The bitterness was genuine and indicative, perhaps, of the course cricket will take if it is played for money and a television sponsor.

The continued glaring and swearing which was so much a part of World Series Cricket, and which seemed to be admired and highlighted by those responsible for the television transmission, was setting an appalling example to the many young spectators his games were attracting. As a keen golfer one would have thought he would have noticed how immaculate is the behaviour of the golf champions who play for even higher stakes before an even more close-up television coverage, yet whose fortune depends upon their keeping control of their emotions.

An enjoyable day at Geelong was squeezed between the two internationals, and the hospitality afforded to every visitor made one wish that the match had been the three-day affair originally scheduled rather than a forty-over match sandwiched between two coach journeys. The only exceptional feature of the game was its ending. Randall, who had enjoyed a typical day in the 'country' (the atmosphere was that of a country match although Geelong is now a very large town), was the innocent cause. He had been out attempting a reverse-handed sweep and then spent much of the time in the field with a red woolly hat on his head, borrowed from one of the cheerful crowd of 5,000; with a few overs of the Geelong innings left and the last-wicket pair facing a hopeless task, he came on to bowl. After four balls of his second over, the 39th, a horde of schoolchildren – several hundred of them – invaded the field and Brearley, feeling that it would take a long time to clear the ground, had a brief word with one of the umpires before leading his team off. England were still adjudged the winners on the grounds that their score was 48 runs the greater at the comparable stage of their innings.

The following day Australia beat England in a one-day international for the second time in four days and thus took the Benson and Hedges Gold Cup and the bulk of the prize-money. England played like a tired and stale side, and a newcomer might have been forgiven for thinking that Australia were the team 4-1 up in the series. Brearley lost the toss again but this time the pitch could hardly be blamed for the fact that the first three batsmen were caught in the slips. Only Brearley himself batted well until Edmonds (15) and Botham (13) gave him some support. Brearley was seventh out for 46 but England's total of 94 was woefully inadequate, and after the excitement of Sunday a midweek crowd of more than 12,000 watched Australia coast to a six-wicket win with Wood, Yallop and Toohey playing the main parts.

Dymock, who had taken the first two wickets to start the England collapse (and to assure himself of another visit to England for the World Cup), was announced as Man-of-theMatch at the presentation ceremony afterwards, at which Brearley gave a rather unfortunate impression to viewers watching on television. They were unaware that he had been abused by a few 'okkers' before going to the microphone. When someone said as he began to speak: 'We can't hear', he replied angrily: 'If you'd shut up you might learn something.' It was not 'sour grapes' but rather looked like it, which was a pity. Brearley, like everyone else, needed a rest, but there was one more demanding match to come.

It was difficult to get very animated about the sixth Test match, yet the first day's play was an excellent one and it was the greatest shame that the Saturday crowd was a mere 8,601. They saw the innings of the series, played by Graham Yallop, an effort made all the more glorious by the colourless and feeble batting produced by most of the other Australian batsmen.

Yallop won the toss as usual, to Brearley's dismay. He was understandably becoming increasingly exasperated by the pressures of captaining a touring side, and he ruffled further feathers later in the day when he dismissed the President of the Australian Primary Club from the dressing-room. (The Club was holding a dinner that evening for the 1948 Australian team and he had come in to see if any players needed transport.) Brearley walked off alone after the toss whilst Yallop stayed to discuss the pitch with the ABC commentator. Of the nine tosses Yallop had won against Brearley out of eleven during the tour, this was clearly one of the better ones and he had no hesitation about batting first. There was some dampness in the pitch but its colour was brown and it seemed certain to give the spinners increasing assistance. It was in fact exactly the same strip which had been used for the fourth Test; almost certainly it is unique for the same pitch to be used for two Tests in one season, but the Sydney Cricket Ground had been saturated with cricket throughout the season because of the additional demands made by WSC.

However, the pitch was blameless on the first day and the outfield the fastest of the series, which enabled Australia to get away to a businesslike start as Wood took eleven runs from Willis's first six balls, including boundaries to fine-leg and third-man.

England were unchanged for the fourth successive Test, while Australia's eleven showed two changes from the Adelaide Test, with Hilditch replacing the unfortunate Darling to gain his first cap and Toohey returning for the equally unfortunate Border. Two Tests before on the same Sydney pitch, Darling had made 91 and 13, Border 60 not out and 45 not out.

Hilditch's first ball in Test cricket was a bouncer from Willis. But this pleasant, fresh-faced young opener, whose mature approach and clean-cut appearance already give him the look of a future Test captain (if his batting continues to improve), solidly glanced his second ball for two to square-leg. Thirteen runs off the first over represented a very good start, but Hendrick was not so easy to score from and in his second over there was a sudden jolt to Australia's progress from which, for all Yallop's brilliance, they never really recovered. Hilditch steered the ball well to the right of Gooch at third slip and set off optimistically for a run as the big man from Essex arrested the ball with a ponderous dive and quickly flicked it back to the wicket. Wood, rightly refusing the run, did so too late and Hilditch was run out by Emburey, who had come in from short-leg, after an agonised juggle. It was the latest in a succession of disastrous Australian run-outs, all but one involving the man they knew as the 'kamikaze kid', Graeme Wood. The sorry facts were that one or other of the Australian openers had been run out in every Test, Cosier in the first innings at Brisbane, Darling in the first innings at both Perth and Melbourne, Wood in the second innings at both Sydney and Adelaide, and now Hilditch at Sydney. One run later Wood was out to a brilliant diving right-handed catch at second slip by Botham off Hendrick.

Yallop and Hughes settled in with determination to retrieve another dangerously crumbling position. Hughes, a different man from the free strokeplayer of a week before, was beaten frequently outside the off-stump by Willis, Hendrick and Botham, but Yallop greeted Botham with three fours in his first over, all cuts through the gully region to balls pitched just short of a length. The challenge was on and Yallop never looked back from this sudden burst, settling in to play shots all round the wicket with a freedom, touch and confidence which made a nonsense of the struggles of his fellows.

Hughes finally got a fatal touch outside the off-stump, giving Willis his only wicket and Botham a second, more straightforward catch. The wicket came at a good time for England, in the last over before lunch, and they must have thought during the interval that if they could dismiss the dangerous Toohey early on they would be halfway home. In the event Toohey settled in safely although he could not trust himself to play the sort of strokes which Yallop was cheerfully displaying at the other end: on-drives, off-drives, cuts and every now and then a hook. His fifty included six fours, but at 101 Toohey pushed forward around his off-stump in the first over of a new spell by the irrepressible Botham and Taylor took his first catch of the match. Enter Carlson, with an opportunity on an easy-paced pitch to prove he was of Test class. He did not take it. Botham got a ball to lift on the off-stump, the batsman failed to get over it, and Gooch held a straightforward catch at third slip.

Willis and Hendrick had finished their afternoon stints by now, and Emburey, who had been given three overs in the morning, was already embarked upon a long and steady spell. At 116 he bowled Yardley, who left the ball, expecting it to turn, and lost his leg-stump, and at 124 he had Wright comfortably stumped as he danced down the pitch and missed.

One can only guess at Yallop's consternation as this sorry procession continued back and forth from the old green-roofed pavilion, but he was playing so well himself that a third Test century looked certain if only someone could stay with him long enough. Hogg and Higgs provided the assistance he needed, but his trust in them was not so great that he did not feel it necessary to accelerate. Hogg, at loggerheads with his captain at Adelaide, watched in admiration as Yallop drove Willis on the up for two majestic fours through mid-wicket off successive balls, then glanced him square and cut him to third-man. At tea Australia were 157 for 7 and soon after Yallop reached his second hundred of the series with a risky single to extra-cover. He deserved his moment of triumph. He had hit ten fours in his century and survived a skied catch to Brearley off Miller at 105 before hitting three more boundaries and eventually being ninth out, hitting Botham to mid-wicket with a cross-bat. Hogg had been caught at short-leg, but Higgs had played another staunch innings which he was unable to extend because Hurst was bowled first ball. Botham had now taken 87 wickets in seventeen and a half Test matches.

Left with an hour to bat, Brearley and Boycott underlined the quality of the pitch by dealing confidently with all that Hurst and Hogg could hurl at them, and by the close England had made 24 without loss, of which the captain had made an excellent 18. The strength of the England position and the intense humidity of a typically hot February day in Sydney kept the Sunday crowd down to only a little above 8,000. England, their skipper very much at the helm, made 74 for two in the morning and all four batsmen who went to the crease looked thoroughly comfortable on the placid brown pitch.

Brearley began so cautiously that it took him 54 minutes to score his first run of the morning, but there was none of the suspicious prodding of many earlier innings and instead of rapping the pads the ball was generally running smoothly off the middle of his defensive bat. Boycott, in contrast, gathered runs busily and efficiently and had just overhauled his captain when his fallible technique around the off-stump undid him again. Hurst, now tormenting him more than Hogg, got a ball to lift a little more than usual and Boycott jabbed a low catch to second slip. Hilditch, his hands pointed downwards, instantly claimed that he had caught the ball fairly but Boycott held his ground until umpire Crafter gave him out from the bowler's end. The television playback showed that it was a very close thing, but whilst one fully appreciated why Boycott had waited Hilditch was clearly sure that he had caught the ball fairly. The fielder usually knows best and batsmen and umpires are often obliged to take these matters on trust, especially when, as in Hilditch's case, the fielder is a solicitor!

Randall looked equally unhappy when two overs later, and after one solid hook, his notorious shuffle across the stumps led to his dismissal as Hogg got a ball to nip back and hit his pads. Randall's moody dissension did him no credit. It was a pity his tour should end thus. However, at 46 for two, the burly figure of Graham Gooch walked out to play an innings which may have transformed his career. Certainly at this late stage of the tour his future as a Test cricketer was being questioned, but for the first time he was able to develop a promising innings and though he fell at a time when his first Test hundred seemed a distinct possibility, he showed Australians at last exactly why he was so highly rated by his colleagues.

Gooch, in fact, made quite a tentative start, although it was clear from the way that he hit the ball and from his generally confident bearing that he knew at last he was on a pitch he could trust. He moved into top gear in an over from Yardley, during which he unleashed a succession of handsome drives and cuts. Yardley was bowling to a six-three English-style off-spinner's field but without the control that was necessary, and, ironically, he was punished a good deal more severely than Border had been two Tests before. (Border was condemned to the job of carrying out the drinks this time.)

Brearley in his own quiet way had begun to pick up runs after his slow start, hitting two particularly sweet drives through the covers against Carlson, who was unable to swing the ball as he had done at Adelaide. At lunch England were 98 for two, Brearley 41 not out, Gooch 29 not out. The session which followed was to produce two more wickets for Australia, both to the admirable Higgs, but it was also to see batting domination of a kind which was all too rare in this series. England, in fact, scored at a run a minute, and with two spinners operating in harness for much of the time the cricket was highly entertaining. Hogg shared the attack with Higgs for a while but he could manage only three overs in the humid heat of the early afternoon, and though he bowled straight only the occasional ball was especially fast. Gooch and Brearley played him with confidence but the captain had got a little bogged down before, driving at a subtle, looping delivery from Higgs, he lofted the ball to cover where Toohey moved in smartly to take a neat, low catch. Brearley, who had briefly swapped his helmet for a cap, symbolic of his relative comfort at the crease, collected the former from the square-leg umpire with an air of resignation. 46 was a big improvement on the Test average of 11 with which he had started the match, but a century was there for anyone's taking today.

Gower, of course, was the man most likely to get one. He had a brief look at Higgs, then swept him off his off-stump for an impudent four, drove the next ball through extra-cover for four more, and drove the next ball into the same gap for three. All at once the Sydney Cricket Ground was vibrant again. A genius was at large. In fact, Gower played one or two streaky strokes, once edging Hurst to the third-man boundary and another time slashing outside the off-stump without making contact. If anything Gooch compared favourably on this occasion; he was relishing every moment of his innings and it was good to see him doing so after all his tormented defence against the rising ball in earlier matches. He dealt capably with Hurst before greeting the returning Yardley with another splendid array of strokes. Surviving one appeal in the twenties when the Australians believed he had dislodged a bail as he cut a ball to third-man, he reached his fifty, off only 98 balls, in the grand manner, hooking Hurst powerfully to the half-built Brewongle Stand. Soon after this he danced down the pitch to straight-drive Yardley over the sightscreen for a majestic six. This brought up the fifty partnership between Gower and Gooch in only 43 minutes. It was heady stuff which seemed to prove the case for the batsmen of both sides. *We are more sinned against than sinning*, was their plea: *give us the pitches and we will play the strokes*.

Gower had a narrow escape when he cut Higgs past Hughes at slip, but it was Gooch who gave Higgs his second wicket when he moved out of his ground again to drive through the covers and as the ball spun away from him he saw Wright make a perfect stumping, a swift, decisive piece of wicket-keeping. Gooch must have been disappointed, for he was threatening at this stage to tear the bowling to shreds. He had hit seven fours and a six in his stay of

less than two and a half hours, and the sight of Botham walking
out to replace him can hardly have encouraged the Australian
bowlers and supporters. But Botham had been fallible against
Higgs throughout the series, and he twice edged him past slip
during his first few minutes at the crease due to his tendency to
play 'half-cock' rather than right forward or back.

Gower, noting, no doubt, how the ball which dismissed Gooch
had turned and knowing that the size of England's first-innings
lead would decide the outcome of the match, seemed to concentrate more sternly now, although he still drove, swept and pulled
with the sweetest timing as tea approached to the sound of boom-
ing thunder in the west. Almost as soon as the players had left the
field, the storm which had been raging over Botany Bay for some
time erupted with sudden violence over the Sydney Cricket
Ground. Rain cascaded off the old pavilion roof like spume from
huge waves breaking against a rocky coast, and within minutes
there were puddles on the outfield. The groundstaff did a noble
job in battening down the tarpaulins over the pitch as the wind
blew strongly enough to rip the Union Jack flying above the pavilion into tatters. But there was no protection for the edges of the
square and at five o'clock, by which time the sun was shining
brightly again, the umpires ruled that play should be abandoned
for the day. England, 216 for four, were 18 ahead, with Gower 47
not out and Botham 17. They were strongly placed but no more so
than Australia had been after two days of the fourth Test. There
was much work to be done yet before the dream of winning five
Tests in a series against Australia for the first time came true.

The mood of the game had changed when play began on a
steamy hot Monday morning. Gower and Botham, who had been
preparing themselves for an evening assault against tired bowlers,
had to get their adrenalin flowing again and before a small crowd
(it grew a little during the day to reach 4,159) it was not so easy.
The new ball was due after seven overs, but Higgs presented
enough problems in the early overs and a timely wicket by
Yardley persuaded Yallop that he should stick to his spinners.
Botham had added six to his overnight score when, in the 65th
over, he lofted a drive to mid-off where Carlson held on well to a
hot chance.

Gower was forced by the flight, accuracy and considerable spin
of Higgs to cut down on his attacking strokes and he had hit only
one four, a crisp square-cut, when he tickled a ball which turned

and lifted into the safe gloves of Wright. England's lead was a mere 49 when Miller and Taylor renewed acquaintance. Both had played enough cricket in the East to be experienced players of spin, and Miller inspired confidence with his ability either to stun the spin with a dead bat and a turn of the wrists or to play a full-blooded attacking shot. It is the prod and the poke, or the checked attacking stroke, which undo most batsmen against good spin bowling. Not that either batsman was able to make much progress and the total had merely crept up to 265 for six when Hogg took the new ball in the 81st over.

Both batsmen survived l.b.w. appeals before, in the last over before lunch, Miller was beaten for pace and palpably l.b.w. to Hurst. But it took a long time for the Australian bowlers to finish the job afterwards. England's tactics were clearly to occupy the crease for as long as possible in the belief that the longer the brown pitch was exposed to the burning sun, the more it would aid the spinners. At the same time they were tiring and frustrating their opponents. These were perfectly legitimate and logical tactics for a Test, but they won England no new friends amongst the small crowd, and it was certainly almost as wearying to watch as it was for those footsore Australian fielders. Emburey fell quickly to Hurst, Hilditch taking a fine, fast catch at second slip, but Taylor and Willis put on 26 in 69 minutes before Willis swept a ball from Higgs onto his stumps. Hendrick succumbed more quickly, driving a return catch to Yardley, and Australia went in with two hours and twenty minutes of the third day to go, facing a deficit of 110.

The most appreciated entertainment during the afternoon came from a trumpeter on the thinly populated Hill. His repertoire included 'Oh when the Saints', 'Have you seen my little Willie', 'Oh Sir Jasper', 'The Last Post', and the old and new Australian theme songs (or popular national anthems) 'Waltzing Matilda' followed by 'C'mon, Aussie, C'mon'.

If the entertainment value of England's approach was in doubt, the wisdom of it was not. Australia's innings was soon in a state of total disarray. Hilditch again fell a little unfortunately when he edged Hendrick towards Taylor who dived to his right to take a low catch which Hilditch, like Boycott before him, believed had not carried. Hughes was unable to smother sharp spin, and off bat and pad gave Gooch the first of two good catches at backward short-leg. The second of them was Toohey, out second ball, and

Above Yallop pulls Willis for four during his century in the sixth Test at Sydney—undoubtedly the most commanding innings played by any batsman in the series. *Below* Boycott is caught by Hilditch off Hurst in the same Test. Boycott indicates that he believes the ball landed before being taken by the fielder.

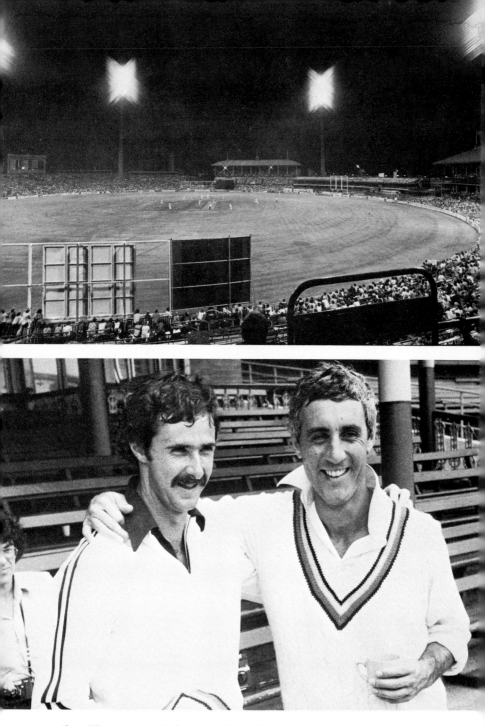

Above The 'new sport' of night cricket, WSC-style, at the VFL Park, Melbourne. The success of one-day cricket played at night led the Australian Board to decide to stage night matches of their own after 1979. *Below* Brearley and Yallop together at the end of the series; generally speaking they had ensured that the cricket was sensibly and honourably contested.

Carlson was also out second ball, turning another sharply turning Emburey off-spinner to Botham at forward-short. Wood played soundly and well against both the new ball and the spinners to make 29 before he was out to a well-judged catch off Miller by Willis, running from mid-off to extra-cover. But after three wickets had fallen at 48 Yallop, making the two off-spinners look much less dangerous through some positive batting, and Yardley, as usual meeting the crisis with aggression, saw Australia to 70 for five by the close of the third day.

By 2.40 p.m. on the fourth day it was all over. The temperature the previous day had been only a little short of 100° F in Sydney and as much as 110°(44° C) at the historic Macarthur Onslow house at Campden where the first-ever fixture played in Australia by the Free Foresters Club took place against the Australian I Zingari. Serious bush-fires were raging in the country areas of New South Wales and it was a clear case of mad Aussies and Englishmen playing cricket in the mid-day sun. It was mercifully cooler next morning as Miller and Emburey resumed their devastating partnership in gloomy light before the small but enthusiastic crowd who had come to watch the last rites.

Australia had added only twelve more runs when Miller got a ball to turn so sharply to Yallop that he was, within a split second, caught behind the wicket and stumped. But Yardley, moving his feet boldly and hitting hard whenever he got to the pitch or received a ball short enough to cut or pull, saw to it that England would have to go in a second time. Wright stayed with him for 54 minutes to underline his promise before sweeping Miller to backward square-leg; Hogg lifted his curly head and was bowled; Higgs gave forward-short a simple catch off bat and pad, and Hurst presented Miller with a caught-and-bowled off the ninth ball after lunch. Miller's figures after an immaculate spell of off-spinning on a pitch which Yallop described as a minefield and Brearley as a road, were 5 for 44 in all and 15.1-3-28-4 on the fourth day.

England took only forty minutes to score the necessary 34 runs after a delayed start to their innings whilst the inexperienced umpires (both of whom had so far done well) decided whether or not Yallop was entitled to use an old ball. They wrongly allowed him to do so and Yardley and Higgs opened the bowling, turning the ball as sharply as England's off-spinners. But Brearley, with no helmet and less armour than usual to weigh him down, played carefree cricket – partly *because* he was less encumbered – and hit the winning runs, a lofted drive to the mid-wicket boundary, soon after Boycott had spooned a square-cut to cover. The triumph of the scholar-captain was complete.

AUSTRALIA v ENGLAND (Sixth Test)

Sydney, February 10, 11, 12, 14. England won by nine wickets.

Australia *First Innings*

		Second Innings	
G. M. Wood c Botham b Hendrick	15	c Willis b Miller	29
A. M. Hilditch run out	3	c Taylor b Hendrick	1
K. J. Hughes c Botham b Willis	16	c Gooch b Emburey	7
*G. N. Yallop c Gower b Botham	121	c Taylor b Miller	17
P. M. Toohey c Taylor b Botham	8	c Gooch b Emburey	0
P. H. Carlson c Gooch b Botham	2	c Botham b Emburey	0
B. Yardley b Emburey	7	not out	61
†K. J. Wright st Taylor b Emburey	3	c Boycott b Miller	5
R. M. Hogg c Emburey b Miller	9	b Miller	7
J. D. Higgs not out	9	c Botham b Emburey	2
A. G. Hurst b Botham	0	c and b Miller	4
Extras (lb3, nb2)	5	(b3, lb6, nb1)	10
Total	198	Total	143

Fall of Wickets
1 – 18   2 – 19   3 – 67   4 – 101   5 – 109   6 – 116   7 – 124   8 – 159   9 – 198
1 – 8   2 – 28   3 – 48   4 – 48   5 – 48   6 – 82   7 – 114   8 – 130   9 – 136

Bowling	*First Innings*				*Second Innings*			
Willis	11	4	48	1	3	0	15	0
Hendrick	12	2	21	1	7	3	22	1
Botham	9.7	1	57	4				
Emburey	18	3	48	2	24	4	52	4
Miller	9	3	13	1	27.1	6	44	5
Boycott	1	0	6	0				

England *First Innings*

		Second Innings	
G. Boycott c Hilditch b Hurst	19	c Hughes b Higgs	13
*J. M. Brearley c Toohey b Higgs	46	not out	20
D. W. Randall lbw b Hogg	7	not out	0
G. A. Gooch st Wright b Higgs	74		
D. I. Gower c Wright b Higgs	65		
I. T. Botham c Carlson b Yardley	23		
G. Miller lbw b Hurst	18		
†R. W. Taylor not out	36		
J. E. Emburey c Hilditch b Hurst	0		
R. G. D. Willis b Higgs	10		
M. Hendrick c and b Yardley	0		
Extras (b3, lb5, nb2)	10	(nb2)	2
Total	308	Total (for 1 wkt)	35

Fall of Wickets
1 – 37   2 – 46   3 – 115   4 – 182   5 – 233   6 – 247   7 – 270   8 – 280   9 – 306
1 – 31

Bowling	*First Innings*				*Second Innings*			
Hogg	18	6	42	1				
Hurst	20	4	58	3				
Yardley	25	2	105	2	5.2	0	21	0
Carlson	10	4	24	0				
Higgs	30	8	69	4	5	1	12	1

Umpires: D. G. Weser and A. R. Crafter. Toss won by Australia.

Chapter Ten
CONCLUSIONS

The 1978–79 series in Australia provided the latest and most striking evidence that the character of Test cricket has changed in recent seasons and that it has now become essentially a bowler's game, especially indeed a fast bowler's game. In the Ashes series of the 1960s, 25 Tests were played between England and Australia and 15 of them were drawn. Australia, who won six matches in that period between 1961 and 1968 to England's four, held the Ashes throughout. There was a strong feeling at the time that much of the cricket played was sterile and it was often suggested that the Ashes themselves should be scrapped. Now the records present a sharp and happy contrast: in the last two series between the countries there have been nine results out of eleven matches.

At least now there is no lack of action or spectacle. Tumbling wickets make for entertainment of a kind, and there was always much brilliant fielding to be admired on both sides in this series, especially by England, whose recent successes have all stemmed from the confidence the bowlers have derived from the fitness, swiftness and sure hands of the fielders supporting them. But the general lack of runs and the slow rate at which they were scored were clear evidence of the changing trends in Test cricket, and one longed to see more strokes and more batsmen capable of dominating the bowlers.

The lack of hard, true pitches is without doubt the main reason for this development. If anyone doubts that pitches have indeed declined or tends to believe that modern batsmen use this as an excuse for poor technique, one has only to point to the number of batsmen now getting hit around the head and body. In the space of twelve months the batsman's helmet has changed from being a ridiculed gimmick to a piece of equipment reluctantly accepted as necessary. It is sad that this should be so. Again, his greater age and his mental worries cannot wholly explain why Geoff Boycott should have averaged 93 in the series of 1970–71 and only 21 eight years later. Boycott was only one of a number of experienced cricketers who believe that pitches in Australia now have more grass left on them and a less reliable bounce than in days gone by.

There are other reasons why the bowlers generally remained on top from the moment that Yallop's young Australian side collapsed to 27 for six on the first morning of the first Test at Brisbane. The most obvious one is that some very good bowlers were supported, as I say, by excellent fielding. In England's case they were shrewdly used, bowling with great discipline to a carefully planned campaign of attack. They were helped also by slow outfields on most grounds. The use of fertilisers and the modern groundsman's tendency to water outfields plentifully, combined with a reluctance to set the mower low enough, made countless good strokes worth less than they should have been.

But the shortcomings of the batsmen themselves cannot be ignored. The art of building a long Test innings was rarely in evidence in this series – perhaps because of habits begun in limited-over cricket, or because with the pace of life so much hotter spectators themselves are less inclined to stand for slow batting. Whatever the reason Test batsmen set their sights lower than past players. The intense concentration and the discipline to eliminate dangerous shots which marked the approach of a Ken Barrington or a Bobby Simpson was rarely to be found during the series. On the other hand there was also a reluctance by many players to bat in a positive way or to look for runs all the time. Commenting on the absence of initiative and the iniquities of the forward prod, Sir Donald Bradman pertinently quoted A.C. MacLaren's dictum: 'If you can't drive you should play back.' In England's case the failures came more often than not in the first innings, which suggests that when they had a definite target, as in the second innings at Sydney, the batsmen found it easier to overcome the hectic, frenetic atmosphere in which much Test cricket is now played and to get into the right mood and rhythm to keep the score moving calmly along without resorting to strokeless defence on the one hand (a state of mind which often prevents the batsman from hitting the bad ball) or feverish attack on the other. The few long stands in the series – between Yallop and Hughes at Brisbane; Brearley and Randall at Sydney; Miller and Taylor at Adelaide – all achieved this balance. In each case the batsmen were fighting to retrieve what appeared to be losing situations. The threat of defeat often makes it easier for batsmen to concentrate singlemindedly. Conversely Australia had an outside chance of victory at the start of their second innings in both the fourth and fifth Tests but were

bowled out cheaply on the final day of each. If they had set their
minds to saving them they would probably have been capable of
doing so. All of which confirms what everyone knows, that cricket
is a game played as much in the minds of the players as on the
fields of conflict. Most of the leading batsmen of both sides undoubtedly had the talent to make them worthy Test cricketers.
What many lacked was the right mental conditioning – what
Bobby Simpson referred to as the computer programming of the
mind – to make them regular high scorers.

England won the series for all the reasons one had expected:
they were shrewdly led by Brearley, as wise and tough a leader as
England has ever had. Their team spirit, created during a succession of successful series, was equal to a critical period in the
middle of the tour when Australia won at Melbourne and looked
likely to level the series at Sydney. They enjoyed themselves very
much off the field, yet remained superbly fit. The management
team of Insole, Barrington and Thomas worked with great sympathy and efficiency. The batsmen scored just enough runs to get
by despite a worrying vulnerability at the top of the order against
Hogg, whose 41 wickets in six Tests at 12 runs each represent
an even more amazing appearance on the Test scene than
Jeff Thomson's four years before; and Hurst, who has always
looked a top-class fast bowler and has now learned to believe in
himself. Despite the success of these two opening bowlers, and
some admirable bowling by Higgs, the best Australian leg-spinner
since Benaud, Gower proved his genius, making batting look a
simple, natural and amiable business. He scored more runs at a
higher average than any player on either side. Randall and
Botham each played brilliantly at times, and at critical points both
played decisive and responsible innings.

Botham, with 23 wickets, was the joint leading wicket-taker. He
has now taken 87 wickets in 17 Test matches and may well get 100
in fewer Tests than anyone else. Miller, who also took 23 wickets
and batted consistently, established himself as a senior member of
the team. Emburey confirmed himself as an off-spinner of the
highest class. Edmonds was disappointing but also unlucky, and
will surely come again. Willis took 20 Test wickets despite illness
and loss of form; Hendrick had everyone in Australia marvelling
at his extraordinary accuracy. He took 19 wickets in five Tests but
also helped others take wickets at the other end.

Faced with this attack, it is not surprising that an Australian

side containing some talented but relatively inexperienced batsmen failed to get enough runs. On better pitches they would have
had more chance but they also had to contend with the best fielding side England has ever sent to Australia. In Yallop (whether
or not he remains captain in the long term), Wood, Border,
Wright, Hogg, Hurst and Higgs, there is the nucleus of a talented
side needing better direction and a little more experience to produce success. Hughes, Darling and Toohey also have great innate
ability, and other bowling attacks might not expose their technical
frailties as England's did.

England, of course, had relative failures too, although without
exception all of those who played in Test matches made a vital
contribution at some time or other. In the other matches Radley,
Tolchard and Bairstow, the only three not to win a Test place at
any time, each had his moments. Radley and Tolchard were the
most unlucky members of the party. Radley bore the mental scars
of being hit on the head long after his physical injury had healed,
and Tolchard, who could easily have taken a batting place from
Gooch at one stage, still looked like a boxer who had been ten
rounds with Muhammad Ali several weeks after his cheekbone
had been shattered. He never once complained.

The most striking disappointment of the tour was Boycott,
whose distinguished Test career is clearly nearing its end. In addition to his worries about the Yorkshire captaincy, his technique
has lost its infallibility, although his obsessive need to practise
never wavered. One day at Melbourne late in the tour, when the
temperature was 105 degrees and almost unbearably oppressive,
Boycott insisted on having a net in both the morning and the afternoon. But for all his amazing dedication his tendency to move his
feet sideways rather than forwards or back, to play across the line
of flight when going back to the quicker bowlers, and to nibble
outside the off-stump without getting his feet far enough across,
all contributed to his run of low scores. Yet such is his zeal for the
game that it would be foolish to write him off just yet.

The England team kept a happy balance between the good life
and the need to retain a disciplined approach. Ken Barrington
was as keen to please everyone in his role as assistant manager as
he had been when manager on previous tours. He has an endear-
ing habit of sometimes saying what he does not exactly mean; in
the past, for instance, he has referred to 'a great performance in
anyone's cup of tea' and of Boycott's batting being 'second to any

batsman in the world'. He once told a gathering of dignitaries in Sri Lanka that they hadn't 'fallen down on any failings', and referred to a crowd invading a field in the Orient as 'coming on like a swarm of lotuses'. Referring once to the time when he got dropped by England for scoring too slowly during a century he explained to a journalist that all had gone well until he had got hopelessly bogged down. That, he said, was when all the 'paraphernalia' started.

On this tour I began an interview by confronting him with an awkwardly phrased question. 'That century stand by Randall and Brearley,' I suggested, 'can't have done England's morale any harm, can it?' 'Yes, Christopher,' said Ken, 'a tremendous amount.' But the wittiest remark of all came from Bob Willis, whose thoughtful approach to the job of vice-captain had as much to do with the team's success as his bowling until he lost form late in the tour. Brearley was consoling his team during the Western Australian match when his batsmen were in desperate trouble on a green wicket. 'Don't worry,' said Brearley, 'we'll bowl them out even more cheaply. Even Bradman would struggle to make any runs against us on this pitch.' 'I should darn well think so,' said Willis. 'He's 70.'

Finally, back to the second of the two battles to which I referred at the start of the book. Although World Series Cricket gained ground upon traditional cricket in the civil war, there are good reasons for believing that, for all their widely believed publicity, the pirates were no better off than the establishment players. Though the gates for the Ashes series were cut by almost half compared with the numbers who had watched Australia beating England four years before, they still compared favourably with World Series Cricket. In all, 375,414 watched the Ashes series, bringing receipts of 757,580 Australian dollars. Bob Parish, the chairman of the Australian Board, said that there was no question of the Board making a loss on the England tour (the touring side itself had a guaranteed profit) but that the profit would be much less than had been hoped for and that this would seriously affect the distribution of income to youth and state cricket on which the future of the whole structure of cricket in Australia depended. The crowds obviously declined for two main reasons: the rivalry from World Series Cricket, creating an excessive amount of cricket for spectators to watch both on television and in the flesh; and the defeat of Australia in the Ashes series. Australian crowds had always tended to fall away when their national side was being beaten.

World Series Cricket continued to plough nothing back into the grass-roots of Australian cricket, yet their activities spread to the West Indies and India in 1979. The apparently philanthropic payments made by WSC to the West Indies Cricket Board were not pure charity. The members of the West Indies Board, like its major players, were so placed financially that they saw the payments made by Packer as 'offers they couldn't refuse', and they apparently accepted the strings attached with resignation, believing that they had no alternative but to welcome WSC to the Caribbean, where the crowds were so eager to see their star players again.

It is unlikely, in any case, whether in its second year WSC made any profit. It is more likely that the vast financial empire over which Kerry Packer presides, Consolidated Press Holdings, was still having to feed the growing baby World Series Cricket. Since the assets of Consolidated Press were 165 million dollars in June 1977 and had risen to 192,657 million in June 1978, whatever losses made in the second year of WSC's operations can have been of no financial concern at all to Mr Packer. He refused to discuss the financial details but after the estimated loss of 3.7 million dollars on the first year (the amount calculated in Eric Beecher's authoritative *The Cricket Revolution*) Packer merely claimed to be 'ahead on budget'. That he had budgeted for a loss is certain but in a business of this size tax losses can be cheerfully borne, and in any case by showing so much cricket Channel Nine was helping to solve the problem of being obliged by law to fill a certain number of hours each day with programmes of 'Australian content'. The Australian Broadcasting Tribunal imposes a points system on TV stations and the cricket matches were a relatively cheap method of meeting this demand.

WSC's outgoings were less in the second year of their operations, largely because the amount spent on preparing grounds was only a fraction of the estimated one million dollars in the first year. In addition advertising revenue from the television programmes was up, and what were claimed to be 'very good' ratings ensured more support from advertisers in the year 1979–80.

Gate receipts also went up, although no figures were published until the end of the series when they were claimed to have reached

1.5 million dollars. There were times during the matches at the Sydney Cricket Ground when spectators could come and go as they pleased through unattended gates and free tickets were available at stores for people who bought certain products. Thus one must be careful before accepting the 'official' attendance figures, but there was no doubting the increase on the first year. According to the WSC figures, 354,933 people went to watch 73 days of Packer cricket in 1977–78 and approximately 700,000, almost double that amount, watched 85 days cricket in the second year. This is still an average of only 8,235 spectators a day. The seventeen days of the four-day 'Supertests' drew 159,190, an average of 9,364 a day. This compares with an average crowd of 12,945 for the 29 days of the Ashes Tests, a figure depressed by the inevitably low crowds for the last Test at Sydney after the series had been decided. Yet at the height of the cricket boom in Australia in 1975–76, shortly before Packer's dramatic entry, 736,984 people watched the six Tests between Australia and the West Indies. This was 202,380 more spectators, in six matches, than WSC and establishment cricket between them could raise for *eleven* matches only three years later. The inescapable conclusion is that now Australian spectators are being so saturated with cricket, and so much of it is televised, they are going to watch it less.

It is only partly an explanation to say that the figures for limited-over cricket are more impressive, because there is now so much more one-day cricket in Australia and it is clear, as I have written elsewhere in the book, that a new kind of audience has been attracted to one-day, and especially to night, cricket. The majority of Packer's one-day games were well attended, as were the three Benson and Hedges Cup international matches, which drew crowds of 15,000, 11,000 and 12,000 at a time when the public had rather lost faith in the Australian team. England's matches in the country areas were all enjoyable and exceptionally well supported, far better than the Cavaliers' games played by the World Series second elevens. These games seem certain to be eliminated, or drastically reduced, in future WSC programmes.

Speaking in the Americanised jargon which characterised much of the publicity emanating from World Series Cricket, Mr Packer claimed at the close of the second year of his cricketing operations: 'We've had a dramatic growth situation in two seasons' (*Melbourne Age*, February 1979). Significantly he added: 'It has probably been one of the most successful launches of a new *sport* ever seen.' The italics are mine for in many ways World Series Cricket *was* like a new sport.

The time still seems far off when WSC and official cricket will be married harmoniously to the 'old' sport of cricket. One must hope that whilst the Australian Board greatly increases their revenue from television they will not fall into the WSC trap of running cricket primarily as a television exercise. If they do, the worst features of World Series Cricket – an obsession with money, obtrusive advertising, an emphasis on show-business rather than on straightforward competitive sport, play-acting, gamesmanship, displays of bad temper, blood and thunder preferred to subtlety and character, fawning commentators building moderate performances into superlative ones – will quickly spread through establishment cricket too.

But let me end on a more optimistic note, for two reasons. First, all the evidence which one gleans from schools and amateur clubs both in England and Australia is that participation in cricket is increasing, not declining. Second, much of the traditional goodwill between professional cricketers of all nationalities, *on both sides of the fence*, still exists. There is still time for this goodwill to assert itself – both to bring the two sides together and also to ensure that the example the leading players set for their young admirers is not that set on the final day of the 'Supertests' but at Melbourne on the same day when Graham Yallop spent several minutes setting his field to do his best in the tough but fair spirit of the game to prevent David Gower hitting four off the last ball of the innings to reach his hundred. When Gower's genius prevailed, and he somehow threaded the ball through the deep offside field, every Australian player and spectator rose to applaud him.

Compare this with the words of Maryna Procter, wife of Mike Procter, about the crowds at World Series Cricket. 'If a batsman doesn't get runs he is booed, and the sight of Tony Greig sends them into a frenzy. When someone gets hit, you think you are in a bullring. The sight of blood seems to arouse them and they howl for more.'

Histrionics for the benefit of television will always elicit this sort of reaction. The players will get the crowds they deserve.

The Ashes 1978-79

A statistical survey compiled by Patrick Allen

(1) THE TEAMS

England Touring Team to Australia

Players	County	Date of Birth
BREARLEY, John Michael (Captain)	Middlesex	28 April 1942
WILLIS, Robert George Dylan (Vice-Capt.)	Warwickshire	30 May 1949
BAIRSTOW, David Leslie	Yorkshire	1 September 1951
BOTHAM, Ian Terrence	Somerset	24 November 1955
BOYCOTT, Geoffrey	Yorkshire	21 October 1940
EDMONDS, Phillippe Henri	Middlesex	8 March 1951
EMBUREY, John Ernest	Middlesex	20 August 1952
GOOCH, Graham Alan	Essex	23 July 1953
GOWER, David Ivon	Leicestershire	1 April 1957
HENDRICK, Michael	Derbyshire	22 October 1948
LEVER, John Kenneth	Essex	24 February 1949
MILLER, Geoffrey	Derbyshire	8 September 1952
OLD, Christopher Middleton	Yorkshire	22 December 1948
RADLEY, Clive Thornton	Middlesex	13 May 1944
RANDALL, Derek William	Nottinghamshire	24 February 1951
TAYLOR, Robert William	Derbyshire	17 July 1941
TOLCHARD, Roger William	Leicestershire	15 June 1946

Manager:
INSOLE, Douglas John	ex-Essex and Cambridge University	18 April 1926

Asst. Manager:
BARRINGTON, Kenneth Frank	ex-Surrey	24 November 1930

Physiotherapist:
THOMAS, Bernard

D. L. BAIRSTOW flew out on 17 January as a replacement for R. W. TOLCHARD who suffered a depressed fracture of the cheekbone.

Their Australian Opponents

Players	State	Date of Birth
YALLOP, Graham Neil (Captain)	Victoria	7 October 1952
BORDER, Allan Robert	New South Wales	27 July 1955
CARLSON, Phillip Henry	Queensland	8 August 1951
COSIER, Gary John	Queensland	25 April 1953
DARLING, Warrick Maxwell	South Australia	1 May 1957
DYMOCK, Geoffrey	Queensland	21 July 1945
HIGGS, James Donald	Victoria	11 July 1950
HILDITCH, Andrew Mark	New South Wales	20 May 1956
HOGG, Rodney Malcolm	South Australia	5 March 1951
HUGHES, Kimberley John	Western Australia	26 January 1954
HURST, Alan George	Victoria	15 July 1950
LAUGHLIN, Trevor John	Victoria	30 January 1951
MACLEAN, John Alexander	Queensland	27 April 1946
TOOHEY, Peter Michael	New South Wales	20 April 1954
WOOD, Graeme Malcolm	Western Australia	6 November 1956
WRIGHT, Kevin John	Western Australia	6 November 1956
YARDLEY, Bruce	Western Australia	7 September 1947

G. J. COSIER was Vice-Captain for the first two Test Matches.
J. A. MACLEAN was Vice-Captain for the 3rd and 4th Test Matches.
K. J. HUGHES was Vice-Captain for the 5th and 6th Test Matches.

(2) THE RESULTS

Match record of official MCC teams in Australia

Season	Captain	P	First-class matches			
			W	D	L	T
1903–04	P. F. Warner	14	9	3	2	—
1907–08	A. O. Jones	18	7	7	4	—
1911–12	J. W. H. T. Douglas	14	11	2	1	—
1920–21	J. W. H. T. Douglas	13	5	2	6	—
1922–23	A. C. MacLaren	7	0	4	3	—
1924–25	A. E. R. Gilligan	17	7	4	6	—
1928–29	A. P. F. Chapman	17	8	8	1	—
1929–30	A. H. H. Gilligan	5	2	1	2	—
1932–33	D. R. Jardine	17	10	5	1	1
1935–36	E. R. T. Holmes	6	3	2	1	—
1936–37	G. O. B. Allen	17	5	7	5	—
1946–47	W. R. Hammond	17	1	13	3	—
1950–51	F. R. Brown	16	5	7	4	—
1954–55	L. Hutton	17	8	7	2	—
1958–59	P. B. H. May	17	4	9	4	—
1962–63	E. R. Dexter	15	4	8	3	—
1965–66	M. J. K. Smith	15	5	8	2	—
1970–71	R. Illingworth	14	3	10	1	—
1974–75	M. H. Denness	15	5	5	5	—
1977	A. W. Greig	2	0	1	1	—
1978–79	J. M. Brearley	13	8	3	2	—
Totals		**286**	**110**	**116**	**59**	**1**

Australia v England—in Australia

Series	P	Tests			Adelaide			Brisbane			Melbourne			Perth			Sydney		
		E	A	D	E	A	D	E	A	D	E	A	D	E	A	D	E	A	D
1876–77	2	1	1	—	—	—	—	—	—	—	1	1	—	—	—	—	—	—	—
1878–79	1	—	1	—	—	—	—	—	—	—	—	1	—	—	—	—	—	—	—
1881–82	4	—	2	2	—	—	—	—	—	—	—	1	1	—	—	—	—	1	1
1882–83	4	2	2	—	—	—	—	—	—	—	1	1	—	—	—	—	1	1	—
1884–85	5	3	2	—	1	—	—	—	—	—	2	—	—	—	—	—	—	2	—
1886–87	2	2	—	—	—	—	—	—	—	—	—	—	—	—	—	—	2	—	—
1887–88	1	1	—	—	—	—	—	—	—	—	—	—	—	—	—	—	1	—	—
1891–92	3	1	2	—	1	—	—	—	—	—	—	1	—	—	—	—	—	1	—
1894–95	5	3	2	—	—	1	—	—	—	—	2	—	—	—	—	—	1	1	—
1897–98	5	1	4	—	—	1	—	—	—	—	—	2	—	—	—	—	1	1	—
1901–02	5	1	4	—	—	1	—	—	—	—	—	2	—	—	—	—	1	1	—
1903–04	5	3	2	—	—	1	—	—	—	—	1	1	—	—	—	—	2	—	—
1907–08	5	1	4	—	—	1	—	—	—	—	1	1	—	—	—	—	—	2	—
1911–12	5	4	1	—	1	—	—	—	—	—	2	—	—	—	—	—	1	1	—
1920–21	5	—	5	—	—	1	—	—	—	—	—	2	—	—	—	—	—	2	—
1924–25	5	1	4	—	—	1	—	—	—	—	1	1	—	—	—	—	—	2	—
1928–29	5	4	1	—	1	—	—	1	—	—	1	1	—	—	—	—	1	—	—
1932–33	5	4	1	—	1	—	—	1	—	—	—	1	—	—	—	—	2	—	—
1936–37	5	2	3	—	—	1	—	1	—	—	—	2	—	—	—	—	1	—	—
1946–47	5	—	3	2	—	—	1	—	1	—	—	—	1	—	—	—	—	2	—
1950–51	5	1	4	—	—	1	—	—	1	—	1	1	—	—	—	—	—	1	—
1954–55	5	3	1	1	1	—	—	—	1	—	1	—	—	—	—	—	1	—	1
1958–59	5	—	4	1	—	1	—	—	1	—	—	2	—	—	—	—	—	—	1
1962–63	5	1	1	3	—	—	1	—	—	1	1	—	—	—	—	—	—	1	1
1965–66	5	1	1	3	—	1	—	—	—	1	—	—	2	—	—	—	1	—	—
1970–71	6	2	—	4	—	—	1	—	—	1	—	—	1	—	—	1	2	—	—
1974–75	6	1	4	1	—	1	—	—	1	—	1	—	1	—	1	—	—	1	—
1977	1	—	1	—	—	—	—	—	—	—	—	1	—	—	—	—	—	—	—
1978–79	6	5	1	—	1	—	—	1	—	—	—	1	—	1	—	—	2	—	—
Totals	**126**	**48**	**61**	**17**	**7**	**12**	**3**	**4**	**5**	**3**	**16**	**22**	**7**	**1**	**1**	**2**	**20**	**21**	**3**

206

(3) THE AVERAGES

Tour Averages First-Class Matches
Batting

	M	I	NO	HS	Runs	Av	100's	50's	c
D. W. Randall	10	18	2	150	763	47.68	2	3	6
R. W. Tolchard	3	5	1	72	142	35.50	—	2	13
J. M. Brearley	11	21	5	116*	538	33.62	1	2	11
D. I. Gower	12	20	1	102	623	32.78	1	3	7
G. Boycott	12	23	3	90*	533	26.65	—	4	5
G. Miller	11	18	3	68*	398	26.53	—	2	5
I. T. Botham	9	14	0	74	361	25.78	—	3	14
G. A. Gooch	13	23	1	74	514	23.36	—	3	13
R. W. Taylor	10	15	2	97	230	17.69	—	1	35c. 6st.
P. H. Edmonds	7	9	2	38*	115	16.42	—	—	8
C. M. Old	6	6	1	40	81	16.20	—	—	2
C. T. Radley	6	9	0	60	138	15.33	—	1	2
R. G. D. Willis	10	13	3	24	115	11.50	—	—	3
J. E. Emburey	9	12	2	42	101	10.10	—	—	9
J. K. Lever	6	7	0	28	67	9.57	—	—	—
M. Hendrick	8	12	4	20	68	8.50	—	—	6

Substitute fielders took 2 catches.

D. L. Bairstow did not bat in a first-class match.

Bowling

	O	M	R	W	Av	B/B	5W/I
M. Hendrick	184.4	40	399	28	14.25	5–11	1
G. Miller	277.1	78	607	36	16.86	6–56	2
J. E. Emburey	261.1	73	563	31	18.16	5–67	1
I. T. Botham	239.3	44	848	44	19.27	5–51	2
R. G. D. Willis	210.3	34	696	34	20.47	5–44	1
C. M. Old	138	24	452	21	21.52	6–42	1
J. K. Lever	118.1	18	377	13	29.00	4–28	—
P. H. Edmonds	149	34	397	11	36.09	5–52	1
G. A. Gooch	26	2	80	1	80.00	1–16	—
G. Boycott	3	0	11	0	—	—	—

Also bowled:
D. W. Randall 2 – 0 – 9 – 0; C. T. Radley 1 – 0 – 4 – 0.

5 wkts in an Innings:

I. T. Botham (2)	5–51	v. N.S.W. (Sydney)
	5–70	v. Queensland (Brisbane)
G. Miller (2)	6–56	v. N.S.W. (Sydney)
	5–44	v. Australia (Sixth Test) (Sydney)
P. H. Edmonds (1)	5–52	v. South Australia (Adelaide)
J. E. Emburey (1)	5–67	v. South Australia (Adelaide)
M. Hendrick (1)	5–11	v. Western Australia (Perth)
C. M. Old (1)	6–42	v. Tasmania (Hobart)
R. G. D. Willis (1)	5–44	v. Australia (Second Test) (Perth)

Centuries (first-class matches only)

D. W. Randall (2)	150	v. Australia (Fourth Test) (Sydney)
	110	v. New South Wales (Sydney)
D. I. Gower (1)	102	v. Australia (Second Test) (Perth)
J. M. Brearley (1)	116*	v. Victoria (Melbourne)

The only century scored against England outside the Test matches was by J. E. Nash, 124 for South Australia in Adelaide.

TEST MATCH AVERAGES

England—batting

	M	I	NO	HS	Runs	Av	100's	50's	c
D. I. Gower	6	11	1	102	420	42.00	1	1	4
D. W. Randall	6	12	2	150	385	38.50	1	2	4
I. T. Botham	6	10	0	74	291	29.10	—	2	11
R. W. Taylor	6	10	2	97	208	26.00	—	1	18c. 2st.
G. Miller	6	10	0	64	234	23.40	—	1	1
G. A. Gooch	6	11	0	74	246	22.36	—	1	9
G. Boycott	6	12	0	77	263	21.75	—	1	2
J. M. Brearley	6	12	1	53	184	16.72	—	1	5
J. E. Emburey	4	7	1	42	67	11.16	—	—	6
R. G. D. Willis	6	10	2	24	88	11.00	—	—	3
M. Hendrick	5	9	4	10*	34	6.80	—	—	3

Played in one Test: J. K. Lever 14, 10; C. M. Old 29*; P. H. Edmonds 1.

England—bowling

	O	M	R	W	Av	B/B
G. Miller	177.1	58	346	23	15.04	5–44
M. Hendrick	145	30	299	19	15.73	3–19
J. E. Emburey	144.4	49	306	16	19.12	4–46
R. G. D. Willis	104.3	23	461	20	23.05	5–44
I. T. Botham	158.4	25	567	23	24.65	4–42

Also bowled: J. K. Lever 15.1 – 2 – 48 – 5; C. M. Old 26.7 – 2 – 84 – 4; P. H. Edmonds 13 – 2 – 27 – 0; G. A. Gooch 6 – 1 – 15 – 0; G. Boycott 1 – 0 – 6 – 0.

Australia—batting

	M	I	NO	HS	Runs	Av	100's	50's	c
A. R. Border	3	6	2	60*	146	36.50	—	1	3
G. N. Yallop	6	12	0	121	391	32.58	2	—	3
K. J. Hughes	6	12	0	129	345	28.75	1	—	5
G. M. Wood	6	12	0	100	344	28.66	1	1	6
W. M. Darling	4	8	0	91	221	27.62	—	1	4
B. Yardley	4	8	1	61*	148	21.14	—	1	4
P. M. Toohey	5	10	1	81*	149	16.55	—	1	5
G. J. Cosier	2	4	0	47	52	13.00	—	—	2
J. A. Maclean	4	8	1	33*	79	11.28	—	—	18
K. J. Wright	2	4	0	29	37	9.25	—	—	7c. 1st.
R. M. Hogg	6	12	0	36	95	7.91	—	—	—
J. D. Higgs	5	10	4	16	46	7.66	—	—	—
P. H. Carlson	2	4	0	21	23	5.75	—	—	2
G. Dymock	3	6	1	11	28	5.60	—	—	—
A. G. Hurst	6	12	2	17*	44	4.40	—	—	1

Played in one Test: T. J. Laughlin 2, 5; A. M. Hilditch 3, 1.

Australia—bowling

	O	M	R	W	Av	B/B
R. M. Hogg	217.4	60	527	41	12.85	6–74
A. G. Hurst	204.2	44	577	25	23.08	5–28
J. D. Higgs	196.6	47	468	19	24.63	5–148
G. Dymock	114.1	19	269	7	38.42	3–38
P. H. Carlson	46	10	99	2	49.50	2–41
A. R. Border	31	13	50	1	50.00	1–14
B. Yardley	113.2	12	389	7	55.57	3–41

Also bowled:
T. J. Laughlin 25 – 6 – 60 – 0; G. J. Cosier 12 – 3 – 35 – 0.

(4) THE SCORES

South Australia Country XI v England XI (not first-class)
Renmark, November 1. Match Drawn.
England XI 199 – 4 declared (G. A. Gooch 47, C. T. Radley 64, J. M. Brearley 29)
South Australia Country XI 137 – 6 (B. J. Sampson 37, I. J. Fillery 35)

South Australia v England XI
Adelaide—South Australia won by 32 runs.
November 3, 4, 5 and 6

South Australia *First Innings*

			Second Innings	
J. E. Nash lbw Miller	124		st Taylor b Miller	33
W. M. Darling c Miller b Willis	17		c Edmonds b Old	1
I. R. McLean c Taylor b Edmonds	30		c Randall (sub) b Miller	52
B. L. Causby c Brearley b Miller	20		c and b Edmonds	4
J. L. Langley st Taylor b Edmonds	1		st Taylor b Edmonds	0
*R. K. Blewett c Taylor b Willis	22		b Edmonds	12
P. R. Sleep c Taylor b Lever	45		c Taylor b Edmonds	3
†T. J. Robertson c Taylor b Willis	2		b Edmonds	24
R. M. Hogg b Lever	11		run out	16
G. R. Attenborough lbw Miller	19		run out	3
A. T. Sincock not out	14		not out	1
Extras (b2, lb2, nb2)	6			0
Total	311		Total	149

Fall of Wickets
1 – 31 2 – 133 3 – 195 4 – 196 5 – 200 6 – 245 7 – 261 8 – 272 9 – 281
1 – 11 2 – 55 3 – 64 4 – 64 5 – 84 6 – 90 7 – 112 8 – 144 9 – 146

Bowling	*First Innings*				*Second Innings*			
Willis	11	1	61	3				
Lever	16	1	67	2	9	0	40	0
Old	18	2	78	0	5	1	20	1
Edmonds	21	5	53	2	21	3	52	5
Miller	18.4	5	41	3	16	2	37	2
Gooch	1	0	5	0				

England XI *First Innings*

			Second Innings	
G. Boycott lbw Hogg	62		lbw Hogg	6
G. A. Gooch c Robertson b Hogg	4		b Sleep	23
C. T. Radley hit wicket b Hogg	4		c Sleep b Sincock	3
D. I. Gower lbw Attenborough	73		c Blewett b Sincock	50
*J. M. Brearley b Sincock	27		run out	25
G. Miller c Langley b Hogg	0		lbw Sincock	5
†R. W. Taylor c Blewett b Sleep	6		c Langley b Attenborough	4
P. H. Edmonds not out	38		c Robertson b Attenborough	0
J. K. Lever c and b Sleep	1		b Hogg	28
C. M. Old c Darling b Sleep	4		c McLean b Sleep	40
R. G. D. Willis (absent injured)	0		not out	0
Extras (lb5, nb8)	13		Extras (b4, lb1, nb7)	12
Total	232		Total	196

Fall of Wickets
1 – 9 2 – 15 3 – 148 4 – 148 5 – 149 6 – 179 7 – 215 8 – 222 9 – 232
1 – 19 2 – 22 3 – 67 4 – 100 5 – 108 6 – 117 7 – 117 8 – 124 9 – 192

Bowling	*First Innings*				*Second Innings*			
Hogg	12	2	43	4	12.4	1	39	2
Sincock	9	0	42	1	10	2	28	3
Attenborough	15	1	49	1	11	2	49	2
Sleep	17.5	3	72	3	12.5	1	49	2
Blewett	10	4	13	0	5	1	19	0

Victoria Country XI v England XI (not first-class)

Leongatha, November 8. England XI won by 71 runs.
England XI 130 – 8 declared (G. Miller 30, G. A. Gooch 29, C. Aitken 4–30)
Victoria Country XI 59 (S. McNamara 20, J. E. Emburey 5–10)

Victoria v England XI

Melbourne—Match drawn.
November 10, 11, 12 and 13

Victoria *First Innings*

				Second Innings	
J. M. Wiener c Edmonds b Lever	48			not out	14
P. A. Hibbert c Tolchard b Old	6			not out	16
D. F. Whatmore c Edmonds b Lever	27				
*G. N. Yallop b Edmonds	10				
P. Melville c Edmonds b Emburey	16				
J. K. Moss c Emburey b Edmonds	73				
T. J. Laughlin run out	37				
†I. L. Maddocks c Radley b Edmonds	8				
I. W. Callen c Tolchard b Emburey	8				
A. G. Hurst b Emburey	1				
J. D. Higgs not out	1				
Extras (lb15, nb4)	19			Extras (nb3)	3
Total	254			Total (0 wkts)	33

Fall of wickets
1 – 11 2 – 84 3 – 93 4 – 113 5 – 129 6 – 213 7 – 239 8 – 244 9 – 249

Bowling	First Innings				Second Innings			
Old	17	5	44	1				
Lever	18	3	52	2	4	1	3	0
Hendrick	11	2	29	0				
Edmonds	22	6	48	3	2	0	3	0
Emburey	26.5	5	56	3	5	0	11	0
Gooch	2	0	6	0				
Randall					2	0	9	0
Radley					1	0	4	0

England XI *First Innings*

*J. M. Brearley not out	116
G. A. Gooch lbw b Hurst	3
D. W. Randall b Wiener	63
D. I. Gower c & b Wiener	13
C. T. Radley c & b Higgs	22
†R. W. Tolchard c Whatmore b Higgs	0
P. H. Edmonds c Melville b Higgs	5
C. M. Old c Maddocks b Hurst	4
J. E. Emburey c Higgs b Laughlin	5
J. K. Lever } did not bat	—
M. Hendrick }	
Extras (lb3, w2, nb5)	10
Total (8 wkts declared)	241

Fall of wickets
1 – 7 2 – 121 3 – 145 4 – 195 5 – 199 6 – 207 7 – 225 8 – 241

Bowling	First Innings			
Hurst	17	4	44	2
Callen	16	4	44	0
Higgs	39	8	82	3
Laughlin	15.7	5	24	1
Wiener	13	3	31	2
Yallop	2	0	6	0

Australian Capital Territory v England XI (not first-class)
Canberra, November 15. England XI won by 179 runs.
England XI 255 – 2 (40 overs) (G. Boycott 123,* R. W. Tolchard 108)
Australian Capital Territory 76 (33.6 overs) (B. Willett 32, R. G. D. Willis 4 – 10,
M. Hendrick 2 – 7, G. Miller 2 – 5)

New South Wales v England XI
Sydney—November 17, 18, 19 and 20. England won by 10 wickets.

England XI *First Innings*		*Second Innings*	
G. Boycott c Border b Lawson	14	not out	4
G. A. Gooch c Rixon b Border	66	not out	0
D. W. Randall c Hughes b Clews	110		
C. T. Radley c Hughes b Border	13		
D. I. Gower b Hourn	26		
G. Miller st Rixon b Hourn	5		
I. T. Botham c Toohey b Clews	56		
†R. W. Taylor c Hilditch b Lawson	9		
J. E. Emburey c Johnston b Lawson	0		
*R. G. D. Willis not out	21		
M. Hendrick b Border	20		
Extras (b17, lb6, w2, nb9)	34		
Total	374	Total (0 wkts)	4

Fall of wickets
1 – 20 2 – 145 3 – 173 4 – 250 5 – 252 6 – 276 7 – 305 8 – 313 9 – 336

Bowling	*First Innings*				*Second Innings*			
Lawson	17	5	39	3	0.5	0	4	0
Watson	18	2	61	0				
Clews	13	1	88	2				
Hourn	32	4	114	2				
Border	12.1	2	38	3				

New South Wales *First Innings*		*Second Innings*	
J. Dyson c Boycott b Miller	67	c Gooch b Willis	6
*A. M. Hilditch c Taylor b Willis	4	b Botham	93
P. M. Toohey c Gower b Hendrick	23	c Gooch b Botham	20
A. R. Border c Taylor b Miller	11	c Taylor b Botham	12
D. A. H. Johnston c Hendrick b Miller	16	c Gooch b Botham	3
G. C. Hughes c Hendrick b Miller	27	b Emburey	11
M. L. Clews st Taylor b Emburey	1	run out	5
†S. J. Rixon c Hendrick b Miller	10	c Botham b Emburey	24
G. G. Watson c Boycott b Emburey	2	not out	14
G. F. Lawson not out	0	c Miller b Willis	7
D. W. Hourn c Emburey b Miller	0	b Botham	0
Extras (lb1, nb3)	4	(b6, lb4, w1, nb4)	15
Total	165	Total	210

Fall of wickets
1 – 5 2 – 47 3 – 65 4 – 107 5 – 142 6 – 146 7 – 162 8 – 165 9 – 165
1 – 18 2 – 57 3 – 82 4 – 87 5 – 119 6 – 124 7 – 173 8 – 192 9 – 209

Bowling	*First Innings*				*Second Innings*			
Willis	8	3	16	1	15	3	39	2
Hendrick	12	2	33	1	4	2	4	0
Botham	9	2	41	0	17.2	6	51	5
Miller	18.4	3	56	6	24	6	56	0
Emburey	10	4	15	2	22	5	44	2
Gooch					1	0	1	0

211

Queensland Country XI v England XI (not first-class)

Bundaberg, November 22. England XI won by 132 runs.
England XI 259 – 5 (35 overs) (R. W. Tolchard 74, J. M. Brearley 59, D. W. Randall 37,*
G. A. Gooch 32*)
Queensland Country XI 127 (31.6 overs) (K. Maher 47, P. H. Carlson 31; J. K. Lever 4 – 17,
G. Miller 2 – 15, P. H. Edmonds 2 – 6)

Queensland v England XI

Brisbane—November 24, 25, 26 and 27. England XI won by 6 wickets

Queensland	First Innings			Second Innings	
M. J. Walters c Gower b Willis			0	retired hurt	4
W. R. Broad c Taylor b Old			41	lbw b Willis	0
A. D. Ogilvie retired hurt			43	(7) c Gower b Willis	45
G. J. Cosier c Taylor b Botham			32	(3) b Willis	0
P. H. Carlson c Miller b Old			1	(4) b Botham	37
T. V. Hohns c Taylor b Willis			3	(5) c Old b Botham	43
*†J. A. Maclean c Boycott b Botham			1	(8) c Gooch b Old	94
G. K. Whyte c Brearley b Old			10	(6) b Botham	0
G. Dymock c Brearley b Botham			13	c Taylor b Botham	16
L. F. Balcam not out			10	b Botham	21
G. W. Brabon lbw b Old			2	not out	2
Extras (nb16)			16	(b4, lb2, nb21)	27
Total			172	Total	289

Fall of wickets
1 – 4 2 – 90 3 – 97 4 – 100 5 – 129 6 – 135 7 – 158 8 – 159 9 – 172
1 – 0 2 – 0 3 – 83 4 – 83 5 – 121 6 – 169 7 – 214 8 – 268 9 – 289

Bowling	First Innings				Second Innings			
Willis	11	1	40	2	11	1	46	3
Old	14.7	4	33	4	14.2	3	63	1
Botham	12	1	66	3	20	3	70	5
Gooch	3	0	11	0	1	0	8	0
Edmonds	5	2	6	0	8	1	35	0
Miller					11	1	40	0

England XI	First Innings			Second Innings	
G. Boycott c Cosier b Brabon			6	c Maclean b Balcam	60
G. A. Gooch c Brabon b Dymock			34	c Ogilvie b Carlson	22
D. W. Randall c Maclean b Balcam			66	b Whyte	47
†R. W. Taylor c Maclean b Dymock			2		
*J. M. Brearley not out			75	(4) not out	38
D. I. Gower b Balcam			6	(5) c Cosier b Hohns	1
G. Miller c Maclean b Dymock			18	(6) not out	22
I. T. Botham c Maclean b Dymock			6		
C. M. Old lbw b Balcam			2		
P. H. Edmonds c Maclean b Cosier			14		
R. G. D. Willis b Brabon			6		
Extras (b1, lb3, w1, nb14)			19	(b7, lb2, nb9)	18
Total			254	Total (4 wkts)	208

Fall of wickets
1 – 14 2 – 75 3 – 90 4 – 129 5 – 148 6 – 188 7 – 201 8 – 208 9 – 241
1 – 42 2 – 117 3 – 165 4 – 168

Bowling	First Innings				Second Innings			
Balcam	13	1	56	3	12	2	25	1
Brabon	10.1	1	45	2	5	0	31	0
Carlson	14	1	48	0	9.3	1	29	1
Dymock	19	3	46	4	17	5	38	0
Hohns	2	0	3	0	8	5	13	1
Cosier	4	0	19	1	5	2	10	0
Whyte	7	3	18	0	15	3	44	1

AUSTRALIA v ENGLAND (First Test)

Brisbane. See scorecard on p. 78.

212

Western Australia v England XI

Perth. December 9, 10, 11. England XI won by 140 runs.

England XI First Innings		Second Innings	
G. Boycott lbw b Clark	4	c Marsh b Yardley	13
G. A. Gooch c Wright b Alderman	3	c Wright b Porter	15
C. T. Radley b Alderman	2	c Marsh b Yardley	18
*J. M. Brearley c Wright b Porter	11	b Yardley	18
D. I. Gower c Wright b Alderman	0	c Marsh b Porter	4
†R. W. Tolchard not out	61	b Yardley	3
I. T. Botham c Charlesworth b Porter	4	c Marsh b Yardley	4
P. H. Edmonds lbw b Porter	21	c Wright b Alderman	27
J. E. Emburey c Wright b Clark	22	not out	7
J. K. Lever c Wright b Mann	2	b Alderman	1
M. Hendrick c Charlesworth b Mann	6	b Clark	8
Extras (b1, lb2, nb4, w1)	8	(b7, nb1)	8
Total	144	Total	126

Fall of Wickets
1 – 7 2 – 7 3 – 13 4 – 17 5 – 25 6 – 31 7 – 69 8 – 115 9 – 121
1 – 23 2 – 41 3 – 58 4 – 63 5 – 69 6 – 73 7 – 98 8 – 115 9 – 117

Bowling	First Innings				Second Innings			
Alderman	12	4	18	3	9	2	26	2
Clark	16	4	50	2	12	2	22	1
Porter	17	4	37	3	16	9	16	2
Yardley	2	0	7	0	13	1	54	5
Mann	8.3	2	24	2				

Western Australia First Innings		Second Innings	
G. M. Wood b Lever	2	lbw b Botham	15
R. I. Charlesworth c Tolchard b Botham	3	lbw b Lever	6
K. J. Hughes b Botham	8	lbw b Botham	1
G. R. Marsh c Tolchard b Botham	0	c Tolchard b Hendrick	9
*R. J. Inverarity c Tolchard b Hendrick	9	lbw b Botham	2
A. L. Mann c Botham b Hendrick	3	c Tolchard b Botham	0
G. D. Porter c Brearley b Hendrick	8	c Tolchard b Hendrick	2
B. Yardley c Tolchard b Hendrick	8	not out	38
†K. J. Wright c Brearley b Botham	0	b Hendrick	0
W. M. Clark not out	2	run out	1
T. M. Alderman c Botham b Hendrick	1	run out	2
Extras (lb3, w1, nb4)	8	(lb2)	2
Total	52	Total	78

Fall of Wickets
1 – 4 2 – 6 3 – 10 4 – 16 5 – 28 6 – 39 7 – 48 8 – 49 9 – 49
1 – 22 2 – 22 3 – 28 4 – 32 5 – 32 6 – 35 7 – 48 8 – 64 9 – 69

Bowling	First Innings				Second Innings			
Lever	8	3	10	1	7	3	16	1
Botham	9	3	16	4	13.5	4	37	4
Hendrick	5.4	2	11	5	7	2	23	3
Gooch	2	0	7	0				

Western Australia Country XI v England XI (not first-class)

Albany (40 Over Match)
December 13, 1978. England XI won by 69 runs.
England XI 208 – 4 wkts. (G. A. Gooch 112)
Western Australia Country XI 139 (34·3 overs) (B. Miguel 53, R. Ditchburn 31;
P. H. Edmonds 6 – 53, G. Miller 4 – 68)

AUSTRALIA v ENGLAND (Second Test)

Perth. See scorecard on p. 104.

213

South Australia v England XI

Adelaide. December 22, 23, 24. Match drawn.

South Australia First Innings		Second Innings	
J. E. Nash c Tolchard b Old	10	lbw b Emburey	25
W. M. Darling c Tolchard b Old	19	(7) not out	41
I. R. McLean c Tolchard b Gooch	7	(2) c and b Emburey	25
B. L. Causby b Old	87	(3) c Randall b Emburey	7
R. Parker c & b Edmonds	51	(4) c Randall b Emburey	42
*R. K. Blewett c Old b Emburey	19	c Brearley b Emburey	51
P. R. Sleep not out	31	(5) c Tolchard b Old	18
†S. R. Gentle lbw b Lever	1	not out	21
A. T. Sincock not out	12		
Extras (lb3, nb1)	4	(lb1)	1
Total (7 wkts dec)...	241	Total (6 wkts dec.)...	231

Did not bat: G. R. Attenborough, D. A. Johnston.

Fall of Wickets
1 – 25 2 – 36 3 – 38 4 – 129 5 – 174 6 – 220 7 – 221
1 – 45 2 – 57 3 – 58 4 – 96 5 – 140 6 – 184

Bowling	First Innings				Second Innings			
Lever	16	1	63	1	10	1	33	0
Old	18	2	55	3	5	0	21	1
Gooch	6	1	16	1	4	0	11	0
Emburey	17	3	48	1	26	3	67	5
Edmonds	17	3	55	1	28	9	91	0
Miller					4	1	6	0
Boycott					1	0	1	0

England XI First Innings		Second Innings	
G. Boycott c Gentle b Sincock	4	(11) not out	7
G. A. Gooch st Gentle b Causby	20	(5) st Gentle b Blewett	64
C. T. Radley c Gentle b Attenborough	60	lbw b Attenborough	1
†R. W. Tolchard run out	72	lbw b Johnston	6
D. W. Randall c Gentle b Attenborough	47	(2) c Blewett b Johnston	45
*J. M. Brearley not out	18	(1) c Parker b Johnston	26
G. Miller not out	2	(6) not out	68
C. Old		(7) b Attenborough	2
P. H. Edmonds ⎫		(8) lbw b Blewett	2
J. E. Emburey ⎬ Did not bat		(9) b Blewett	0
J. K. Lever ⎭		(10) c Darling b Attenborough	11
Extras (b3, lb4, nb4)	11	(b1, lb2, nb3)	6
Total (5 wkts dec.)...	234	Total (9 wkts)...	238

Fall of Wickets
1 – 26 2 – 32 3 – 138 4 – 186 5 – 231
1 – 65 2 – 68 3 – 74 4 – 91 5 – 180 6 – 187 7 – 196 8 – 202 9 – 223

Bowling	First Innings				Second Innings			
Attenborough	13	5	41	2	16	1	92	3
Johnston	8	2	21	0	7	0	44	3
Sincock	5	0	27	1	5	0	39	0
Causby	6	0	34	1				
Sleep	12	1	58	0	2	0	22	0
Blewett	8	1	41	0	7	0	35	3
Nash	1	0	1	0				

AUSTRALIA v ENGLAND (Third Test)

Melbourne. See scorecard on p. 127.

AUSTRALIA v ENGLAND (Fourth Test)
Sydney. See scorecard on p. 153.

BENSON AND HEDGES (First Match) **ONE-DAY INTERNATIONAL** (Sydney)
13 January. Match abandoned and rearranged. Australia 17 – 1 (7.2 overs).

Northern New South Wales v England XI (not first-class)
Newcastle, January 14, 15, 16. England XI won by 9 wkts.
Northern N.S.W. 223 – 9 dec. (C. Beatty 62, J. Gardner 59; P. H. Edmonds 3 – 66) and 166
  (C. Evans 64, R. Neal 44; C. Old 4 – 30, J. K. Lever 3 – 24, P. H. Edmonds 3 – 49).
England XI 163 (J. M. Brearley 66; R. Holland 4 – 60, K. M. Hill 3 – 49) and 230 – 1 wkt.
  (G. Boycott 117*, C. T. Radley 55*, J. M. Brearley 50).

Tasmania v England XI
Launceston (40-Over Match), *January 18.* England XI won by 163 runs.
England XI 240 – 8 wkts (I. T. Botham 61, D. W. Randall 60, C. T. Radley 44).
Tasmania 77 (34.4 overs) (G. Miller 3 – 3).

Tasmania v England XI
Hobart, January 19, 20 and 21. Match drawn.

Tasmania *First Innings*

			Second Innings	
M. J. Norman c Taylor b Old	13		b Emburey	43
G. W. Goodman c Taylor b Old	1		c Taylor b Willis	1
S. J. Howard c Taylor b Old	13		b Lever	20
J. H. Hampshire c Taylor b Old	0		not out	46
†R. D. Woolley b Old	4		c Radley b Miller	0
T. W. Docking b Emburey	39		not out	2
*J. Simmons c Miller b Old	1			
D. J. Gatenby b Willis	1			
G. J. Cowmeadow c Edmonds b Willis	10			
M. B. Scholes b Miller	10			
G. R. Whitney not out	0			
Extras (b5, lb3, nb5)	13		Extras (b2, lb1, nb3)	6
Total	105		Total (for 4 wkts)	118

Fall of Wickets
1 – 6 2 – 20 3 – 20 4 – 36 5 – 47 6 – 60 7 – 61 8 – 75 9 – 105
1 – 3 2 – 34 3 – 102 4 – 107

Bowling	First Innings				Second Innings			
Willis	10	1	24	2	4	1	9	1
Old	14	3	42	6	5	2	12	0
Lever	7	3	18	0	8	0	27	1
Emburey	4	3	1	1	6	1	15	1
Miller	3	1	7	1	5	1	18	1
Edmonds					12	3	27	0
Boycott					1	0	4	0

England XI *First Innings*

G. Boycott not out	90
G. A. Gooch c Goodman b Whitney	14
C. T. Radley c Woolley b Cowmeadow	15
D. I. Gower b Gatenby	30
†R. W. Taylor b Whitney	1
G. Miller b Gatenby	44
P. H. Edmonds not out	7
Extras (b4, lb2, nb3)	9
Total (5 wkts dec.)	210

Did not bat: C. M. Old, J. E. Emburey, J. K. Lever, *R. G. D. Willis

Fall of Wickets
1 – 30 2 – 54 3 – 99 4 – 102 5 – 187

Bowling	First Innings			
Cowmeadow	16	2	64	1
Whitney	26	3	73	2
Scholes	10	4	40	0
Gatenby	5	1	22	2
Simmons	1	0	2	0

BENSON AND HEDGES ONE-DAY INTERNATIONAL
(First Match, rearranged) *Melbourne, January 24*. England won by 7 wickets.
Australia 101 (M. Hendrick 4 – 25, I. T. Botham 3 – 16)
England 102 – 3 (G. Boycott 39*)
Man of the Match: M. Hendrick.

AUSTRALIA v ENGLAND (Fifth Test)
Adelaide. See scorecard on p. 182.

Tasmania (Gillette Cup Winners) v England XI (not first-class)
Melbourne (48 6-ball Overs), February 3. England won by 3 wkts.
Tasmania 131 – 6 wkts (G. W. Goodman 36)
England XI 134 – 7 wkts (43.4 overs) (R. J. Sherriff 3 – 16)
R. J. Sherriff won Man of the Match award.

BENSON AND HEDGES ONE-DAY INTERNATIONAL
(Second Match) *Melbourne, February 4.* Australia won by 4 wickets.
England 212 – 6 (40 overs) (D. I. Gower 101*)
Australia 215 – 6 (38.6 overs) (P. M. Toohey 54*, K. J. Hughes 50, J. K. Lever 3 – 51)
Man of the Match: D. I. Gower.

Geelong and Districts XI v England XI (not first-class)
Geelong (40-over match), February 6.
England won by 48 runs (their total was 148 – 8 at 38.6 overs)
England XI 165 – 9 wkts (40 overs) (P. Caulfield 3 – 28)
Geelong and Districts XI 100 – 9 wkts (38.6 overs)

BENSON AND HEDGES ONE-DAY INTERNATIONAL
(Third Match) *Melbourne, February 7.* Australia won by 6 wickets.
England 94 (J. M. Brearley 46, G. J. Cosier 3 – 22).
Australia 95 – 4.
Man of the Match: G. Dymock

AUSTRALIA v ENGLAND (Sixth Test)
Sydney. See scorecard on p. 196.

216

(5) TOUR NOTES

v SOUTH AUSTRALIA at *Adelaide*
South Australia's victory by 32 runs was their first win over an MCC/England team since A. E. R. Gilligan's side of 1924/25 suffered defeat. It was also the first time since before the First World War that an England side had lost its first match on an Australian tour.

v VICTORIA at *Melbourne*
J. M. Brearley's 116* against Victoria was his first century since 20 July 1977 when he made 145 v Gloucestershire at Lord's.

v AUSTRALIA at *Brisbane (First Test)*
G. N. Yallop, in recording a century in his first match as captain of Australia (102), joined W. L. Murdoch, G. H. S. Trott, M. A. Noble, W. W. Armstrong and H. L. Collins in recording the feat against England. C. Hill and A. L. Hassett achieved it against South Africa.

W. L. Murdoch	The Oval	1880	0 & 153*
G. H. S. Trott	Lord's	1896	0 & 143
M. A. Noble	Sydney	1903–04	133 & 22
W. W. Armstrong	Sydney	1920–21	12 & 158
H. L. Collins	Sydney	1924–25	114 & 60
G. N. Yallop	Brisbane	1978–79	7 & 102

C. Hill v South Africa at Sydney, 1910–11   191.
A. L. Hassett v South Africa at Johannesburg, 1949–50   112.

K. J. Hughes recorded his maiden Test century.
R. M. Hogg had figures of 6 – 74 on his first Test appearance.
D. W. Randall was declared Man of the Match.
England's victory was their first at Brisbane since 1936–37.

v WESTERN AUSTRALIA at *Perth*
Defeat for Western Australia ended a run of 31 matches unbeaten, and their first-innings total of 52 was only two runs higher than their previous lowest first-class score since the war (50) recorded v N.S.W. at Sydney in 1951–52.

v AUSTRALIA at *Perth (Second Test)*
When G. Boycott reached 47 during his first innings of 77 he became the eighth Englishman to reach 2000 runs in Tests v Australia in his 24th Test Match.

	Tests	Runs
J. B. Hobbs	41	3,636
W. R. Hammond	33	2,852
H. Sutcliffe	27	2,741
J. H. Edrich	32	2,644
L. Hutton	27	2,428
M. C. Cowdrey	35	2,186
K. F. Barrington	23	2,111
G. Boycott	24	2,053

He took 9½ hours to make 100 runs in his two innings (77 and 23) and failed to reach the boundary during the first day's play, which left him 63* at the close.
D. I. Gower with 102 scored his first Test century v Australia.
R. M. Hogg with match figures of 10 – 139 (5 – 65 & 5 – 74) was made Man of the Match in his second Test match.
The umpire Tom Brooks announced his retirement on the last day of the match following adverse comment on his decisions during the Test.
England's victory was their first in a Test match at Perth, previous results being a draw in 1970–71 and an Australian victory in 1974–75.

v AUSTRALIA at *Melbourne (Third Test)*
G. M. Wood and W. M. Darling with opening partnerships of 65 and 55 gave Australia two opening partnerships of more than 50 in the same match for the first time since K. R. Stackpole and I. R. Redpath v West Indies at Kingston in 1973.
R. M. Hogg with 5 – 30 and 5 – 36 (10 – 66 in the match) took five wickets in an innings for the fifth time in six innings.
G. Miller in his innings of 7 during England's first innings batted 108 minutes for 3* at stumps on the second day (8 minutes longer than J. T. Murray, who batted 100 minutes for 3* at Sydney in 1962–63 whilst suffering a shoulder injury).

Man of the Match was G. M. Wood, who registered his first Test century against England.

J. M. Brearley suffered his first defeat in 16 Test matches as England's captain.

The only England captain to have bettered Brearley's record of 10 wins and 5 draws is R. Illingworth, who had 8 wins and 11 draws in a run of 19 matches before defeat.

v AUSTRALIA at Sydney (Fourth Test)

A. G. Hurst (5 – 28) took five wickets in an innings for the first time in a Test match.

G. Boycott's dismissal for 0 by R. M. Hogg in the second innings was his first 'duck' in 68 Test innings since the second Test v New Zealand at Trent Bridge in 1969 when he was dismissed by R. C. Motz.

J. D. Higgs (5 – 148) in his marathon spell of 478 balls took five wickets in a Test innings for the first time.

D. W. Randall with his innings of 150 in 9 hours 50 minutes was Man of the Match.

v AUSTRALIA at Adelaide (Fifth Test)

R. M. Hogg took his 37th wicket of the series when he had R. G. D. Willis caught by W. M. Darling and beat A. A. Mailey's record number of Test wickets – 36 in a series against England in 1920–21.

W. M. Darling when hit under the heart by Willis at the start of Australia's first innings was given the 'kiss of life' by J. E. Emburey.

G. Miller (64) and R. W. Taylor (97) put on 135 for the 7th wicket, only 8 fewer than the record in England v Australia Test matches held by F. E. Woolley and J. Vine, Sydney 1911–12. Their partnership for the 7th wicket was the highest in England v Australia Tests at Adelaide, surpassing the record of J. B. Hobbs and E. Hendren of 117 in 1924–25.

R. W. Taylor's 97 was equal to his previous highest score in first-class cricket – for International Wanderers v South African Invitation XI at Johannesburg, 1975–76.

I. T. Botham was declared Man of the Match for his 74 and 4 – 42.

v AUSTRALIA at Sydney (Sixth Test)

G. N. Yallop, in scoring 121 out of 179 in 4 hours 27 minutes whilst at the wicket in Australia's first innings, scored 67.59% of the runs scored.

J. M. Brearley during his first innings of 46 reached 1,000 runs in Test cricket when he had made 19.

G. Miller (5 – 44) in his 20th Test took five wickets in an innings for the first time in his Test career.

In England's second innings, with 34 runs needed for victory, umpires D. Weser and A. Crafter, both standing in their first Test, together with G. N. Yallop, the Australian captain, were in breach of Law 5, which states that 'subject to agreement to the contrary either captain may demand a new ball at the start of an innings'. J. M. Brearley objected unavailingly to the use of an old ball.

G. N. Yallop was declared Man of the Match.

At the conclusion of this Test J. M. Brearley's captaincy record was
Played 19   Won 13   Drawn 5   Lost 1.

Only J. W. H. T. Douglas in 1911–12, A. P. Chapman in 1928–29 and D. R. Jardine in 1932–33 had previously won four times in Australia in a five-Test series. J. M. Brearley had won eight out of 11 Test matches against Australia.

R. M. Hogg, with 41 wickets in the series, surpassed all other bowlers in Test cricket history with the exception of S. F. Barnes (49), J. C. Laker (46), and C. V. Grimmett (42), and his figures are the best of any Australian bowler in Test matches against England.

Rodney Hogg's Test Wickets

Boycott:	c Hughes ...	13	Botham:	c Maclean	49	Taylor:	c Maclean	2
	lbw	23		c Yallop .	59		bowled ...	1
	bowled	1	Miller:	lbw	27		c Maclean	5
	lbw	0		bowled ..	40		c Wright ...	97
Gooch:	c Laughlin ...	2		bowled ..	7	Willis:	c Yallop ...	2
	c Yardley ...	2		lbw	17		c Yallop ...	3
	c Maclean ...	1		lbw	31		c Darling...	24
	lbw	43	Gower:	bowled ...	102		c Wright ...	12
	lbw	40		c Maclean	12	Hendrick:	bowled ...	0
	c Hughes	1		c Maclean	34	Edmonds:	c Maclean	1
Brearley:	c Maclean ...	6	Randall:	c Wood ...	0	Emburey:	bowled ...	42
	c Maclean ...	0		lbw	2			
	lbw	1		lbw	150			
	c Maclean ...	0		lbw	7			
	bowled	17						
	c Wright	2						

				AVERAGE:	12.85 per wicket
FIRST TEST:	6/74	1/35	7/109		
SECOND TEST:	5/65	5/57	10/122	SUMMARY:	Bowled 8
THIRD TEST:	5/30	5/36	10/66		Lbw 11
FOURTH TEST:	2/36	4/67	6/103		Caught 22
FIFTH TEST:	4/26	3/59	7/85		
SIXTH TEST:	1/42		1/42		
				Maclean took 10 catches and Wright 3	
TOTALS:	23/273	18/254	41/527	of the 22 catches shown above.	